addiction
reform

addiction
reform

THE ORGANIC PROCESSES
OF SUBSTANCE USE BEHAVIOR

brett sondag

addiction reform
THE ORGANIC PROCESSES OF SUBSTANCE USE BEHAVIOR

Windy City Publishers
2118 Plum Grove Road, #349
Rolling Meadows, IL 60008

www.windycitypublishers.com

Published in the United States of America

ISBN#:
978-1-941478-83-7

Library of Congress Control Number:
2019911077

WINDY CITY PUBLISHERS
CHICAGO

contents

part 1

Getting Started

What's the problem?

I WAS COMPLETING A BEHAVIORAL health internship in the West Side of Chicago when I facilitated an assessment on a person who gave me an epiphany about addiction. He was a Puerto Rican man in his sixties who did not speak English. I had to use a phone translator to complete the assessment. The man was describing the tension and some type of fear that he was experiencing. He was very eager to see a doctor to get a refill for his medication. Halfway through the assessment, I realized that the man was going through opioid withdrawal. I don't think he understood what he was undergoing. The man had worked all his life until a recent injury took him out of work, and led him to be prescribed an opioid pain medication. He became dependent on the medication, ran out, and began experiencing the uncomfortable side effects of opioid withdrawal.

He didn't know what it was. He just knew that more medication would provide him relief and take away his discomfort. There was no prior substance abuse history in his life. I made a recommendation for him to receive medical detox and follow-up with his primary care physician for pain management. Even though this was the correct recommendation, I felt uneasy about it. I felt uneasy that this man had no idea that he was experiencing an addiction. Then he was going to be exposed to a culture where he would be labeled an "addict" and directed to attend support groups for the rest of his life. The epiphany I had was that many people do not understand addiction, and they will not receive the individualized care that they need and deserve if they seek out help. This man comes from a different culture, and may have a completely different outlook about what addiction is. He will be taught concepts about his behavior that may feel like a life sentence and not resonate with him. This can lead him to resist help altogether, and further keep him trapped in a cycle of addiction.

This man just needed to be educated about what he was experiencing, the substance-use behavioral process in general, and then to work towards a plan to get rid of his chemical dependency. How we do that will depend on the individual experience. This man's story was an amplified version of what millions of people experience every day with addiction. They don't have knowledge about the reality of their substance-use behavior. Then culture comes in, to impose its preferences and preconceived notions about what they're experiencing and how they should experience help. Many people will run the other way, and never come to understand their substance-use behavior for what it is. I think about that man from time to time, hoping that he received the proper help and that he's found joy in his life. I not only want people to overcome their addiction, but I also want them to understand their behavior for what it is and address it with a lifestyle as they see fit.

The world is a puzzle that has many problems and solutions. We're always trying to make the world more efficient by developing new inventions, rewriting policies, and finding convenient new shortcuts. We need to be able to challenge the norms and the traditional ways we do things if we want progress. People may feel uncomfortable about that. But it's necessary when making applications in the world function more smoothly, and if we want to be all-inclusive.

Substance use means something different for every person. This can be based on cultural practices, peer interest and personal benefit. This will impact how we help people with substance use issues, and affect what they will need to live a quality life. Then again, quality of life will mean something different for every person as well. Living a quality life is not in itself related to substance use exclusively, but particular substance-use patterns can negatively impact various areas of our lifestyle. Then what needs to be considered is the underlying properties that are driving this behavioral pattern with substances. Do you think we paid this close attention to our behavioral patterns thousands of years ago? We have the gift now to do so, and we will only get better at understanding our behaviors and learn new ways to change them to maintain a quality life.

Our identity is a fluid construct that assists on the production of behavior, which in turn impacts our quality of life. Identity changes in various ways throughout our lifespan, and there are dynamic components shaping it. When we start to have a relationship with substances, the world starts molding our identity based on the relationship with substance use. Some may identify us as an "alcoholic," "stoner," "social drinker" or "straight-edged." So then we are expected to act or get help in a certain way, based on the culture's current approach to the problem identity. Our behavior starts to be misinterpreted, and we're treated like an identity that became generalized to our existence. The actual substance-use behavior gets lost in the shuffle and is not considered as an individual experience. However, we can effectively modify a person's problematic substance-use behavior once we consider the individualized experience, and then we don't need to construct an identity for that person that limits their understanding of their behavioral pattern and overall behavioral potential for the future. Did we need to manufacture an identity for the man I did an assessment on to better understand him and his behavior? I don't think so. Substance-use behavior is complex, so culture is quick to create associated identities as a shortcut. We can unmask these identities by observing the organic processes of substance-use behavior, and realize its malleable ability to change.

chapter 1

Vision

How do we visualize the resolution of the problem?

THE WHOLE LIFE OF HUMANS is embedded into a stream of actions or *behaviors*. Our behaviors vary in the degree of motor action and conscious effort involved. Some behaviors take more conscious effort, such as completing a chain of mathematical tasks to achieve a single goal at work or following a food recipe. Other behaviors are more procedural, such as exiting a room or the process of folding laundry. Many times behaviors present with clear physical action patterns that signal someone is *behaving*, while other behaviors are sometimes presented as a state of inaction. This could be in the case for a person with severe depression who vegetates and stays in bed, which only maintains depressive symptoms.

Behaviors are also highly contextual. The behavior can be influenced by general life circumstances, environmental stimuli, internal states related to thinking, emotions, and other sensations. This includes the whole context of a single behavior. Due to prior learning or conditioning, *pairing* the fear of pain, sounds of drilling, blood and the anticipation of bad news with the sight and smell of a dental office, many people may feel anxious and tense right when they walk into their next dental appointment. In this context a person may behave in a nervous manner by asking the dentist a hundred questions before a procedure, or become more sarcastic than usual to help lower their tension. While environmental conditions directly affect behavior based on prior learning, internal states can also influence behaviors directly within the environmental context. Sitting in the dentist's office, a person can produce realistic self-talk about the evidence that in all the years they've been coming to the dentist, their worst fears never came true. They can also focus their attention on the stimulating art in the room or close their eyes and imagine themselves leaving the dentist's office feeling relief and a sense of accomplishment. Shifting the context directly through internal states in this situation, the person may feel more relieved and now behave in more pleasant ways by talking casually with the staff and expressing interest what's on TV during the dental procedure.

It's a general notion that most behaviors aim to maximize pleasure, while others try to minimize pain. The subtle behavior of exiting a room may be a sub-goal to achieve the pleasure of going home and taking a nap to relax, while humor at the dentist helps escape the discomfort of the anxiety. Reinforcement and punishment shapes behaviors, and further influences what behaviors come out in specific contexts. A set of social behaviors become "reinforced" during a dinner party, such as laughter, spontaneous chatter, and picture-taking, while the same set of behaviors may be "punished" and inhibited in a classroom context.

Behaviors are a manifestation of the complex interplay between the universe of the mind and the immediate external environment. This view of behavior becomes more three-dimensional and complete when you consider the internal processes, contextual features and reinforcing properties of the behavioral experience. Some foundations of behavior are based on instincts and reflexes, as seen in spontaneous physical movements with infants in response to their environment, such as eye gaze with their caregiver or grip action with objects. As the brain develops in early childhood, children's behavior becomes more motivated by their emotional experiences trying to influence their environment, as seen in tantrums and imaginative re-enactments. As the brain further develops in late childhood, the mind does a more adequate job of inhibiting inappropriate social behaviors, and self-control to consciously manage more challenging environments. This developmental sequence presents how sophisticated behaviors become as the given brain configurations become available through development. These varying levels of sophistication are also present throughout the lifespan, based on the difficulty of the behavioral task, available mental resources and environmental demands. If someone yells, "Watch out!" it only takes a physical reflex to look over, sit up and move our legs in a walking motion to get out of the way. Other behaviors may be more motivated by our emotional world, such as saying comments in an aggressive tone during an interpersonal conflict, while more sophisticated states of mind may activate higher cortical areas in the brain to reduce physical arousal and think things through to help us behave more assertively during the interpersonal stressor. Furthermore, the new assertive behavior becomes reinforced by a desirable response from the other person, and this behavior may be expressed again with less conscious effort in a future stressful context. These various learned behavioral processes develop a string of habitual behavioral patterns throughout our lifespan that makes up the self.

As behavior patterns are a fluid process throughout everyday life and across our lifespan, many of us are achieving *behavioral health* as a goal in various areas of our lives. We are trying to eat healthier, commit more consistently to exercise routines, manage time better, improve intimate relationships, and many other things that are beyond the scope of this book. We find behavioral health everywhere in our lives and throughout our cultures. The concepts of "behavioral" or "mental" health have been used interchangeably in the field of clinical psychology. It's understood that engaging in healthy behaviors promotes a state of a healthy mind, while engaging in healthy states of mind promotes a state of healthy behavior patterns. Mental or behavioral health has traditionally been viewed as a field concerned with alleviating abnormalities or deficits. This view places an unjustified negative stigma on behavioral-mental health as a whole, because any person can work on achieving more mental-behavioral health. New wave behavioral health places more emphasis on improving individualized areas in a person's lifestyle to promote a fully functioning self. Since this chapter opened up with the groundwork about behavior in general, we can build on that to better understand the targets for change with some of the most challenging behaviors.

This book takes a close look at addiction and substance-use behavior as a whole. Substance-use behaviors, whether involving alcohol, heroin, or caffeine use, strive to achieve or maintain behavioral health in a variety of ways. This may be to enhance physical energy, social fulfillment, creativity, boredom reduction or to relieve depression. An issue occurs when substance-use behaviors create consequences and end up disrupting individual mental health in the long run. Substance misuse has long been considered a societal issue in our culture. The twentieth century faced the alcohol prohibition era, the crack epidemic in the 1980s, issues with opioid pain medications, and the debate about the "war on drugs." People discuss the annual multi-million-dollar cost of addiction in our country, while the impact of substance abuse, from drug-related violence to tragic automobile accidents and overdoses, touches many communities throughout the U.S. Families watch loved ones experience the devastating consequences of addictive behaviors and often feel sad, angry and confused. But we also have to remember, as the neuroscientist Carl Hart emphasizes in his research, that the majority of people who use illicit substances do not abuse them or ever develop an addiction.[1] Substance use will always be a subject of interest in culture, and "just saying no" and fear signaling are unhelpful narratives to project, as we will explore.

The varying levels of social platforms related to substances trickle down from culture to the foundation of the individual who engages in the direct substance-use behavior. The individual can experience some of the most devastating consequences related to substance use, which may vary in severity. A brief glance at individual consequences includes the annoying hangover on a Sunday morning for a person who drinks casually, to social shame, to unreasonable felony drug convictions and severe health issues. This book is about the individual who engages in substance-use behavior, whether they experience severe consequences, minimal consequences or no consequences at all and they would just like to grow a better understanding about the processes of substance-use behavior in general. While we may feel powerless to solve the war on drugs or advocate for new drug conviction policies, my goal as a behavioral health professional is to take a bottom-up approach to addressing society's relationship with substance use. This approach with the individual grasps the authentic relationship between a person and the substance, which drives the uproar in the higher social platforms related to substance use. The euphoria the individual experiences when their biological systems ingest a substance is a robust force that flares into the stream of culture. As we better understand human behavior, the bottom-up approach can produce more effective solutions to preserve the array of resources that substance use costs in our societies and within the individual.

Substance misuse behaviors have a historic reputation of being highly challenging to change compared to other behavioral health concerns. Many people who experience issues with anxiety or depression do not find any part of the experience pleasant, but continue to engage in behaviors and mental states that maintain the unpleasant experience without realizing it. The unpleasant experience can help someone be a little more motivated to change their behaviors compared to substance-use behaviors, since a major component of the behavior is a pleasurable one. Other mental health issues also have a clearer formulation of *what it is*, and how to effectively overcome it.

Many people with depression engage in behaviors that maintain symptoms, such as self-isolating, lying around, and giving up, while engaging in negative self-talk and rumination about themselves, the future and past failures. Much of the treatment works on monitoring symptoms, deliberately engaging in new behaviors that target the maladaptive behaviors, and restructuring of thought processes that perpetuate mood discomfort. Engaging in new behaviors will help people with depression feel more accomplished in themselves and see the future as more worthwhile. Then thinking in more realistic ways will enhance motivation to engage in healthier behaviors, and these behaviors will further encourage healthy mental states. This enriches a healthy mood cycle, reducing depressive symptoms and building up mental–behavioral health.

The primary behavior that maintains anxiety issues is called "avoidance," often carried out while simultaneously engaging in unhelpful thinking patterns about a feared stimulus. A person who experiences panic attacks may avoid situations that may enhance anxiety symptoms, and further misperceive or catastrophize that their mild anxiety symptoms are actually a medical concern, which further develops into a panic attack. Then the person engages in "safety behaviors," such as gripping the wall, which only perpetuate the thinking that they are going to have a heart attack, and then the panic continues. In simple terms, the treatment includes intentionally exposing oneself to anxiety-provoking stimuli, reappraising the anxiety symptoms with a more realistic view, and dropping safety behaviors.

On the other hand, substance abuse behaviors are highly rewarding, which makes it more difficult to change them, because they bring some type of enhanced immediate benefit. Many times substance use does not need to be changed. A person who has a daily coffee habit may not experience a significant amount of consequences or lifestyle impairment to need a change in their behavior. A person who is engaged in a daily heroin habit continues to experience reinforcement, whether it's the excitement of preparing the syringe, experiencing euphoria from the effect, or just using to escape the discomfort of withdrawal symptoms. While they continue to experience immediate reward, they may have ongoing consequences related to health risks, financial costs, social isolation, mood difficulties, and preoccupation with using. These are the emblematic aspects of substance abuse behavior. The behavior is achieving some type of reward, whether it is enhancing pleasure or escaping pain, while continuing a spiral of negative consequences. Using any substances is not necessarily a "bad" thing in itself; but the context of the behavior can make it negative. Doing an insignificant dose of pure cocaine for a healthy functioning adult is not necessarily bad, although cocaine is illegal in the U.S., so just possessing it puts you at risk of receiving a felony conviction. You would also have to put yourself in physical danger buying from a drug dealer, and then you would not know what type of substance or dosage you were actually getting. For the individual, the effect of cocaine can put them at risk of engaging in other high-risk behaviors, potentially experiencing acute health risks, and the risk that the person may come to like the effect after the single dose *too much*. This can be the case for any existing substances or rewarding behaviors, but cultures place various restrictions on different behaviors, and each individual has a different relationship with the substance or behavior. This connects to the other challenges of changing substance abuse behaviors, such as the complex relationship between biological, psychological and environmental components that impact the behavioral pattern. The more the behavior becomes rewarding for an individual, the higher the likelihood that it could be repeated, and in turn have more potential consequences in health, emotional, financial, social and legal areas of lifestyle functioning.

Substance use should be celebrated and enjoyed in cultures, but at the same time should be appreciated and approached earnestly. Substance use is major part of the culture here in the U.S. Alcohol use is popular in routine social activities throughout the week, and the cannabis culture has been booming ever since states have legalized cannabis for recreational use. A 2012 study by Christensen and colleagues examined the drug- and alcohol-related lyrical content of 496 Billboard Top 100 songs from 1968 to 2008. The authors found that alcohol- and drug-related lyrical content in music has been steadily increasing since 1968, and has dramatically increased since 1998.[2] They also found that the songs with such content portrayed a significantly more positive image than a negative one. These findings imply that substance use has become more popular and accepted in U.S. culture. While culture influences human behavior, human behavior influences what culture and the media are motivated to portray in different forms of entertainment and advertising. As society at large plays a major role in guiding individual behavioral patterns, the goal of this book is to place more resources within individuals to guide their own behavior and to achieve behavioral health. Cultural messages trickle down to individual behavior, as we take an upward approach, transforming individual behavior to ultimately change our entire culture's relationship with substance use and addiction.

A separate challenge regarding substance abuse behaviors being difficult to change is that the current treatment paradigm in North America is not effective for everyone who can benefit from some type of behavioral health intervention. Substance abuse behaviors are highly pathologized in the treatment industry, where *everyone* who comes to seek treatment is said to have a "disease," labeled an "addict" or "alcoholic," and expected to strive towards the same goal of abstinence for the rest of their lives, or else the person is considered "resistant." According to an American Psychological Association (APA) source, 23 million people in the U.S. each year meet the criteria for a Substance Use Disorder, while only 3 million of them get treatment.[3] This means that 87% of people who have issues with substance use do not seek or receive some type of help. One of the factors that I believe is impacting this trend is our culture's current approach to overcoming addiction.

It's been estimated that 74 to 90% of treatment centers in the U.S. rely on a 12-Step model approach, while encompassing other forms of treatment interventions. In fast, 12-Step self-help support programs such as Alcoholics Anonymous (A.A.) and Narcotics Anonymous (N.A.) have a lot of beneficial and effective components for helping issues with substance use, which I will flesh out later in this book. Still, there continues to remain a language in the addiction industry adopted from the 12-Step philosophy that contributes to the very low treatment initiation rate. The 12-Step programs have been around since the 1930s and their original principles have greatly influenced the current treatment approach to substance abuse; they have become universal concepts in the industry. Consequently, every substance abuse pattern is considered diseased, individuals acquire the label of an addict, and every person is expected to have the same treatment goal. It's not surprising that people with minimal to mild consequences or severity will not seek any type of treatment, to avoid being labeled and assigned a universal goal for the rest of their lives. A large portion of these 23 million people will only meet the criteria for a *mild* Substance Use Disorder. Moreover, people will not seek treatment until their substance use becomes more *severe*, so that they fit the highly pathologized description of substance misuse. This approach plays off the expired idea that behavioral health only addresses abnormalities or deficits. A lot more responsibility needs to be placed on the treatment industry and its providers to change the language related to substance misuse, and deliver a variety of treatment options to improve the rate of treatment initiation in our culture.

Over the past century, the field in substance abuse has been deliberating about what theory best describes what addiction is. An early approach to addiction is that it's a "moral failing." This view is understood to mean that people who abuse substances possess a character flaw or defect that motivates their addiction. Naïve as it is, people understood addiction as a moral failing to make sense of the paradoxical observation of engaging in substance abuse behaviors despite their creating consequences and impacting those around them. But morality is highly subjective, and not every person who misuses substances or has an addiction engages in "immoral" behaviors that violate the moral standards of other people. Substance misuse is not an immoral action in itself. Therefore, the moral failing approach could not explain the varied cases of addiction, nor could it explain substance-use behavior in general. We now understand that addiction has many facets, including a component at the biological level. Emerging from the neuroscience revolution of the late twentieth century, the Disease Model of addiction has become the primary view of what addiction *is*. The "disease versus moral failing" debate of the past has become deflated. So we can cease to consider the moral failing or character defect explanation completely.

But then is addiction or substance abuse really a disease? First, the main premise that drives the disease concept is that the brain experiences plastic changes through repeated substance use, enhancing compulsion despite nega-tive consequences. This is true, but the brain changing does not make it a "dis-ease" *per se*, but merely a natural process that occurs in the brain when a person learns something new or develops habits. Neuroscientists in the field have been reinterpreting the neurobiological data pertaining to addictions and substance abuse. They have come to debunk the idea that it's a disease, and see it more as mere *learning*. This is depicted in the neuroscientist Marc Lewis's book *The Biology of Desire*. Second, saying that it's a disease because people keep using or cannot stop despite negative consequences is a false blanket statement. While some people do continue to use substances despite negative consequences, many people quit or reduce their consumption due to consequences all the time, as well. We will discuss more about the disease concept in a later chapter, and readers can draw their own conclusions. The American Psychological Association (APA) describes addiction as a *chronic disorder* and not as a dis-ease: the disorder description is informed by the complex relationship between biology, psychology and the environment. But if developing an addiction is a natural learning process, is it still considered a "disorder," or is it a disorder as a result of the behavior's consequences? The *self-medicating* approach is a popular view as well, but is not complete enough to explain every substance abuse pattern. So what theory or understanding best describes addiction? Well, we can start by saying it's a *behavior*.

This book will introduce a Behavioral Approach to substance use and addic-tion. In the argument over what addiction *is*, there has never been any con-sideration given to the concept that addiction is simply a robust behavioral experience. The behavioral model may seem like an obvious oversimplification of the complex and perplexing aspects of substance abuse; however, the model that will be discussed is a comprehensive approach towards addiction and *all* substance use in general. It's not so important what we call or label this behav-ioral health concern; what's important is how we conceptualize it and under-stand its complete features in order to best overcome it.

I have developed the Vacuum Approach – M.E.R. Model, which is a strictly behavioral formulation for substance abuse and substance-use behavior in any form. This model unmasks the complexity of addiction in a concise manner, encompassing all the necessary features that make up a substance-use behavior. M.E.R. stands for *Mindfulness, Exposure,* and *Reinforcement.* These three concepts represent the organic processes or components that make up the substance-use behavior itself, whether it's an addiction or healthy use of substances. The Mindfulness component represents the *habitual* aspects of the behavior; Exposure represents the *contextual* features of the behavior; and Reinforcement represents the *pleasurable* properties of the behavior. Calling addiction or substance abuse a "behavior" suffices as long as M.E.R. explains all the parts that make up the mere behavior, while attending as well to the challenges of modifying addictive behaviors.

The Vacuum Approach uncovers the key developmental or underlying components that contribute to the output of the behavior. The Vacuum posits that there are five primary developmental factors that manufacture a person's unique substance-use behavioral pattern, which we will break down later. These five factors that make up a total person flow into a single *vacuum* of the reward system in the brain as the substance-use behavioral process begins. Then this "vacuum" filters the output of M.E.R., which makes up the single overt substance-use behavior. This whole model is an integrative approach that combines the understanding of various parts of the human experience, from genetic molecular functioning to the observable behavior within the person's unique environment during any moment of their total lifespan. This model places importance on the behavior itself and the function of it. We will examine this model in more depth in the coming chapters.

Meeting many people in my personal and professional life over the years that use substances in a variety of ways has shed light on the fact that everyone is truly different in some way. This truth influenced me to ask questions about the traditional approaches to addiction treatment. It has made me curious about the various features that contribute to these differences in behavioral patterns with substances. Here we will consider some examples that inform necessary questions.

I think it's safe to say that adolescent and young adult substance use *generally* looks different than use by later adulthood cohorts. A set of college-aged individuals who possess the same substance abuse behavior pattern throughout college may have very different trajectories with substance use later in life. While some of these individuals naturally reduce or change their substance abuse behavioral pattern when they leave college, others may continue their behavior pattern throughout their adulthood. I have worked with a person who was a truck driver and would only abuse substances during the periods when he was not working. He would not use any substances when he was truck driving for weeks at a time, but he would binge use cocaine when he was home for weeks with nothing to do. I've met many people who developed a daily habit with heroin, but could take or leave alcohol and let it sit in their fridge for weeks without touching it even if they were sober from heroin. Some people may misuse alcohol to cope with their trauma and escape everyday life, but later in their life they learn to use alcohol at healthier levels. Also, why is it that many people who have an extensive trauma history and have a lot of current life stress never develop a substance abuse pattern? What about the housewife who starts to drink a little more wine during the day after dealing with the stresses of raising children when her mother died, but as time passed she was able to get back to her healthy level of alcohol use? Another important example to consider is the person who seems to have an ongoing struggle with either reducing their substance use or maintaining sobriety no matter how much help or treatment they get for their addiction. While many of us have felt this to be a hopeless circumstance, the importance in helping the person lies in the precise features within their behavioral pattern. What *exactly* is happening between them being sober and having the first drink, between the first drink and six drinks, and then between that day and the next day of substance misuse? Why can some people achieve wellness without any type of treatment, while others have multiple treatment episodes without personal success? These individual cases pose questions about why something turned out the way it did and then how and why it changed, or how some people's experiences were similar but the results turned out different or similar. Whatever the behavioral pattern is, each individual case encompasses a wide array of elements that contribute to the behavior. So it's not logical to consider a single-way approach.

Other behavioral health concerns, such as unhealthy eating habits, sex addiction or excessive buying can provide insight into substance abuse behaviors. People who developed food addictions cannot focus on abstinence as goal because humans need to eat to survive. So people with unhealthy food habits that they want to change utilize strategies to change individual behaviors with food. Their goals may be to limit themselves to one sweet a day, cut out sugar all together, eat more meals throughout the day in small portions or deliberately abstain from eating when they feel bored or stressed. A person's goal with sex addiction may only be to quit engaging in extramarital affairs, while another's goal could be to reduce their viewing of pornographic material to fill a void in their intimate relationship. When we break down these various addictions into the form of a behavioral approach, it is no longer necessary to label a person an "addict," saying they have a "disease," and supposing that everyone should achieve the same goal. Other behavioral addictions demonstrate how the individualized behavioral pattern holds the primary significance, and that each person has their own vision for behavioral health achievement.

The vision of this book is to contribute to the paradigm shift that is occurring in the field of substance abuse and addiction as a whole. This shift is happening through the development of alternative recovery programs, such as S.M.A.R.T. Recovery and Refuge Recovery, TED Talks about shaping our culture's view on drugs, journalists rebranding addiction, and clinicians utilizing progressive practices to manage substance use. There have been a lot of great ideas and new approaches in the field in the recent years, but we have yet to capture a complete and comprehensive framework on what addiction *is*. Part of this challenge is trying to develop a model that is not limiting, while addressing all of the complex features of an addictive pattern. Right now we have a lot of isolated concepts that are not integrated into a needed framework. We currently have several substance abuse treatment modalities, including Cognitive-Behavioral Therapy (CBT), Dialectical-Behavior Therapy (DBT), Motivational Interviewing (MI), recovery support programs, and Medication-Assisted Treatments (MATs), all gathered under the disease umbrella. The Vacuum Approach conceptualizes a behavioral model for substance use that integrates principles from established concepts in psychology, while welcoming the use of new practices.

This book is written for a wide range of audiences from mental–behavioral health professionals and policy makers, to families, individuals and philosophers. I hope this model can help clinicians view substance abuse in an innovative way, and can be used as a blueprint for program development and integration. A self-help feature of this book can assist individuals and families in achieving behavioral health through their own autonomy. This can be especially beneficial for people who do not have access to treatment due to lifestyle, geographical location or finances. Some of the language that will be used to explain concepts may sound technical. This is so professionals can easily recognize and understand concepts, and others will be able to put a name to what they experience and what tools are needed. Using jargon and special terms for behavioral health is equivalent to utilizing the names and functions of household tools and processes to address other areas of lifestyle health. The goal of this is for people to become masters of their own behavioral health. This is crucial. Just as we know the technical functions of personal dental care to address dental hygiene, know how to prepare multiple meals for nutritional benefit or navigate common medical recommendations, people should understand how to influence the processes of healthy mind and behavior states. The next part of this book will be more technical and mechanical, while the last part of the book will tie major concepts of addiction in with the presenting model. The ideas in this book will be expressed in a versatile way. Some ideas will be expressed through established scholarly research, while other ideas may be presented through clinical anecdotes or my professional and personal opinions. Therefore, this book has a strategy to accomplish many feats, from individual meaning to cultural shifts, through education and discussion. You are encouraged to read this book multiple times or use it as a reference to really grasp its concepts and make the skills applicable if you're addressing your own substance use.

While substance misuse is an issue that will never be eliminated, I envision that there will be an overall severity reduction of substance-use behaviors with increased treatment initiation. I believe a way to achieve this is by treatment providers and professionals helping to change the cultural and therapeutic language related to addictions. Also, the industry needs to offer more varied treatment options and alter the overall attitude about behavioral health. As the approach of behavioral–mental health changes, people will feel less shame seeking help and view behavioral health as being as routine as addressing any other lifestyle concern. This implies that people will seek treatment a lot earlier on to adjust their substance-use behavior pattern as a result of minimal to mild consequences, instead of higher severities. Furthermore, as more people seek treatment sooner, the cost of treatment can decrease and availability can become more widespread in communities. Substance abuse and behavioral health as a whole needs continuing reform to capture its essence from within the falsehood of cultural narratives.

part 2

The Approach

chapter 2

Origins
Why does the behavior occur?

EVERYDAY BEHAVIORS COME FROM FARAWAY places. These places stretch as far back as anywhere from a moment ago to life events throughout our lifespan, including early childhood experiences and the embryo, to genetic mutations from biological parents, intergenerational dynamics, and the last hundred thousand years of human evolution. Single behaviors are influenced by a combination of these different routes through human history, while various facets of the total individual influence their present behavior. For example, a person's *people pleasing* behaviors are a result of this complex interaction. It can be assumed that people pleasing, along with its closely connected emotion *shame,* could have been naturally selected over thousands of years because it favored group living. This created more opportunities for reproduction, and further shaped cultural and family values. Therefore, a person's single people pleasing occurrence can result from the relationship between their genetic propensity, cultural background, personality characteristics, history of experiencing social shame, and current social functioning. This complex process of behavior development can be seen in the common observation, "nature versus nurture." Nature is considered the mere inherited genetic influence on behavior, in which genes have been developed, refined, and replicated across thousands of generations. On the other hand, nurture is considered to be all the factors that may affect behavior after conception, within the limits of genetic endowment.

Various theories of human development have considered a multidimensional approach to how a number of factors, and their interactions, contribute to the development of various aspects of human functioning. These interactions may begin in the womb. D.F. Swaab, in *We Are Our Brains,* asserts that girls exposed to high levels of testosterone due to an adrenal gland disorder in the womb, as well as being exposed to other chemicals, have higher chances of becoming bisexual or lesbian.[1] Maturationists are interested in how biological milestones greatly affect early human development, such as physical capability to start walking around twelve months of age; neural expansion to be able to produce language; and cognitive development throughout early years of school. Information processing, integrated with punishment-reward learning theories and biological temperament, can have profound explanatory power regarding social, emotional, and overall personality development. Later, throughout the stages of adulthood, cultural expectations, natural disasters, changes to the social environment, personal milestones, and mere aging may have more influence on human development than earlier processes. It would take a lot of discussion to explore the depths and various directions of behavior development as a whole, but for our purposes, the current conversation sets out the context of how complex it can be to understand the developmental factors of addictive behaviors.

One psychotherapy modality in particular demonstrates the challenges of working with the depth and complexity of human development. Psychoanalysis or psychodynamic therapy, as set out by Freud, focuses on making the unconscious part of the mind conscious and reducing the use of primitive defense mechanisms in the hope of relieving emotional distress and enhancing insight, so as to further empower healthy behaviors. As a person provides a stream of consciousness narrative of their week, daily concerns, and reactions to the therapist, the person is providing clues about relatable experiences from their past or important personal themes that are embedded in the neural structures of their unconscious memory. Our unconscious manifests itself in everyday behaviors and overt expressions upon the canvas of present life. The unconscious consists of biological instincts, earliest emotional experiences that we have long forgotten, repetitious messages that were received from prominent figures in our life, all our behaviors that reinforce unconscious material, and other dynamics that cannot be brought into awareness by the conscious mind at once. Throughout counseling, the therapist makes interpretations and provides feedback about the themes and associations that the person produces in conscious language so as to better understand who they are and the behaviors that lie within their developmental history. I've worked with a man who seemed to frequently get irritated and oppose me when I would introduce concepts during sessions. I'd often feel frustrated, but as I caught on to this theme I began to point out, "It seems that you're irritated with me right now and you have gotten irritated with me before when I introduced new ideas. What do you think about that?"

He said, "Well, you're insinuating that I don't know what I'm doing. I told you in the past, as long as I'm working, things will work out."

I continued, "Oh. You're taking it as I'm telling you how to do things. I'm wondering if you have experienced this in the past?"

He stated, "Well, you kind of remind me of my father. He always used to say how I could do this or that differently."

Even though I'm thirty years younger than this man, the way I behaved during sessions elicited an unconscious memory of how his father used to act towards him. This unconscious material that became activated made the man respond in an emotionally distressed way and he was completely unaware of its origin. After he uncovered this insight he was able to work with me more freely, and was able to recognize how he could be rough around the edges with others, which further led him to behave in more flexible ways. Psychoanalysis can be a long dynamic process, but it validates the point of how developmental factors in mental-behavioral health are never fully captured. Due to human development being such a diverse process, we can never be one hundred percent certain as to the exact developmental nature and origins of our behaviors.

It has been commonly understood that many views on the development of addictive behaviors consider that a combination of genes and environment play a role. Much of the field stresses the idea that a person can have around 50% genetic probability that they will develop an addiction if they have a close biological relative with an addiction. However, some addiction experts believe that all addiction is rooted in trauma or emotionally painful experiences, and that genes do not matter as much as these other factors. While both of these claims contain some truth, they may not explain every case of substance abuse and do not target all the pertinent factors in developing an addiction. Also, while many people with substance abuse behaviors have some type of trauma history or other mental health issues, in many cases their use of substances may not be directly related to these issues, but related to other factors that can be commonly overlooked.

As I attempted to portray earlier, the development of human behavior can be a complex process and substance-use behaviors are not so simple, either. Here I will introduce the five primary factors that I believe contribute to the development and presentation of all substance-use behaviors. This Five Factor approach hopes to explain the individualized patterns of substance use and address the significant factors across the lifespan as a person's substance-use behavior changes throughout their life. Every person will experience these five factors differently, and the magnitude of the effect of each factor on their behavior will differ from person to person. While these factors can be connected to each other, the factors are very precise and distinct from one another as they relate to the influence on substance-use behaviors.

FIVE FACTOR DEVELOPMENT FOR SUBSTANCE-USE BEHAVIORS
FACTOR ONE: GENES

Our genetic blueprint that we all inherited creates a foundation for how our personal genes influence our behavior with substances in general and with specific substances respectively. Many of us know someone who always seems to get sick or experience significant side effects whenever they take a dose of an opioid pain medication. A particular gene variation that modifies the process of the enzyme CYP2D6, which helps break down and metabolize common analgesics, plays a substantial role in this effect.[2] While there are some people who can take enough painkillers to kill a small village, there is also a population that processes medications in different ways. I've heard some people talk about how a shot of espresso makes them too jittery, while other people notice they can easily go to sleep after having a cup of coffee. I have worked with a handful of people who did not enjoy the effects of cocaine, and would only desire cocaine if they first got intoxicated with alcohol. So although it's not always clear how much of our behavior with substances is impacted by environmental elements, we do know that genes alone do have an impact. The Gene factor for the development of substance-use behaviors will be laid out in this section as a distinct factor that emphasizes the baseline effect of genes on behavior.

There is no "addiction gene," but there are certain genes that could make a person more vulnerable to developing substance abuse behaviors, while other genes may help inhibit substance misuse. As the Learn.Genetics Science Learning Center so eloquently put it this way, "Not every addict will carry the same gene(s), and not everyone who carries an 'addiction gene' will exhibit the trait."[3] This indicates that genes are not a predetermination that a person will develop addictive behaviors based only on DNA, and that there are other factors to consider, which we will get to later in this chapter. Also, some specific genes that influence substance-use behaviors may have a direct effect on organs that process the substances, such as liver enzymes, while others may have a direct impact on neurotransmitters and other chemical processes in the brain. Genetics can also play a complex role at different stages of the substance use experience, such as the quality or euphoric effect of a single use of the substance, rate of tolerance and sensitization, and severity of withdrawal symptoms.[4] Therefore, since genes play a diverse role in behavior, substance-use behaviors present in diverse ways in diverse people.

There are some common genetic variations that can impact a person's substance-use behavior. People who abuse cocaine or alcohol are more likely to have an A1 allele of the D2 dopamine receptor gene, or to lack the Htr1b gene for a serotonin receptor.[3] People who experience negative side effects from smoking tobacco are more likely to have a protective genetic variation of CYP2A6.[3] A mutation of the PER2 gene can increase drinking behavior three times more in rats, while the presence of a multiple variation of ALDH2 is common in a population that does not abuse alcohol.[3] Other research studies have found a difference in frequency and level of substance use intake among individuals with different genetic variations.[5, 6, 7] With some people this can result from the genetic variants impacting the effects of a substance, for example, people without a particular opioid receptor gene may experience alcohol as having more of a sedative effect, while others who have the gene variant experience alcohol as having more stimulating effects.[8] The implications: that people who abuse substances may present different substance-use behaviors, and could be motivated to use substances for different reasons, based on their genetic make-up. Furthermore, a person who abuses alcohol can be more likely to drink excessively to cope with stress or block out painful memories if they experience more sedative effects, while a person who experiences the stimulating effects may be more likely to binge drink when they go out with their friends, for example. Therefore, the relationship between genes and individual substance use can play a role in the context of the behavior. The former person may be more at risk to abuse alcohol at home alone while naturally drinking less when out with co-workers, whereas the latter person with the opioid gene variant may dislike drinking at home during the week but look forward to nights of drinking on the weekend. Most of this is speculative, due to the complexity of individual behaviors and other genetic circumstances that impact behavior. But this demonstrates how genes alone have a bearing on the motivation and inhibition of substance use.

The use of medications for addiction provides some insight into how altering gene expression can influence overt behavior expression related to substance use. Naltrexone has been found to help people reduce excessive drinking behavior and reduce cravings for alcohol.[9, 10] The primary way this medication works is by blocking the effects of particular opioid receptors that modulate dopaminergic-reward activity, which influences "reward" processing of alcohol and further alcohol abuse potential. Naltrexone has typically been paired with alcohol use for the goal of stopping or reducing drinking through the practice known as the Sinclair Method.[11] This method works by taking a dose of Naltrexone one hour before a person starts drinking, and as they drink they will experience the intoxicating effects of the alcohol but not necessarily the rewarding aspects of the substance. Therefore, drinking behavior should naturally lessen, since the rewarding effects are absent, as the person continues taking the medication, which is a process called "behavioral extinction." Medication assistance for substance misuse has been traditionally associated with the medical-disease model of addiction due to the nature of this intervention, but that outlook is not necessary. Simply put, the use of these different medications helps alter gene and neurobiological expression, therefore producing different *behaviors* with substance use.

Genetic testing in the treatment of substance abuse can be highly benefi-cial for understanding the foundation of individual substance-use behavior. Many people who abuse substances are polydrug users as well, that is, they use a combination of two or more substances. Having insight into genetic markers can help us better understand the nature and context of polydrug use behavior. Also, genetic testing can help inform treatment implications for moderation management success or the use of medication assistance. Geneticists are encouraged to work with the field of addiction treatment to develop a taxonomy of specified gene variants. A taxonomy system can be used to help identify genetic profiles of individual vulnerabilities and then safeguards against developing addictive behavioral patterns with substances. Genes are carved out as a distinct factor that forms the groundwork for how the combinations of genes impact behavior through an inherent attraction and as a natural phenomenon with a substance.

FACTOR TWO: PSYCHOLOGICAL

The second factor that I have identified is the *Psychological* factor; as a distin-guishable element this can often be overlooked and not viewed exclusively (i.e. on its own), the way other developmental factors of substance-use behavior are viewed. This factor does not include mental illness or emotional health in particular. Instead, it focuses on other psychological processes, which include personality traits, impulsivity, executive or cognitive functioning on self-reg-ulation, features of the developing brain, and other psychological character-istics that can contribute to substance use. Many people may be engaging in substance misuse, not due to "mental health" issues or because of trauma, but because there are other psychological factors that could be a primary influence on their behavior.

Executive functioning includes processes located in the frontal lobe of the brain, or more specifically the prefrontal cortex (PFC), which is responsible for planning, decision-making, impulse control, attention functionality, processing speed, and other sophisticated cognitive processes. Impulsivity is acting out of whim without foresight or reflection about the behavior or its consequences, which can be highly recognized in addictive behaviors. Impulsivity for some individuals can be exclusively related to executive or cognitive functioning, while for others impulsivity can be more a part of their personality structure. Personality traits that will be pertinent in our discussion include novelty- or sensation-seeking, adventurousness, grandiosity, and extroversion. Attention-Deficit/Hyperactivity Disorder (ADHD) is also considered to be under the category of the Psychological factor, due to the nature of its symptoms and how it can potentially impact substance use. ADHD most commonly presents during childhood development. But adults with ADHD may present with a cluster of symptoms, such as hyperactivity, fidgeting, forgetfulness, disorganization, difficulty with focus or hyperfocus, risky behavior, and experiencing boredom easily. We will now consider some of the research related to the Psychological factor.

It's been demonstrated in multiple studies through neuropsychological testing that lower executive functioning has been a risk factor preceding substance abuse behaviors, while other studies did not find a connection between executive functioning and substance abuse.[12] This implies that not everyone who develops addictive behaviors or misuses substances has lower executive functioning, but for some people this can be one risk factor among others. A disposition of lower executive functioning in a person who receives some type of benefit or reward from substances could mean some risk for substance misuse related to attention inflexibility on substance-related stimuli, leading to challenges with decision-making for substance use related behaviors. General executive functions are closely tied to impulse control concepts, related personality traits, and other psychological factors, such as ADHD.

A 2014 study with 297 individuals had a significant finding that people who did not regularly use substances scored lower on impulsivity and thrill-seeking traits.[13] Others, who regularly used cannabis and nicotine, scored higher on thrill-seeking and lower on the executive functioning characteristics.[13] Having more impulsivity or sensation-seeking personality traits may have a greater impact on a person's attitudes, expectations, and willingness to use substances in the future.[14] This relates to the concept of "delay reward discounting," which is a concept that helps measure a person's impulsivity. Delay reward discounting looks at whether a person can delay an immediate reward to receive a similar or larger reward later. Obviously the more difficulty a person has delaying the reward for the future, the higher they may measure for impulsivity. It has been consistently found that people without addictive patterns are able to delay rewards more easily than others with addictive behavioral patterns. [15, 16] At the same time, impulsivity can be a process in itself, associated with executive functioning. Personality traits can potentially have an indirect impact on impulse control, delay reward discounting, and attitudes about future substance use. It's possible that some people's grandiose personality traits make them feel overly confident, leading them to be more open to new experiences or to justify the risk potential related to substance use. This can further influence them to act impulsively. Also, being more extroverted can have a similar impact, perhaps making people more likely to put themselves in social contexts where others are using substances.

I do not like the concept of the "addictive personality," because this idea seems too rigid, and creates more stigma. It carries a connotation that someone is predetermined to develop an addictive pattern. Also, I do not consider there to be a standard personality of addiction. I believe it is more productive to break down the specific traits or psychological factors as they relate to the behavioral patterns. Maybe someone is simply poor at delaying gratification for something they enjoy that is available to them (e.g., chocolate), or their novelty-seeking or adventurous personality traits motivate them to seek out potentially high-risk substances because it provides them a stimulating and fulfilling experience. Unlike direct personality characteristics, ADHD can have a relationship with developing addictive behavior patterns.[17, 18] The understanding that people with ADHD generally have lower levels of dopamine in the brain helps explain why 10 to 30% of people who abuse cocaine also have ADHD.[19] Stimulant drugs often prescribed for ADHD, like Ritalin, mimic the effect of cocaine, increasing dopamine levels in the brain and so helping people with ADHD to be more focused, calm, and regulated. On the other hand, a person without ADHD who takes cocaine may experience the effect of the stimulant with more mental intensity and physical arousal. Consequently, a person with ADHD could be at risk for developing an addictive pattern by directly enhancing the dopamine in the brain through the use of a stimulant drug, while others with ADHD may use other substances that increase stimulation and help reduce boredom.

The last *Psychological* characteristic that we will consider as contributing to developing substance-use behaviors is related to the features of the developing brain. Having a brain younger than 25 to 30 years old automatically puts a person at risk for developing substance abuse due to the frontal lobe not being fully developed until the mid- to late 20s. This is represented by the peak of impulsivity, sensation-seeking and possible risk-taking behaviors in adolescence through emerging adulthood because of premature personality and executive functioning.[20] This can explain why substance-use behaviors *generally* present differently in adolescence and emerging adulthood than in later adulthood cohorts. Adolescents and young adults can be more curious about experimenting with different types of substances, and may engage in binge use, along with other high-risk experimenting behaviors. Substance-use behaviors may change drastically throughout a person's lifespan, and the developing brain is a major characteristic that needs to be considered, especially if young people seek treatment.

Again, the characteristics here do not predetermine the development of addictive behaviors, but they can be an influence, among the other factors discussed in this chapter. In fact, concepts like delay reward discounting and other psychological characteristics can be a mere result of a developed addiction due to changes in the brain. But the Psychological factor as a whole in this section looks at the person's general disposition in terms of these characteristics that contribute to the behavior. The *Psychological* factor was difficult to name, because I wanted to make sure to encompass all the necessary characteristics that I believe are pertinent in this category. I did not think it was advantageous to limit the category to only "executive functions" or "cognitive processes." "Personality functioning" does not address other characteristics that have been discussed as well. Then, concerns like Traumatic Brain Injuries (TBI) or lack of fulfillment will be associated with this factor. It can also be difficult to distinguish this factor from other mental health issues in general, and avoid the slippery slope of the addictive personality concept. This factor needs to be recognized as a separate entity for the sake of understanding the precise developmental features of substance use, and to become more pragmatic about the way we approach the nature of the behavior.

FACTOR THREE: TRAUMA/AFFECT

The next factor of importance is related to emotional trauma and affect issues, which have been familiarly related to the development of substance-use behaviors. Emotionally related *trauma* can consist of acute trauma, such as being exposed to a natural disaster, combat at war, a community crisis, or episodes of neglect, or physical, sexual and emotional abuse. While acute trauma is related more to experiencing a single episode of a traumatic experience, complex trauma is related to experiencing repetitive occurrences of trauma or being exposed to multiple types of trauma over a period of time. A person can experience trauma directly or vicariously, such as becoming emotionally distressed when hearing about another person's traumatic experience. The *affect* component of this factor relates to issues with depression, anxiety, and other mental health concerns connected to difficulty managing anger and resentment, and issues with self-esteem. While trauma can precipitate affect issues, affect issues can also complicate later trauma impact, or the affect and trauma components can be somewhat separate entities. This single factor for developing substance-use behaviors primarily focuses on mental health disorders, current emotional impact of trauma history, and issues with emotional regulation in general.

The concept of dual-diagnosis has long been a recognized term in the field, as substance use disorders have been routinely seen co-occurring with other mental health issues within individuals. Large epidemiological studies with community and clinical populations in the last fifteen to thirty years have found some general trends and patterns in the prevalence of mental health and issues related to substance use. They found 18 to 39% of people with major depression, 11 to 19% of people with anxiety, 36% of people with panic disorder, 33% of people with obsessive-compulsive disorder (OCD), 26 to 36% people with social phobia, 25% people with binge eating, 34 to 72% of people with Bipolar Disorder, 84% of people with Antisocial Personality Disorder (APD), 38 to 47% of people with schizophrenia and as high as 80% of people with post-traumatic stress disorder (PTSD) have also met the criteria for a substance use disorder in their lifetime or had substance use that co-occurred.[21] Thirty-seven percent of people with a alcohol use disorder and 53% of people with a drug use disorder have a comorbid mental disorder, and another study found that 20 to 41% of people with a substance use disorder met the criteria for a mood disorder, while 18 to 30% of them met the criteria for an anxiety disorder.[21] These findings demonstrate that mental health issues have a substantial relationship with substance abuse behaviors. It must be said that there is still a large population of people with substance abuse issues who do not have any related mental health disorders, and there are many people with mental health concerns who do not have any substance use issues, as well.

One of the biggest questions in dual-diagnosis is which came first, the substance use issue or the mental health issue. Many people who developed a mental disorder earlier in their life, later developed a substance abuse pattern as a response to cope with the affect issue developed earlier. I have completed mental health evaluations for a psychiatrist at a substance abuse treatment center, and it was not uncommon to see a person meet the criteria for a mental disorder as they were getting sober while coming to treatment. But they did not meet the criteria at any other period of their life. Many times the person's mental health issue is merely a consequence of their addictive behavioral pattern. If a person goes to the hospital for detox, a physician may slap a Major Depressive Disorder label on them because they're experiencing low motivation, poor sleep, and flat affect due to withdrawal from substance use. It's important for clinicians to provide a thorough evaluation of a person's mental health history, and monitor mental health symptoms as a person maintains sobriety early on to gauge the nature of the mental health and affect issues. They may find that the person who was given the major depression diagnosis in detox naturally reduced in depressive symptoms as they stayed sober, but the generalized anxiety symptoms remained. Others may continue to abuse substances to cope with the resultant mood issues of their addictive pattern, which many call a "vicious cycle." Another idea that needs to be considered is how much of a person's Trauma/Affect issue and substance-use behavioral pattern operate independently of one another. A person may not always be using substances as a response to their trauma or to relieve their emotional health issues.

It can be tricky to classify some mental health issues in the appropriate category of the Five Factor Developmental model due to the complexity of mental health issues and of detecting what part of the issue drives the development of a substance-use behavior. For instance, the prototype characterization of Bipolar Disorder is presented as having episodes of minimal to severe depression and, in between, episodes of experiencing manic or hypomanic periods characterized as having an excessive elevated mood, decreased need for sleep, rapid speech, psychomotor agitation, racing grandiose ideas or plans, and impulsivity. It gets blurry when trying to categorize a person's Bipolar Disorder, because this disorder has multiple features and each person's substance-use behavior can present differently with the same mental disorder. Person A may only misuse alcohol during the episode of major depression after a hypomanic episode, while person B only engages in binge use with cocaine and alcohol during their manic phase. Then person C is motivated to use heroin and cannabis during the manic phase and depressive state. Therefore, I would categorize Person A and C's Bipolar Disorder primarily within the *Trauma/Affect* category, because the affect or emotional component, as well as the dynamic between the two episodes of their disorder, impact the presentation of their substance-use pattern. On the other hand, I would categorize Person B's Bipolar Disorder with the *Psychological* factor, because their disorder primarily drives the development of substance use through the impulsivity and distorted short-term planning that is highly characteristic of the Psychological factor.

A similar discourse should be considered with personality disorders or related personality features. A person with Borderline Personality Disorder (BPD) may be at risk to misuse substances if they're going through an emotional crisis or perceive an abandonment threat; whereas a person with Antisocial Personality Disorder (APD) may be more driven to misuse substances out of grandiosity, irresponsibility, or adventure-seeking. Without much deliberation, one person's APD may fit better with the Psychological factor, while another person's BPD may fit better with the Trauma/Affect factor. You may ask: what does it matter? It matters because it's important to understand how the exact features of a total person precisely influence their substance-use behavior. Many people may look at a person and see "Cannabis Use Disorder" and "Generalized Anxiety Disorder," and make automatic assumptions about the relationship between these two diagnoses without thoroughly examining the person's history. If we take a closer look, we can see behavioral patterns and relationships among behavioral experiences. Like the surgeon's scalpel, we can use the Factors to dissect the natural facets of a person so as to understand the true nature of their behavioral development.

Diagnostic labels are somewhat arbitrary, because the importance lies within the individual's actual symptoms and the formulation of the cognitive and behavioral factors that produce and maintain their symptoms. It's not as important for a person to fit a diagnostic criterion, as it is to understand the features that manufacture a person's affect issue and their individualized approach to regulating emotions. A person simply having anger issues, experiencing situational depression, or feeling inadequate in social settings can potentially contribute to the development of substance-use behaviors. Yelling or ruminating about a provoking situation may maintain feelings of anger and ultimately influence a person to abuse substances to self-sabotage themselves and find immediate relief. Binge using alcohol while isolating during a state of situational depression can create shame and guilt the next day, which further influences isolative behaviors and negative thoughts, perpetuating depressive symptoms and alcohol abuse. Social inadequacy is highly related to self-esteem, and to further impacting social anxiety and avoidance behaviors, which maintain low self-esteem and potential substance abuse. Unaddressed affect issues and engaging in behaviors that complicate emotional health can put an individual at risk for developing a substance misuse behavior. But again, this is not predetermined, and we have to understand that affect issues do not *cause* substance abuse.

Many of the current affect issues people experience have been established through earlier life development. The "attachment style" between a primary caregiver and their response to their infant when emotionally distressed can create a foundation for how effectively the infant can self-regulate later in life. A person develops core beliefs about themselves, other people, and various situations via information processing through the workings of attention and memory systems in the brain, by absorbing various life and interpersonal experiences throughout early development. A child in a family system who perceived subtle actions from parents indicating that they are "not as good" as the other siblings, may develop a core belief of "inadequacy" or "worthlessness." So, later in life, if the person does not get the job promotion that they anticipated, this maladaptive core belief becomes activated in the current context, leading them into a state of potential depression. The person's depressive state with the current situation about their career is not necessarily a direct response to early interpersonal experiences, but *is* a direct response to the activated implicit core belief that was developed through the early experiences.

On the other hand, affect issues related to PTSD may be a direct response to early maltreatment or a traumatic event. I worked with a man who witnessed his father tragically die in front of him when he was fifteen years old. Over thirty years after the event he continued to experience flashbacks as if the event was happening again. He would experience hyperarousal, intrusive thoughts of the event, visualize bloody images of his father, and experience extreme guilt, thinking there was some way he could have prevented the accident, since he was present at the time. These activated traumatic memories prohibited him from being able to fully live in the present moment and further motivated him to use heroin to relieve his somatic symptoms, distressing thoughts, and chronic guilt. Consequently, his assumed responsibility to take care of his family and addictive pattern since his father's death enhanced more of his experienced shame, which further increased his *Trauma/Affect* factor. Affect and trauma issues are complex within themselves, and this man had to work on multiple levels to finally gain relief. It's important to understand the exact nature of a person's affect issues, while having accurate insight into its relationship with substance-use behaviors or lack thereof.

FACTOR FOUR: LIFE STRESSORS

The *Life Stressors* factor shares some parallels with affect issues, as suggested by their labels. But life stressors are distinctly carved out in relation to a person's external stressors throughout their lifespan, compared to their core affect. Experiencing various stressors can influence a person's substance-use behavioral pattern. These life stressors may include, but not be limited to, chronic medical issues, the death of a loved one, going through a divorce, retirement, academic studies, withdrawal symptoms, a stressful career in the corporate world, or being homeless. It should be considered on an individualized basis, by evaluating the acuteness and circumstantial characteristics, before deciding whether the lifestyle experience or situation should be categorized under the

Trauma/Affect or Life Stressors factor. For example, if a person has a herniated disc from a car accident and this medical concern creates a relative amount of emotional distress during most days, this medical issue may be primarily categorized under the Life Stressors factor. If the same issue leads to the onset of chronic depression, then the medical issue will be exclusively classified as a Life Stressor and the depression will be classified under the Trauma/Affect factor, even though they have a relationship. Likewise, the depression can be alleviated as a separate entity, while the stresses of the medical concern may persist. For instance, while receiving news of a terminal cancer diagnosis or anticipating an amputation procedure can be highly traumatic for many people, these medical concerns could be categorized as Trauma/Affect and further classified as such if this medical status leads to the onset of chronic or severe mental health complications, while the everyday maintenance with the medical issue would be the primary feature for the Life Stressors factor.

Understanding the characterization for the Life Stressors factor within the Five Factor Model provides insight into the onset and trajectory of individualized substance-use behavioral patterns. Anecdotally, there have been people whose substance-use behavior only consisted of misusing alcohol after a parent died and their misuse subsided when they finished grieving after three to six months. Other people may have a history of substance abuse earlier in their life, but it progressed later in life due to the difficulty adjusting to retirement or after a recent divorce, or with balancing a career while raising children. It has been shown that life stressors alone may contribute to the development of substance misuse behaviors, or may complicate substance misuse and move it farther along in its behavioral course.[22, 23]

A major concept that should be considered when discussing the topic of life stressors is coping styles. The two primary categories of coping styles are *avoidant* and *approach* coping. The way a person copes can impact their well-being and life stress in the long run. *Approach* coping includes using a support system, reappraising negative self-talk, and direct problem-solving approaches. *Avoidant* coping styles involve emotionally disengaging from the stressor altogether through actively suppressing thoughts about the stressor, procrastination, or substance abuse. It has been shown consistently that people with HIV who used more "approach" coping styles rather than "avoidant" coping demonstrated better long-term physical and emotional health.[24] Many people who have a history of substance misuse and present with an avoidant coping style may be more at risk to abuse substances in order to cope with life stressors as they occur throughout their lifespan. I have worked with many adults whose substance use has progressed due to homelessness, interpersonal issues, career dissatisfaction, legal stressors, grief and loss, and divorce, which are all categorized within the Life Stressors factor. In many cases a poor coping style for life stress can be a result of early trauma or maltreatment. But the trauma is not important for this factor, as much as the coping style related to present life stressors. The importance of the Trauma/Affect factor would depend on the current significance of the direct trauma itself.

Individual life stressors need to be considered, to better understand the context of a person's substance-use behavioral pattern throughout their lifespan. Erik Erikson's renowned psychosocial stages of human development may be applied to the Life Stressors timeline for the development of substance-use behaviors. According to this human developmental theory, an adolescent can be at risk to misuse substances due to the stresses of role or identity development. A person in late adulthood may experience more despair because of the stresses of medical issues and changes to social support functioning, since friends will be getting older and passing away. Each part of the life course may consist of various psychosocial demands that call for a person to cope in a form that helps them relieve life stress. Life stressors can be just one facet in the development of substance-use behaviors, but still a distinct factor that can contribute to the onset of substance abuse or impact existing substance use.

FACTOR FIVE: ENVIRONMENT

Genes and environment are often seen as a dichotomous view of behavioral development. So it's only appropriate to introduce the *Environment* factor last, or at the other end of the spectrum of the Five Factor Model. The Trauma/Affect and Life Stressors factors can be considered as being highly related to "environmental" influences. But the Environment factor as a feature of the current model is contemplated merely in the sense of a person's immediate environment, related to accessibility to substances, the nature of substance use of others around them, and alternative activities. Environmental influences impact the development of Trauma/Affect issues, Life Stressors, and even Psychological factors. But the Environment factor itself is not so much concerned with these particular environmental influences that underpin the other factors in a traditional sense, but rather more so the direct environmental facets of a person that contribute to influencing substance-use behavior. The Environment factor consists of two primary categories: the environmental elements of a person that *indirectly* and *directly* relate to substance use.

Indirect environmental elements that could impact the presentation of substance-use behaviors may include a work schedule that leaves a lot of free time, having insufficient leisure activities or hobbies, having too much time alone, or not having a fulfilling family life. I spoke earlier about the truck driver who would only abuse substances when he was home not working. This is a good example of how people's immediate environments can shape the development of substance abuse behaviors. While he was truck driving, his mind would be focused on work for weeks at a time, and he was not impulsive enough to use substances on the road. But when he was home and not working for weeks at a time, he experienced more boredom and this environment more likely brought out his substance-use behaviors. A different pattern I've observed with younger people who engage in substance abuse behaviors is that their substance use overwhelmed all of their previous interests. Some young people may not have children, not be engaged in worthwhile careers, or have yet to find fulfilling hobbies and interests that absorb them on a weekly basis. Therefore, without these environmental conditions, and having something in their weekly environment that preoccupies their minds, substance use can become more worthwhile. These are just a few examples of how immediate environmental facets indirectly contribute to the development and presentation of substance-use behaviors.

Merely having access to a substance or behavior is obviously a prerequisite for developing a substance-use behavior. If a person were on a deserted island with no drugs or alcohol available to them, they would measure extremely low on the Environment factor. Without access to the substance, their environmental conditions on the island would inhibit their developing any type of substance-use behavior (even a healthy level of use). But if a person on a boat drops off a crate of whisky; now we're talking! This is what I mean by environmental elements that *directly* relate to substance use. Do we have access to the substance, and how available is it? How are other people using substances around us, in our immediate environment? Looking back when I was doing my undergrad in Minnesota, I noticed that I had a different relationship with prescription drugs than other substances because of the related Environment factor. I would act impulsive and binge more with prescription drugs because of the environment element of not having easy access to them. I ended up getting my second DUI during the night of a friend's get-together where I had initially planned to stay the night so I wouldn't have to drive intoxicated. Someone I knew mentioned they had morphine and he would give it to me if I drove him home. At the time my attitude was, "it's not every day that I get access to this substance." Therefore my high-risk drug-seeking behavior was shaped by this environmental condition of not having easy access to this particular substance, compared to if the person just said they would give me alcohol if I drove them, which was more accessible. This example demonstrates that the immediate environment *directly* relating to substances contributes to the presentation of specific substance use related behaviors.

Another developmental facet of *direct* substance use related environmental conditions is the nature of other people's substance use in a given environment. A person's substance-use behavior can manifest differently depending on the person's social network and how people around them use substances. Some people may be more likely to develop a substance abuse pattern if they primarily use alcohol around other people who are drinking heavily, compared to drinking around family members who don't drink as much. I had a client who thought it was interesting that he may drink significantly less during special occasions or if he was on a date. But he developed more of a binge use pattern when drinking alone or keeping up with old high school friends who drank more excessively. A homework assignment I use with clients who have alcohol-related issues, to help them become more aware of their behavioral patterns, is to have them identify the environmental dynamics for when they abused alcohol versus when they drank at healthier levels. They often find a difference in their pattern between the various environmental facets in their personal life. In other cases, the Environment factor may not relate to fluctuations in their substance-use patterns as much. For that, we have four other factors that are considered from this chapter.

Adolescents present as a good example for being affected by the Environment factor on the basis of peer pressure, being in the presence of common binge use, and using substances in high-risk situations. This can include using substances while driving, because parents and other family members are occupying the home, resulting in a lack of privacy. Adolescents also demonstrate the complexity of developing addictions by automatically measuring high on the Psychological factor because of their underdeveloped frontal lobes, and the Life Stressor of identity development. Thus the Environment factors that an adolescent may experience can have a contingent relationship with the Life Stressors and Psychological factors. On a larger scale, the societal view of substances such as heroin in our country shows how culture can shape the Environment factor for developing substance-use behaviors. This is seen in the example of U.S. soldiers coming home from the Vietnam War. While many of the U.S. soldiers in Vietnam became addicted to heroin or opium, the majority of those who became addicted did not continue their habit upon their return home.[25] The complete environmental shift when returning home changed the substance-use pattern. This was due to the taboo of heroin use in the U.S. at the time and not having as easy access to the substance as they did while in Southeast Asia. Also, the horror of the combat in Vietnam was a major Life Stressor as a separate contributing entity, based on the current model. Environmental conditions are considered at length when discussing how addiction develops. But the current Environment factor drives a specific assembly of substance-use behaviors, and accounts for less breadth than the traditional sense.

These five primary factors establish a comprehensive understanding about what precisely contributes to the development of substance-use behaviors. Any basis of a substance-use behavior can be placed into one or a combination of these five factors. Based on the Five Factor Model, every person has a Five Factor Profile that reflects the presentation of their current substance-use behavioral pattern, or lack thereof. The profile is expressed as a bar graph. The five factors are represented on the x-axis (bottom, horizontally), and the value or level of significance for each factor is measured along the y-axis (vertical) from low to high. There are no current standardized psychometrics to formulate a Five Factor Profile, since there are a variety ways to assess and gather data about the developmental factors for substance-use behavioral patterns. But a profile can be made through clinical judgments from a biopsychosocial assessment or facilitating tests measuring mental health, psychological traits, life stress, and genetic information. Standardized assessments evaluating all the areas of the Five Factor Model will help formulate highly precise profiles. But a collaborative judgment alone with the person seeking help can achieve highly individualized profiles that reflect the presenting substance-use pattern so as to better understand the underpinnings of the behavior and what underlying areas need to be addressed. A Five Factor Profile provides a concise visualization of how substance-use behavior development differs from one person to another.

A given profile portrays the accumulation of the five contributing factors, and reflects the current presented behavior. The level of measure for each factor on the graph may fluctuate as quickly as minutes or days, or as slowly as years, or stay fixed for most of a lifetime. Genes are generally fixed for the majority of the lifespan, but the Psychological factor may naturally lower once a person reaches their mid- to late twenties. The Environment factor can fluctuate in a matter of weeks or hours, depending on changes in social dynamics, hobby engagement, and immediate surroundings. Genes are the most inflexible factor, while Environment, at the other end, is the most flexible. In theory, each primary factor encompasses sub-factors that fall along its own continuum, contributing to the total level of measure for the whole factor. For example, a grandiose personality trait can be a sub-factor of the primary Psychological factor. So the level of grandiosity a person has will impact the total level of the Psychological factor, along with the accumulation of other related sub-factors. This is not represented in the actual visualization of the profile, since it would make it too complicated. But it is understood in theory to capture the complexity of substance-use behavior development, while fitting all the pieces together in a concise manner. Every person has their own individualized profile, even people who have never had issues with substance use. Theoretically, their factors are generally measured lower than people who have developed an addictive pattern. A person may ask, why is it important to consider a profile for a person who never had any issues with substances? It's important because it gives us a fundamental idea that *all* substance-use behaviors come from a similar place. This Model presents the building blocks for developing any level of behavior, from trying a substance and disliking it altogether to the most severe cases of substance use. Then I would hypothesize that people who measure extremely low on the Gene factor for all substances but measure higher on the other factors will engage in other impulsive or addictive behaviors, such as gambling, shopping excessively, self-injury or maladaptive eating in preference to substance use. So, because the Gene factor would naturally inhibit them from enjoying the effects of substances at baseline, they would be fulfilled by other behaviors based on their developmental structure. To close the chapter, I will introduce three brief case studies to demonstrate the idea of the Five Factor Profile for the development of substance-use behaviors.

PERSON ONE presents as a typical social drinker earlier on in her adulthood, without any apparent consequences. She would typically have two to five alcoholic beverages on occasion a few times a week during nights out with friends or co-workers. She has a career as a mortgage broker, divorced in her late thirties, currently lives alone, and most of her family lives out of state, but she has a brother who lives in her area. She is currently going through legal issues for a DUI and is feeling stressed about it due to potential jail time. Her drinking started to progress after her divorce and when she started to live alone away from her son. Currently, at age forty-six, her pattern of substance use is drinking close to a half a fifth of liquor a day, five to seven days a week, where she has been typically drinking alone. Her drinking progressed to this level after she started to deal with her legal issues, became unemployed, and began experiencing moderate levels of depression due to her lifestyle changes and progression in substance use. She denies any current medical complications, and no trauma or extensive prior mental health history. She is not known to have an impulsive disposition or any other significant Psychological sub-factors, but there was enough to lead her to drive over the legal intoxicating limit. As a brief overview of her case, her Five Factor Profile is as follows, reflecting the underlying nature of her current substance-use pattern:

Person One

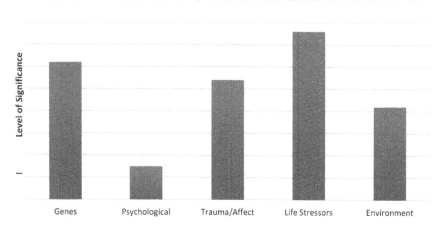

"Person One" Graph

PERSON TWO is a thirty-seven-year-old who has never been married, has no children, and has a history of working in the restaurant industry, serving and managing. He used to drink excessively and party a lot in his twenties, but naturally reduced his heavy drinking as he got into his thirties. During his thirties he has enjoyed trying new alcoholic beverages, but he can take or leave alcohol, and lets alcohol sit untouched in his fridge for weeks at a time. He started to binge use opioid prescription drugs in his twenties, and he started to use heroin intravenously multiple times a day on a daily basis in his late twenties, and continues this currently. He typically uses heroin alone or with his girlfriend, and has lost interest in his old hobbies and the activities that he used to enjoy. Besides continuing to use heroin to avoid withdrawal symptoms, he uses heroin because it's fun and stimulating for him. He has a history of excelling in academics, getting easily bored with different activities, impulsively buying, and identifies as being grandiose at times. He deals well with other life stressors by identifying as a perfectionist and a good problem-solver. He denies any current mental health or affect issues, but when he was growing up, his father was often physically abusive if he made mistakes. He denies that he uses substances to cope with any of his childhood abuse trauma or current affect issues, and describes having a great relationship with his parents currently. But it's a possibility that his trauma history impacted his substance use in an indirect way. Childhood stress and abuse could contribute to experiencing deficiencies in dopamine and endorphin processing later in life.[26] Therefore, his substance abuse can be a response to this neurochemical deficiency, coupled with a high genetic propensity for opioids (the sub-factor gene for alcohol would be measured lower if it was represented in the graph). This is an example of how Trauma/Affect issues may not always play a direct role in substance-use behavior development. But it could *indirectly* impact the Psychological factor by causing a desire for pleasurable stimulation and immediate gratification, due to neurochemical development as a result of trauma:

Person Two

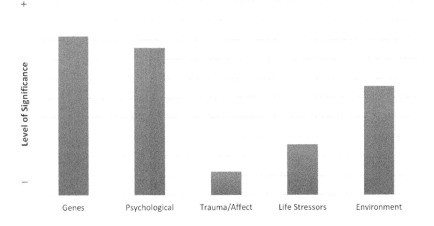

"Person Two" Graph

PERSON THREE is a twenty-eight-year-old who has never been married, has no children, lives with her boyfriend, and currently works for an event planning company. She has a wide array of interests, including travel, exercise, exploring nature, and weekly social activities with her boyfriend and friends. She uses alcohol two to four days a week, drinking one to five drinks per occasion, and uses cannabis one to two times a month with her boyfriend. She typically drinks with other people, and most of the people that she drinks with drink a comparable amount to her. She denies experiencing any issues with her substance use in the past or currently. She is not known to be impulsive and is able to delay immediate gratification, but is somewhat of a novelty seeker, evidenced by her variety of interests and weekly activities. She denies any trauma history and mental health issues, but can often feel entrenched in her mood for the majority of the day if she becomes upset. She does not experience a lot of life stress, but a typical amount for a person who wants to continue to grow in her work life and fulfill developmentally appropriate tasks in young adulthood:

Person Three

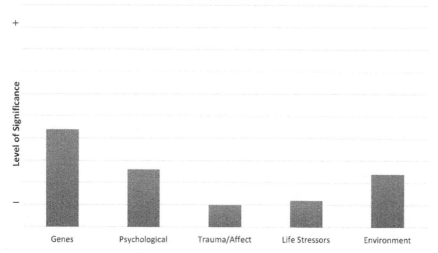

"Person Three" Graph

chapter 3

Behavior

What features make up the behavior itself?

NOW THAT WE HAVE ESTABLISHED the developmental factors of sub-stance-use behaviors, we can explore the nature of the behavior itself. If we understand precisely what makes the behavior function, these processes can be targeted to effectively shrink the behavior and achieve behavioral health.

My model of substance use has been developed over the course of two years. While some of the features of the model came to me spontaneously, other parts came after intentional deliberation about what addiction *is*. One day an ambitious attitude came over me to settle the understanding of what addiction is, which made me ask myself the question: what are the main components that make up any substance-use behavior? Shortly after, I identified the behavior as encompassing *habitual, contextual,* and *pleasurable* ingredients, which make up its whole function. Like a three-dimensional sculpture that holds funda-mental properties that make up its existence, substance-use behaviors feature these three elements that stimulate its existence. *Mindfulness, Exposure,* and *Reinforcement,* also known as M.E.R., relates to the organic processes of the substance-use behavior itself. *Mindfulness* is a way to observe the habitual processes. *Exposure* to an immediate context is a prerequisite for the behavior. *Reinforcement* is the reason for the behavior that seeks to achieve some type of pleasure.

These components are considered *organic,* because they capture the nature of human behavior in a general sense, and they embody the complete proper-ties that are readily measurable or observable during its presence. Therefore, the behavior is non-existent without these components, and their processes display the essence of the behavior with them intact. We observed earlier how simple behaviors could be, while considering all of their dynamic processes. Most behaviors present with an observable physical action of doing, while in conjunction the person is experiencing thoughts or mental activity that influence the physical action. Habits can be observed that are as infrequent as only using cannabis when going to a concert of a favorite band, or a more frequent form, such as picking up a bottle of wine every day after work. All substance-use behaviors occur within a context. We can see in our own lives where we engage in different behaviors depending on the present situational characteristics, life circumstances, and internal sensations that make up the context. We respond to the context; the context may elicit a response in us. I order a beer at a restaurant because this environment manifested an internal desire for it, and I may typically choose to have a drink in this situation, but not so much when I'm at the DMV. Lastly, behaviors can be measured by their rate of occurrence, grounded in their reinforcement properties. It's difficult to assert that substance use is anything other than a behavior. We're also limited in options for how we can conceptualize the behavior, once we get down to its organic nature.

M.E.R.: MINDFULNESS, EXPOSURE, REINFORCEMENT

MINDFULNESS

Addiction or substance-use behavior is a habitual pattern accompanied by mental processes and individual physical actions. The physical action is the overt experience that everybody can observe, while the mental activity is the covert experience that is more observable by the person. Mechanically speaking, a wheel on a car includes a ball bearing that is coinciding with the activity of the wheel by reducing friction, further impacting the quality of the wheel functioning. With that said, the physical action represents the outer wheel, while the mental activity is the ball bearing on the action. The mode of the mental activity will dictate the mode of the outer behavior, just like a rusted ball bearing will impact the wheel to function more coarsely, or a well-tuned bearing will produce a smoothly operating wheel. Whether someone is in an active addiction or does not use substances at all, a mental state is corresponding to an action state, related to the degree of substance use. You cannot have one without the other. You also cannot have an addictive pattern or any substance-use behavior without physical action and mental processes.

The habitual behavior develops after the initial appearance of substance use, whether it's after the first contact ever or repeated occurrences. It has been demonstrated in animal models that underlying neurobiological structures drives habitual substance use actions after repeated substance use.[1] But the sophistication of humans leaves room for ingenuity and variability. All substance-use behaviors hold three phases of physical action. First, the initial physical actions related to *substance-seeking* range from calling different drug dealers to see what's available to driving to Starbucks for a morning cup of coffee. Second, *preparing* actions may consist of preparing a syringe for a dose of heroin or rolling a joint. Third, the last phase is actually *consuming* the substance. Substance-use behavioral habits can be acute, such as occurring during a single episode of substance use, or habitual, that is, across multiple episodes. A person who binge uses may experience an acute habit by typically taking three shots of liquor in the first two minutes of drinking, which are three isolated behaviors accumulating to a habit. A habit can be presented across a longer period of time, such as smoking a cigarette every time you go outside during the day or having two cups of coffee every morning. Even having an alcoholic beverage only on Christmas each year would be considered an annual habit, but obviously this behavior presents much differently than a daily habit of substance use.

Some habitual patterns may contain an impulsive feature, for example, if the behavior occurs despite a high potential for negative consequences, or if the behavior is out of a whim. Some behaviors we discussed in the first chapter may elicit a reflex or involuntary response, such as jumping away from the stove once we notice the flame touching our finger. This would be considered more of an instinctual behavior. On the other hand, substance-use behaviors are not as procedural or "automatic," because there are many individual physical actions that are included, such as substance-seeking, preparing, and then consuming a dose of a substance. Drinking twelve beers in a night certainly can be a habit, but it is surely not an automatic behavior, because there are numerous individual actions in drinking just one beer. Popping a few Vicodin for recreation could be more impulsive than the process of drinking twelve beers, but it is still not an involuntary action like a hiccup. Impulsivity is not a required feature of substance-use behaviors, but can be a catalyst in many addiction-related actions. While mental activity ultimately has a bearing on a behavioral impulse, the mental activity also leads habitual patterns or inhibits substance use related physical actions altogether.

The mental activity that I'm referring to is also known as cognition or cognitive processes; which is the bearing on the overt physical action. Cognition has a root meaning of *to know,* and refers to the mental processes of thinking, perception, attention, memory, knowledge formation, problem-solving, reasoning, and evaluation. These mental activities embrace attitudes of intention and awareness, which relates to "knowing" something. So, to know is to act. Cognition is a common thread throughout the varying levels of human consciousness, from stored unconscious procedural memory to computing complex mathematical equations. Cognition is also an umbrella term for different features of present mental activity, such as what we are thinking or thought content, the direction of our thinking or attention placement, and the speed of our thinking.

There are **five common cognitive processes** that have a bearing on related physical actions related to substance use, from single actions to pervasive patterns of substance use. Cognitive processes are often automatic mental activity, but these processes can be modified through slow and effortful mindful intention.

The **first** cognitive process to consider that is related to substance-use behaviors is **thought content**, which is encoded by implicit memories of previous substance use experiences. These unconscious memories manifest more conscious mental content in the form of linguistic thoughts, images, and attitudes related to substances. These implicit memories and manifested mental activity can motive physical actions or maintain patterns of substance use if positive memories of experiences become activated.[2, 3] *Romancing the high* is an example of cognitive content that can potentially set up the initial action sequence related to substance use if activated. For example, a person may have thoughts and subtle attitudes about how well energized they would feel if they had a nice warm cup of coffee at work, or experience mental images of feeling relaxed and euphoric from heroin. This mental process comes in various shapes and sizes, depending on the person's individual experiences. But the primary criterion is the content of the cognition itself, which will have bearing on the motivation or inhibition of substance use related behaviors.

The **second** cognitive process is "**attention salience**," which primarily relates to the flexible or rigid focus of our mind in regard to substance use. Multiple studies demonstrate that attention salience has a significant relationship with cravings to use substances.[4] Attention salience may be rigidly focused on internal cognition of substance related material, or on external stimuli. I worked with a person who relapsed at a wedding, where he almost blacked out with alcohol. We examined this episode together in great detail to pick up the attention biases that could have contributed to his excessive drinking. He had several months of sobriety at that point, and had no intention of drinking at the wedding until his wife suggested that he could ease up and just have a glass of champagne. He thought, "What the heck" and had the glass. As soon as he finished the glass his attention was not on his wife, good company, gratitude for the weekend, or the entertainment of the wedding anymore. He was laser-focused on where he could get more alcohol. He took multiple shots of liquor at the bar, and then focused on a plan for further drinking. His attention salience for substance-related cues during the wedding took a major hold. His behavioral pattern could have had a much different outcome if his attention biases had been addressed after the first drink. Humans have developed these attention systems to be able to sustain focus for prey, escape danger, and navigate a complex social world to further survive and reproduce. However, our motivational system can direct our attention to behaviors that can produce negative consequences in the long run in our modern world.

Third, the substance-related "**expectations**" is a cognitive process related to prediction and anticipation in regard to substance use. A person may overly expect the benefits of using a substance, leading them to potentially misuse it. At the same time, the person can have expectations that alternative behaviors will be less effective or lead to a less desirable outcome than substance use. Expectations can manifest at varying degrees in mental activity. A person may have a simple expectation that a coffee in the morning will help wake them up before work, motivating them to get a cup. Whereas expectations during a night out on New Year's Eve can be more exaggerated, impacting a person's behavior. They may think, "Tonight is going to be one of the best nights of the year. We're going to have a lot of fun going to different spots, trying different drinks, with all our friends to end the year." Expectations can play a role in various substance-use patterns. A person with depression may have negative expectations as to whether calling one of their friends or getting out for a long walk would help improve their mood. So they just resort to the expectation that drinking alcohol will be the most effective way to relieve their depression.

Another expectation component that should be considered is the anticipation of achieving substance use itself, and not necessarily the expected quality of the experience as just discussed. Our expectations are highly tied to the reward-related neurotransmitter dopamine, by signaling a dopamine release potential when an expectation is made in the mind and then dopamine becomes further released if the expectation is met or exceeded.[5] The magnitude of dopamine release will depend on the discrepancy between expectation and reality. If we were expecting to meet up with a friend to go have drinks but they cancel on us, then the signaled dopamine gets lost. Now feeling displeased, this unmet expectation could now lead us to engage in the initial substance-seeking actions, such as calling up other friends or going to the store to bring back an alcoholic beverage. These overt substance-seeking actions may not have transpired as eagerly if the expectations in the mind had not been created initially. But if, instead of canceling, the person exceeded our expectations by bringing a joint with them as well, the magnitude of dopamine release would be greater, since the original expectation was surpassed. This can lead to further substance-related expectations as to the quality of how the night will go, which will further correspond to the behavioral sequence.

Fourth, "Risk-reward evaluation" relates to expectation and prediction. This cognitive process primarily discerns the subjective outlook of punishment and reward probability for substance use related behaviors. An exaggerated risk evaluation can create more anxiety-related responses, while a very low risk evaluation can lead to more impulsive-related actions.[6] I would further hypothesize that the greater the reward and the lower the risk evaluation discrepancy, the faster our thinking and impulsive physical actions will be. I had a client who had a history of using heroin daily, but only used it two times a week for the two years prior when I started working with him. When we explored his cognitive processes that were associated with his habitual pattern, we discovered that risk-reward evaluation was pretty prominent to his behavior. He discussed how his risk out-look for engaging in his heroin use was always low because he saw himself only throwing away a few days or weeks of sobriety. So his risk perception always maintained a lower level, since he never gave himself a chance to accumulate a larger period of sobriety from heroin. His behavior pattern for those two years reflected a low-moderate risk, while having a moderate reward evaluation prob-ability. Whereas during his period of daily use, his risk evaluation was lower, and his reward probability was much higher, as reflected in his more extensive use. After a few months of sobriety he stated, "It wouldn't make sense for me to use heroin now. I'm working my first forty-hour job in years and I would quickly lose it if I started using. It was so easy to throw away a week or two of sobriety here and there over the years. It was cheap. But now I have a lot invested, and using now would be like putting all my money on one number in roulette." This cogni-tive process can generally manifest in the form of rationalizations.

Fifth, "cognitive errors" are a type of cognitive processing that can impact the behavioral pattern of substance use. The Abstinence Violation Effect is a particular cognitive error that was introduced by Marlatt and Gordon (1985) to characterize a phenomenon that can lead a person to further misuse sub-stances after a reintroduction to using after a period of abstinence.[7] This cogni-tive error suggests that if a person uses a substance after a period of abstinence they could perceive this single use internally as meaning that they have lost all control, they are defective, and their behavior is predetermined. This leads them to further abuse substances. Abstinence Violation Effect is more complex and socio-emotionally developed than the other cognitive processes that we discussed. We will discuss this phenomenon in more depth later, but for now it is enough to recognize the importance of how cognitive errors can influence overt actions based on prior substance use.

Cognition ultimately leads a person to give themselves permission to use substances or not. These cognitive processes can occur in various combina-tions within single episodes of substance use and across a person's behavioral history. A person may also naturally favor one cognitive process over another, depending how their mind works. Cognitive patterns can also be considered habitual, as the recurrent physical action reflects a recurrent cognitive pro-cess. These processes are embedded in the three types of thinking in regard to content, attention, and speed; thus motivating or inhibiting individual actions. Where animal models fall short in relation to substance-use behaviors, we are able to observe how this mental activity plays a direct role in physical actions in ourselves. Every substance-use behavior encompasses the relationship between cognition and action. Then substance use episodes may transform from infrequent habits to more extensive patterns. Generally, the more habitual may reflect an addiction. This demonstrates that healthy substance use is not something completely different or separate from addiction. All of it is behavior, and incorporates these organic processes that just configure differently based on the pattern. Mindfulness is the overarching theme that serves to unwrap these necessary processes of substance-use behaviors.

EXPOSURE

The context is the circumstances that surround all behavior. Like a carbon diamond formed by a multitude of facets, many contextual facets are sewn into substance-use behaviors. Context is inescapable, and without it, behavior does not exist. Context is whole, but has multiple levels consisting of internal states, immediate environmental features, and overall present life circumstances. Substance-seeking, preparing, and consuming behavioral actions of substance use are all immersed within a context. This component of substance-use behaviors is an exclusive process, which maintains a unified function with the previous habitual processes of the behavior.

Triggers are a central concept in addictions, and are a necessary contextual feature of any substance-use behavior. A trigger is a situation, experience, or stimulus that sparks a person to experience a craving or desire to use a substance, which precipitates the related physical actions of substance use. These triggers, or antecedents, present in diverse forms from objects in our environment: smells, being around certain people, or from internal sensations, thoughts themselves, or a combination of these. A person may experience cravings to use substances if they drive past a neighborhood where they got drugs before, while listening to certain types of music, being at a party, having cash on them, during a specific day of the week, or simply from smelling the aroma of coffee beans. Triggers may also present in the form of internal states, such as stress, anger, or boredom. These triggers or other thought associations may stimulate cognitive processes that can also present in the form of a trigger if they produce or maintain cravings. Then if a person continues to experience a craving, they could further experience cognitive processes that will coincide with their physical actions. Cognition is more exclusively related to physical actions, as discussed under the Mindfulness feature. Triggers, whether they present externally or internally, are carved out exclusively as contextual features.

Triggers are developed through the learning process known as Classical Conditioning, which was observed by the work of Ivan Pavlov in the late nineteenth and early twentieth century. Pavlov found that his dogs naturally salivated during the presentation of food, but then learned to salivate to the sound of a bell that was rung right before the presentation of food. The dogs would not naturally salivate to the sound of the bell. But they learned over time that food would shortly follow the sound of the bell. Let's say I've repeatedly experienced the water in my shower turning cold when the toilet flushes. I naturally jump away when I feel the cold water, but over time I become conditioned to jump away when I hear the toilet flush, because I'm anticipating that the water temperature will change. Then let's say we fix the plumbing so the temperature does not change when the toilet flushes. It would then take multiple occurrences without the temperature change before my reflex of jumping away becomes extinct. Triggers for substance use go through the same learning process. A person may experience a craving response or desire to use a substance if they're exposed to the actual substance. But then they start to experience cravings to use substances if they feel stressed, or walk by a bar, or if they're around a specific friend, if these conditions were associated with using substances repeatedly in the past. Therefore, triggers and the linked craving intensity are highly individual, based on the person's culture and the contextual features that were present during their substance use history.[8]

Cravings are purely a sensation and a manifestation of memory.[9] Being exposed to a trigger activates an implicit memory of substance use experiences, which elicits a craving or desire response like the dog salivating at the sound of the bell. Cravings are an automatic response, which can enhance automatic cognition, but as we discussed earlier the physical actions are not automatic responses in themselves. Specific triggers can be associated with positive, negative, or neutral memories of substance use. This demonstrates how a person can continue to experience cravings despite having negative consequences from substance use. Many triggers may elicit cravings that are only encoded in positive memories of the substance use and not associated with the aftermath of the consequences, such as seeing plastic baggies that were associated with the excitement of substance-seeking and acquiring the substance. Other triggers may elicit a *disgust* response, because the trigger activates associated memories of negative experiences with substances. I've worked with many people who are newly sober and describe a disgust response to substance-related stimuli, such as the smell of stale alcohol or seeing other people act unfavorably while intoxicated. While this is an effective reaction to manage substance use, people may not understand that these substance-related cues only elicit a disgust response due to the characteristics of the trigger. All the while, their brain continues to incorporate encoded memories of positive substance use experiences that elicit more of a craving response when activated by a different trigger. So seeing a person eat lunch on a nice sunny day downtown with a refreshing glass of an alcoholic beverage may create a different response. We can observe this months later in the same people who experienced the disgust response towards other substance-related stimuli earlier on. We hear them say something like, "It would be nice to just have a few over the weekend." I know they genuinely mean it, because the nature of the trigger aligns with this thought and desire to only want a few; for that moment at least. So it depends on the presentation of the trigger or context whether a disgust or craving response is elicited. Disgust and craving may be the extreme polar opposites that triggers may naturally elicit, while some triggers may only elicit neutral thoughts about substances without any value either way. Different degrees of trigger responses can fall along a continuum.

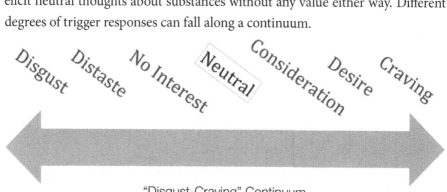

"Disgust-Craving" Continuum

A person may experience less intense cravings,[10] such as a *desire* to use the substance or simply a *consideration* of using the substance. Less extreme than a disgust response, can be a *distasteful* sensation, or simply *no interest* in using a substance. Then, more specific degrees like having an "urge" can fall between desire and craving. Whatever language is used, this continuum demonstrates that triggers and substance-related cues could produce varying automatic sensations, depending on the contextual nature.

Cravings are completely normal experiences, they are a natural effect of a learning process that all humans and many other organisms are included in. I find that some people who are newly sober or have long-term sobriety feel ashamed or feel like they are doing something wrong if they experience cravings. They don't realize that cravings are simply a memory that is activated when they are exposed to a relevant trigger. Also, many people may feel like a "craving" is too extreme and not an accurate description. So they may deny experiencing any level of response whatsoever. But if they were able to use this continuum, they would be able to more accurately identify their trigger responses, like this, "Oh, maybe it was just a consideration but not a craving, and I see how that trigger in particular made me experience distaste for substances." Another important idea to consider is that all people who use substances have triggers and experience a level of craving. Triggers and cravings are not exclusive to people with addictions, but apply to anybody, including the mere coffee drinker. Even people who don't use substances at all still experience some level of response on the whole continuum. A social drinker may experience a *desire* to use alcohol under the right context, while people who do not use any substances may experience *distaste* or *no interest* when exposed to substance-related stimuli. *Cravings,* in particular, may be more prevalent in people who developed an increased habitual pattern of substance use as seen in active addiction, and they may experience more craving associations if they use substances daily. Whereas cravings can still occur with healthy substance use, depending on the circumstances that may produce this response. This understanding normalizes the experience of cravings, and we see that anybody can vary in their natural responses, corresponding to the contextual triggers at a given time.

General life circumstances are always a part of context and contribute to the nature of triggers. Some people may feel like there is nothing to look forward to in their life, which can lead them to experience more desire to use substances when exposed to immediate triggers. Where another person may be out drinking with their friends and decide not to have another drink because they have a career that they value highly and need to wake up early the next day. So sometimes the context of current life circumstances can override or intensify the impact of immediate triggers. I have even worked with people who are living a fulfilling sober lifestyle but can still become acutely triggered to want to use high-risk substances such as heroin or cocaine. This does not mean that the person did something "wrong." But they encountered a trigger in their immediate environment that activated the exclusively positive memory of substance use, despite their current healthy life circumstances in sobriety. Then, obviously, people can experience a trend of negative life circumstances or "red flags" that can lead to desiring a reintroduction of substance misuse. Again, it is all about pinpointing the exact nature and varying levels of context that elicit the favorable or unfavorable sentiments to use substances.

We don't have the entire context if we don't include the nature of substances and substance use in the immediate environment. **Who** are we using substances with? **What** substances are they using? **How** are they using the substance? If I'm using a substance alone, what's going on? How am I taking the substance? I've noticed with myself if I drink alcohol alone or around a girlfriend, I may only drink one to two beers on occasion. But if I'm drinking with friends or just around social company, I'm more motivated to drink extensively until the social encounter ends. So instead of one to two beers, I may drink two to four. I worked with a man who would only use cocaine after he was with a prostitute. He discussed how he would initially fear rejection to date women, further experience loneliness, and then get a prostitute to fulfill his intimate needs. For him, cocaine was merely a supplement. These examples demonstrate how the nature of other people's presence or lack thereof can be a bold contextual feature of our substance-use behavior. Yes, this behavioral feature does go hand-in-hand with the *Environment* developmental factor.

Dosage of the substance also plays a role in the context of the behavior. A beer is much different from a shot of liquor. A person drinking a beer has to drink a lot more liquid to get the same alcohol dose as from only drinking liquor. It can be difficult to judge how much a dose a person gets for substances like cannabis, because the intake of the psychoactive chemical THC (Tetrahydrocannabinol) is inconsistent, due to the diverse strains of cannabis, and different amounts of flower used during preparation, plus the traditional intake process of smoking is difficult to measure. Since the ongoing legalization of cannabis, the mass expansion of edible THC products has greatly helped the classification system of dosing, so people know exactly what kind of dose they are getting from a single edible. This will help eliminate the stigma and create safeguards for people who use cannabis for recreation, social, and medicinal purposes. A person may want to avoid smelling like a joint or becoming "stoned" from the massive amounts of smoke, but just take one or two gummy bears to get the consistent minimal effect they desire. Higher-risk substances like heroin may pose more difficulty with dosing, because these illicit substances may be produced and cut differently by a distributor. Then the effect of different substances plays a contextual role in behavior as well. Someone smoking ten cigarettes a day may function much differently from someone smoking ten joints or drinking ten shots of alcohol a day. The nature of dosing has a highly contextual role in the individual actions of the substance-use behavioral process, as grounded in the complexity of substances and their various administration routes.

Behavior needs to be ultimately viewed in its context. Let's say a person who has five months of sobriety has one beer. The context at face value is that a person is living a healthy lifestyle and they had one beer in five months. There is no substance use problem here whatsoever, and the person is drinking much less than any regular social drinker. However, we still need to consider the potential onset of craving responses if we open that door after or within five months of sobriety. Can having that one beer enhance my cognitions to desire excessive use, or does it simply allow me to realize what I enjoy from my sobriety and appreciate a drink from time to time? Our understanding of these organic processes and the exploration from the last chapter helps us observe how everyone is different. When someone has had ten years of sobriety but based on their life circumstances now maintains social alcohol use one day a week, it does not mean that their whole life has changed or should be viewed as a "failure." We also cannot make assumptions if someone says they drink every day, because they may only drink one beer a day. But we also cannot underestimate the behavioral pattern of someone who only drinks seven days out of a month, because they could be binge drinking and engaging in other high-risk behaviors while intoxicated. Context always matters! If someone seeks help for their substance use, their behavioral pattern needs to be viewed within their individualized context and not compared to the person next to them. We do not take the behavior out of its context. This way, we can better understand the function of the behavior and consider its actual significance.

REINFORCEMENT

The last component that completes the make-up of substance-use behavior is the rewarding properties. Every person who engages in substance use receives some type of benefit. People would not deliberately engage in the behavior if they did not receive pleasure or a payoff. We use substances to relieve trauma, improve emotional health, reduce stress, override boredom, increase social inclusion, to have fun, enhance productivity, generate creativity and for many other reasons. The list of reasons why a person engages in substance use is endless and is different for every person. But they simply like it. To further understand the function of the behavior and its rewarding properties, there are two types of reinforcement that need to be illuminated.

The first type of reinforcement is called *positive* reinforcement. This form of reinforcement increases a behavior to exhibit a wanted experience or stimulus. In other words, a person is primarily motivated to engage in a substance-use behavior if it gives them something more than they already have. This includes a person drinking alcohol at a social gathering to have more fun and create a social camaraderie, or a person using cannabis to stimulate creative thinking and enhance sensory stimulation when listening to music or eating food. Positive reinforcement may be prominent in many substance-use patterns. People may use substances extensively simply because they're extremely fun, give them something to enjoy after work, or heighten their sexuality. Whether a person uses substances once a year or numerous times a day, positive reinforcement enlarges a wanted experience in a person's life. If we magnify the person's behavior, we will be able to observe what the substance-use behavior creates or supplements in their current state of being.

The other type of reinforcement is known as *negative* reinforcement. This mode of reinforcement increases a behavior to remove an unpleasant experience or stimulus. So instead of adding something, the substance use is primarily motivated to subtract something from a person that is non-desirable. Some people may use substances in attempts to remove PTSD symptoms that enhance distress, or eliminate other related emotional health issues, such as depression, shame, or anger. Even a person who does not regularly engage in substance use, but took a prescribed Ativan during a dental procedure to remove anxiety and discomfort is negatively reinforced. This type of reinforcement is commonly seen in people who take prescribed pain medication to remove and manage physical pain as well. Continued substance use to eradicate withdrawal symptoms, as seen in people who are chemically dependent, is negatively reinforced behavior. A lot of us have heard about the daily drinker who uses alcohol in the morning to quiet their shakes. Many people who smoke cigarettes don't realize that they are negatively reinforced to continue their habit to remove the irritability when they miss a smoke break or the withdrawal symptoms that may worsen if they don't smoke. Negative reinforcement's goal is to seek homeostasis. We can look closely at a person's substance use to examine if the behavior is trying to dissolve anything in their life that is unwanted.

A single behavioral occurrence or an episode of substance use may have multiple rewarding properties, and hold a combination of positive and negative reinforcement. Maybe a person uses substances to "escape" their depression, while at the same time it enhances the fun during a social event. Then, if someone becomes chemically dependent, they may continue to use in order to manage withdrawal symptoms, further to remove stress, and then to enrich stimulation or creativity. It can get fuzzy determining whether a behavior is primarily being negatively or positively reinforced, due to the complexity of human behavior. However, of key importance is understanding the function of the two types of reinforcement, and that each behavior may have multiple rewarding properties that can be overlooked. Substances are highly rewarding due to their multifold reinforcing nature. All substances play a direct role in the corresponding neurotransmitters creating the desired effect, while fulfilling personal needs, as we have been discussing. Then many substance-use behaviors will further create a social reinforcement, as is easily seen with alcohol use. The Reinforcement component of substance-use behaviors is vast and multi-layered.

Many triggers can provide a window into what the reinforcing properties are. On many occasions, the initial substance-related actions merely follow a trigger that elicits a craving response, and do not have an exclusive connection to the reward. Substance use may fulfill the internal trigger of stress by removing it when engaging in the behavior. The positive reinforcement of social inclusion during alcohol use may fulfill the external trigger of being around friends or family who are drinking. In other cases, the trigger or triggers may not be necessarily tied to the reinforcing properties, as they are with these examples. A person may use a cigarette to remove the discomfort of an intense craving and enhance relaxation when simply triggered by waking up in the morning with a coffee. The context of waking up in the morning and drinking coffee may not be directly connected to the smoking reward of eliminating craving discomfort and relaxation. Many triggers are simply objects, such as plastic baggies or a smell, which don't have a direct connection to the rewarding nature. Then, as discussed, triggers can present in the form of disequilibrium or unmet circumstances that the substance can help resolve and reinforce. As we understand the contextual nature of substance-use behaviors, we can observe how the combination of triggers and current experiences invent space for a reward potential.

The reinforcement properties of each person's behavior can change and fluctuate over time. With some more chronic cases of substance misuse, I can imagine a general pattern for how the reinforcing nature of their behavior has changed over a span of thirty years. It may start off as a curious teenager just having fun on the weekends, then not meeting socially expected milestones, and the substance use becomes more regular to enhance an unfulfilling life-style. Then, during the latter part of their addiction history, the person may be using substances in a cycle to cope with the consequences of their last binge.

With other people's substance use history, there could be an inverse effect. They may be heavily in substance use with various drugs as a teenager and young adult due to peer pressure or searching for excitement. But when they're in later adulthood they may reduce their substance use to enjoying casual social nightcaps and a joint while they're in California. Many of us have heard of this pattern with our boyfriend or girlfriend's father from high school talking about when he used to take acid, as he is sipping his whisky on the couch with his wife before you go to the movies with their son or daughter. As the reinforcing properties can change throughout a total substance use history, these properties may also change in a matter of months, days, and even hours. The rewarding properties are adjusted to the person as they currently are.

On the other side of the coin, *punishment* decreases the occurrence of a behavior because it exhibits an unwanted experience or it takes away a wanted experience. People quit using substances or reduce their substance use due to punishment or potential punishment consequences. A person losing a job due to their substance-use pattern is an example of *negative* punishment. Then an example of *positive* punishment is if a person receives a felony conviction for having a possession of an illicit substance. Both forms of punishment decrease behavior. While one takes something of value away, the other adds a burden.

I like asking clients what their substance-use behavior looks like right now, because they give me an astounded look, as if being sober is completely detached from their previous substance-use pattern. Many people who become sober or have reduced their substance use are impacted by the punishment properties of the behavior, as presented by their inhibited substance use actions. Then they further experience reinforcement in relation to the benefits of sobriety or reduction. Everything from addictive patterns to nonexistent substance use are linked. As reinforcement increases behavior, punishment decreases it. Many people may not use alcohol because they do not receive any reward from it, and they get "punished" by the undesirable taste and effects of the alcohol if they drink it. Then, as for those who become sober after their addiction, they do not use substances because of their extensive consequences or punishment related to their previous behavioral pattern. All of the other substance-use behavioral patterns that fall within these two extremes acquire a combination of reinforcement and punishment properties that maintain a more balanced functioning. We can see these properties in all of our everyday behaviors, and the essential goal of behavioral health is to maximize reinforcement while minimizing punishment. In total, the cognitive-physical actions through the contextual landscape are the means to the reinforcing end.

Mindfulness *(habitual behavior)*	• Behavior includes three phases of physical actions: substance-seeking, preparing and consuming the substance • Cognitive processes coincide with the physical actions; motivating or inhibiting the actions
Exposure *(context of behavior)*	• "Triggers" include everything from internal states, immediate environmental cues to general life circumstances • Contextual triggers elicit a craving response that is measured along the "disgust-craving" continuum
Reinforcement *(pleasurable behavior)*	• *Positive* Reinforcement: Behavior is present to exhibit a wanted experience or stimulus • *Negative* Reinforcement: Behavior is present to remove an unpleasant experience or stimulus

"M.E.R." Table Description

This table of the M.E.R. (Mindfulness, Exposure, Reinforcement) components is geared towards substance use, while the language **also** implies its opposite, being geared towards the absence of substance use or its inhibition. This includes cognitive processes that keep the related physical actions dormant, contextual features that do not have any desired associations or elicit a "disgust" response, and punishment properties that can be present to reduce the behavior. These components of M.E.R. are all meshed, making up a single behavior or behavioral pattern of substance use. The behavioral process of M.E.R. begins with the exposure to contextual triggers, where automatic cognitive processes co-occur with the craving response. Then cognitive processes continue, eventually driving the three phases of physical action to achieve the reinforcement goal. But if the behavior doesn't occur, or doesn't reach the first phase of physical action, then the behavioral process gets shut down and does not move past the initial trigger-craving and cognitive experience.

M.E.R. can explain *any* substance-use behavior, from people who do not use any substances to people who take medication for a medical issue, to people who use substances socially or engage at the level of severe addiction. Everyone will just present differently within M.E.R. based on the nature of their behavior. This is important, because it demonstrates that, as humans, we all relate by sharing some relationship to substance use. Maintaining rigid divides between addiction and other substance-use patterns only generates more stigma for people with an addiction. All substance-use behaviors exist on the same plane. Every substance-use behavior shares physical actions, cognition, context, and rewarding properties. M.E.R. places no value judgment on *any* substance-use behavioral pattern. M.E.R. simply reveals the behavior as it is, and individuals themselves apply their own values with regard to their behavioral health. The mosaic of the behavior is broken down like atoms of an object by laying out its functional properties to understand the fundamental nature of every substance use occurrence.

chapter 4

Vacuum

How does the behavior occur?

WE HAVE NOW ESTABLISHED THE underlying origins and the processes of the behavior. This embodies the beginning and end of the whole substance-use behavioral experience. We will proceed to bridge this gap between the Five Factor Development and the M.E.R. behavior function by tying the whole model together.

In bridging this gap, we will further examine the central neurobiological mechanism that drives a person's developmental nature into a corresponding behavioral pattern. Many theories and models of addiction are two-dimensional in the sense of viewing and conceptualizing substance use in a single form. Various approaches may only consider a stimulus-response phenomenon, or believe that all addiction is a mere response to trauma, or believe that a biological explanation suffices. These approaches present as scattered ideas. They may explain a fragment of addiction, but they do not capture the universal nature of the behavioral process. This process involves multiple levels and forms, which should be explained in a concise manner. These levels consist of biological processes, activity of the mind, overt behavior, and the encompassing environmental facets. Current models of addiction seem to keep these levels and forms separate as if they cannot be integrated. As if, for example, the rewarding features in the brain have no bearing on overt Operant Conditioning. Tying together these multiple levels of the substance-use behavioral process will create a model that is more three-dimensional, and illuminating what addiction is.

I used to hate learning about neuroscience or biological psychology because it seemed dry and non-relatable. But my whole interest changed when I heard my neuroscience professor say, "Every brain state has a corresponding mind state." This statement stuck with me and tied together everything I knew at the time. This statement creates the perspective that brain processes are occurring at each and every moment, generating a mental state and further leading to our outward actions or behavior. Each level can be targeted to change the other corresponding levels. Psych medication targeting direct neural chemicals will filter out updated mental states and eventually more adaptive behaviors. Mental skills like meditation or cognitive restructuring split off in various directions, changing neurobiological processing while leading to overt behavior. Then, acting in new ways will have a backwash effect, creating new mental activity while firing off a novel neural network that corresponds to it. For example, a person with social anxiety may work on reducing their symptoms through different levels and routes. Taking an SSRI medication may help restore the neurotransmitter serotonin, impacting mood and associated mental states, and further reducing social avoidance behaviors. Creating new self-talk and reframing imagined negative interpretations by others in social settings would influence neural processing in the brain and motivate social engagement. Then, choosing to deliberately act inconsistently with previous socially anxious responses may enhance confident automatic thoughts, which trickle back to the brain. These processes can create a new feedback loop between the three primary levels, with practice, over time.

The brain is composed of various networks that are responsible for exclusive functions. Information is communicated throughout the brain by the firing of neural patterns across these networks, manifesting countless human experiences. The brain has three general levels, composed of the *reptilian brain*, *mammalian brain*, and *rational brain*, which are all interconnected by neural networks. The reptilian brain involves structures like the brainstem, which includes basic functions, such as heart rate regulation and breathing. The mammalian brain, fulfilled by the limbic system, is responsible for our emotional world and unconscious memory systems. The rational brain is illustrated by the outer cerebral cortex, which involves more sophisticated functions of visual processing and locating objects, as well as more complex decision-making. An unfortunate example of how these three levels interrelate during the activation of symptoms is PTSD. Particular systems in the brain may become overactive, while others turn off, making an individual feel trapped in their body.[1]

These networks were discovered in the last century, largely due to the psycho-behavioral effects of damage to different parts of human brains. It was discovered, for instance, that a particular part of the left side of the frontal lobe, now known as the Broca's Area, is responsible for the production of speech and functions related to language comprehension. It was found that people had difficulty speaking after physical damage to this area of the brain. Physical brain trauma is able to provide insight into how different structures in the brain produce specific functions and how others may compensate for damage. But now, through neuroscience research, we are more able to understand how the brain works when a person engages in specific psycho-behavioral tasks while in an fMRI (functioning-MRI). An fMRI observes blood flow and associated neural activity in the various parts of the brain during set tasks. The brain is a highly complex and not fully understood organ, which produces our being and who we are.

DOPAMINERGIC SYSTEM

The central neurobiological mechanism of substance use and addiction is the Dopaminergic System or "reward pathway." In the brain, dopamine acts as neurotransmitter, or chemical messenger, which is involved in a modulatory system for processing rewarding experiences, and promotes learning and motivation. All humans and many animals have a Dopaminergic System in the brain that helps us remember and engage in behaviors that make us feel good. Dopamine is released during the process of a variety of behaviors, such as eating, drinking fluids, buying something new, and having sex. Our dopamine is deeply wired to motivate behaviors that bring us resources, give us social status, produce fulfillment, help us survive, and ultimately maintain the life of our genes through reproduction. This explains why sex is highly pleasurable, despite the fact that most sex today is simply for leisure. The brain is set up as if *all* sex is geared towards reproduction. The more dopamine release that results from a natural behavior, the more the behavior is directly geared toward the long-term survival of our genes. This is a product of natural selection, and the rewarding processes have evolved to motivate us to repeat these behaviors. Various substances are addictive because of their natural chemical structure, and how they mimic various neurobiological processes. The Dopaminergic System ultimately adjusts the importance of substance-use behavior to the level of personal reward output.

The ventral tegmental area (VTA), deep in the brain, projects neuronal connections via dopamine release throughout various networks of the brain, such as the prefrontal cortex (PFC), hippocampus, nucleus accumbens, and other associated areas, enhancing the learning process of substance-use behaviors.[2] At the same time, other utilities, like the opioid system, play a direct role in the pleasure and euphoric experiences of the behavior. During rewarding substance use experiences, system messengers are further discharged to memory systems, like the hippocampus, and cognitive structures like the prefrontal cortex (PFC), so that the brain remembers the importance of the behavior and what it should pay attention to in regard to the association signals for decision-making. One of the primary functions of this dopamine system is to associate rewards with contextual cues, further motivating actions to seek out the rewards. Therefore, dopamine is released before the actual achievement of the reward and experienced pleasure. This is responsible for further motivation enhancement to achieve the reward. Simply put, the Dopaminergic System runs from sub-cortical brain areas to higher cortical structures to attach significance to a reward and its actions so the behavior can be repeated in the future.

All natural rewarding behaviors go through this neurobiological process. But since some substances may release significantly more dopamine than other natural rewards, a person can quickly develop an addiction to substance use. This is what we observe when we say chemical addiction can "hijack" our reward system in the brain. We all have an *implicit reward hierarchy* or "survival hierarchy" in our brain that is tied to our Dopaminergic System. Within this hierarchy we have behaviors such as eating, social contact, working, and exercising. Due to overstimulation of dopamine across repeated patterns, substance-use behavior may be placed higher on the hierarchy in people with addiction.[3] People with the most severe forms of addiction may find their substance-use behavior at the number one spot of the hierarchy, tricking the brain as if the substance is needed to survive. We can observe this in people with severe addiction who neglect eating food or establishing shelter in favor of engaging in substance use. In addition, the isolated actions may be more associated with reward, where getting a drug is exciting or the isolated actions of drinking alcoholic beverages one after another are pleasurable. These isolated actions are seemingly harmless in the moment as well. But the larger behavioral *pattern* in addiction may be more associated with punishment, where a person can lose all of their money in an accumulated drug binge, or where a six-month alcohol abuse pattern creates extensive emotional turmoil and interpersonal stress with a spouse. I worked with a man who would discuss how he would always experience psychoses after taking a dose of crack-cocaine, which made him not understand why he kept using the drug. In his case, the series of physical actions of drug-seeking, preparing, and the initial consumption were highly rewarded through the dopamine system, despite experiencing negative consequences after the initial effect. This is the insidious aspect of the Dopaminergic System; how the brain does a good job at separating the reward anticipation of the ritual in the now, from the potential punishment effect later.

In another example, people who drink socially or use substances at healthier levels may find their substance-use behavior sitting at a lower level of the implicit reward hierarchy. Some people can simply "take it or leave it" when it comes to substance use, as seen in people who use alcohol only on rare occasions. People who have an *accumulation* of activities that are placed at moderate to higher levels of the hierarchy, such as social contact, watching sports, and using alcohol might possess the perfect recipe for being a social drinker. If a social drinker gets a hangover from a night out, this consequence would greatly outweigh this lower-ranked behavior. This will further lead the social drinker to not drink for a while or to be much more mindful next time they drink. The lower the experienced reward of the behavior, the more sensitive a person is to its consequences, while the higher the experienced reward of the behavior, the less sensitive a person is to its consequences. This cost-benefit analysis of our neurobiology at each moment of time reveals the process of behavioral economics. Substance-use behavior has an underlying value for every person, and the reward hierarchy measures this value of personal importance throughout the lifespan.

If a person uses substances more repeatedly and the particular behavior moves to a higher rank of the implicit reward hierarchy, then this can lead into an addictive pattern and the brain will make increasing changes between the pertinent neuronal networks. This process is known as neuroplasticity. We experience neuroplasticity or brain changes throughout our lifespan: whenever we learn something, experience significant events, and develop any kind of habit. People with addictive patterns experience decreased neural connections between sub-cortical structures, such as the limbic-striatum and various cortical structures of the PFC, while neural transmission between structures within its associated neurotransmitters and synapses results in changed gray matter.[4, 5, 6] The Dopaminergic System is the chief mechanism that drives these various neurobiological changes with regard to substance-use behaviors. The complexity of these neuroadaptations in regard to addiction or an extensive substance use is beyond the scope of this book, but it's important to keep in mind when exploring the nature of the behavior. These brain changes reflect the robustness of addiction and the difficulty of the challenges of changing the behavior. These neural changes and behavior robustness also reflect the level of the substance use on the implicit reward hierarchy. If substance-use behavior is located at one of the number one spots of the hierarchy, the brain has been set up into acting as if this is something needed to survive, as seen in more severe patterns. In this case the brain becomes adapted to hyperfocus on substance-related cues, as reflected in these neurobiological changes, further enhancing an intense craving and a continuance of this narrow goal-directed mind state to ultimately take the initial action. While a person likes the use of substances as they repeatedly engage in the behavior, the brain adapts to correspond to the learned motivation to repeat the behavior.

When a person is exposed to relevant contextual triggers, associated memories in the hippocampus and amygdala become activated. Dopamine in the VTA is released to the nucleus accumbens, producing a craving response. Then automatic cognitive processes related to goal-orientation manifest through areas in the prefrontal cortex (PFC), such as the medial-PFC, anterior cingulate cortex, and orbital frontal cortex.[2] This information is projected back to sub-cortical structures of the striatum via glutamate messengers, and dopamine is further released to the nucleus accumbens, *enhancing* the craving. Then the striatum projects messengers to the PFC, continuing the cognitive processes, and eventually to the motor cortex, to set in motion the physical actions related to substance-seeking, preparing, and consuming the actual substance. There appears to be a feedback loop between these brain networks that perpetuates the behavioral process. In a nutshell, once a memory association becomes activated, dopamine is released to the striatum, where the goal-seeking process begins, narrowing attention toward the reward, further producing motivation.[7] Then if a person engages in the substance-use behavior repeatedly, the corresponding synapses between neurons and across networks become strengthened, while synaptic patterns for other behaviors or activities become weakened.[7] As this happens, the substance-use behavior increases on the reward hierarchy as seen in addiction. This covert neurobiological process mirrors the overt behavioral processes of M.E.R. (Mindfulness, Exposure, Reinforcement).

Social drinkers or people with healthier substance-use patterns experience this same neurobiological learning process. But it's hypothesized that people with healthier patterns experience a lower degree of neuroadaptation geared towards substance-use behavior. A Friday night may activate associations in the memory systems related to having a good time drinking with friends. Dopamine is released to the striatum, producing a *consideration-* or *desire*-level response. Then areas in the PFC become active, manifesting cognitive processes that are geared towards low to moderate goal orientation to meet up with friends, which corresponds to the "desire" level response. On the other hand, a person who is more addicted to alcohol may have a larger dopamine release to the striatum after being triggered, producing a *craving* response. This further narrows the person's cognitive attention towards the goal of using alcohol. This can lead them to experience more of a compulsion. So in both cases the person experiences the same neurobiological process, but the users differ in their rate of dopamine release, their level of craving response, and their cognitive flexibility, as reflected in the nature of their biological processing and reward hierarchy. This demonstrates how difficult it is to judge a behavior, because there's a thin line between the varying degrees of substance-use behavioral patterns, and the same neurobiological mechanism produces all substance-use behaviors. This also reminds us about the three levels of the brain state corresponding to a mind state, and how the mind state is further reflected in an action state.

Just as the same neurobiological structures are involved in the broad array of substance-use behavioral patterns, different behavioral addictions share neurobiological processes as well. The Dopaminergic System is embedded within the cortical and sub-cortical networks, which are geared towards reward–seeking and are involved with other behavioral issues related to binge eating, gambling, and sex addiction.[8] While many of these different behaviors share the same reward-seeking mechanism, behaviors like binge eating also include exclusive neurobiological processing, such as the function of the hypothalamus, which is involved with hunger and satiety.[9] These specific behaviors should be considered in terms of their exclusive neurobiological underpinnings to better understand the nature of the behavior and its indirect influences on the Dopaminergic System. Regardless, understanding the universal neurobiological mechanisms in these different behaviors will help us better understand the nature of addiction as a whole and the best way to target the manifested behavior. Then, just as healthy substance use and substance misuse are both derived from a similar neurobiological place, excessive gambling, binge eating, and sex addiction share a common biological basis with their healthier behavioral form as well.

As we delved into the neurobiological nature of addiction and substance-use behavior, we were able to describe these processes without labeling it a *disease*. I believe part of the disease concept comes from good intentions in terms of expressing that people with addictions are dealing with a perplexing issue that has nothing to do with their character. But I also believe the disease concept further creates stigma and makes people feel trapped within a label for the rest of their lives. The disease concept points out that there are measurable changes to the brain when a person develops an addiction. But we have to understand that the brain will always change when we learn something new and develop habits; whether they are good habits, bad habits, neutral habits, or nasty habits. Our brain changes as we develop an addictive pattern, and our brain will continue to change if we reduce our substance use or practice new habits during abstinence.

Is it necessary to call addiction a disease? What does the disease concept really explain? What's the goal of calling it a disease? Exploring these questions makes me realize that calling an addiction a disease may do more harm than good. I know many people who like the disease concept, while I also know many people who feel unsettled about this understanding. So instead of labeling every single problematic substance-use behavior as *diseased*, why don't we just explain the exact nature of the behavior? We can still explain the precise neurobiological processes and how they correspond to the overt behavioral processes without calling any of the processes a disease. Just explain what it is, without the constraints of a label. I have completed many mental health assessments with people who had the label Major Depressive Disorder. Just seeing this label does not mean much to me. It does not explain a whole lot, and simply says they experienced depression or some mood issues at some point of their life. I don't care much about what they were diagnosed or labeled with. But I do care to understand the nature of their symptoms, how their symptoms changed throughout their lifespan, and what processes contribute to the maintenance of their symptoms. The only way to reduce the stigma that occurs in behavioral health is to make more of a conscious effort to minimize the use of labels when we can, and simply explain the organic processes of the behavioral health issue.

The reinterpretation of the neurobiological data pertaining to addiction has been helping to advance our understanding of what addiction is and lay the disease idea to rest.[10] Much of the brain research uses language like "dysfunction" or "impairment" when describing the brain changes in people who have addictions, as if their brain is malfunctioning. But the brain *is* working properly, and is doing what it is supposed to do. Unfortunately, the brain is learning a habit that can cause many devastating consequences in a person's life. Another error of the disease concept is pushing the notion that addictive behaviors are "automatic." If the behavior were automatic, then people would have absolutely zero control and would never be able to quit using substances or reduce their use. Also, a person would use substances every single time they experienced a craving response due to the neurobiological processing, if the behavior were automatic. None of this happens. People reduce their use or abstain from using substances all the time, even if they experience the most intense cravings and associated cognitive processes.

However, what *can* happen is that a person may create a compulsive pattern of substance use after the initial using phase. A compulsion can make you obsess over substances, make you feel like you cannot resist the urge, and eventually create horrible consequences. This experience makes many people feel very uncomfortable and out of control when they're in active addiction. But a compulsion is still separate from automatic or involuntary behavior. These related addictive patterns are reflected in the changed neurobiological processes. The PFC and striatum connection in particular is geared towards rigorous reward-seeking when the behavior is learned. We also need to consider whether the brain changes are primarily a precipitating factor for developing an addiction (as seen in the *Psychological* factor), a result of the learned addictive behavioral pattern, or both. Since these brain changes occur during the development of addictive behaviors, research has shown that people who have a period of abstinence from substance abuse actually enhance the gray matter in the brain that was associated with the underlying processes of their addiction.[11] This implies that people who are sober practice behavioral inhibition, and that not acting on cravings will create new habits and corresponding neural connections.

As humans, we all have a collection of behaviors that we find rewarding. Some are more rewarding than others, and many substance-use behaviors may fall anywhere on a continuum from infrequent leisure use to a compulsive addiction, as measured by the reward hierarchy. Then there are addictive patterns that may not create as many immediate consequences, as seen in caffeine and nicotine addictions. Many people who have these addictions become chemically dependent and engage in a daily compulsive behavioral pattern to use the substance. So do people who are addicted to caffeine or cigarettes have a disease too? This almost sounds silly. Sure, a person with pervasive cigarette use can create a cardiovascular disease. But do they have a "behavioral disease?" If so, then many people are walking around with such diseases; or does the disease concept not include caffeine or nicotine addictions because they don't create as immediate consequences as other substance use? But then the degree of consequences shouldn't set the criteria for a disease, because consequences are relative to each person and are simply undesirable reactions to a behavioral pattern. Various substances and alcohol may *generally* produce a larger release of dopamine throughout the reward system than caffeine; this creates the learned neurobiological connection at a more robust rate. At any rate, behavioral habits go through a learning process in the brain, whether it's brushing our teeth, casual recreational substance use or addiction.

What if we stopped calling physical conditions like cancer "diseases," or anything at all? Would this change anything, or change how we treat these biomedical issues? Calling it a disease or not may not be as important as understanding the exact nature of its etiology and its symptomatic characteristics and how best to treat it. If the disease label made a person with cancer feel more like a defect, I would happily drop the disease characterization if it empowered them. I would almost embrace others labeling their addiction as a disease if it helped them, but we will explore later how holding onto this label can potentially enhance shame and create more harm to behavioral health. I will also eradicate the *progressive* brain disease fallacy later, as we discuss aspects of the concept further. Fundamentally, the Dopaminergic System or the reward pathway is the central neurobiological mechanism that manufactures substance-use behaviors, from occasional social use to severe forms of addiction. The behavior corresponds to a biological brain state.

Some people may think I have been alluding to a Choice Theory of addiction. Choice Theory assumes that people with addictions can easily choose to not engage in the behavior. I find that Choice Theory is at one end of a spectrum, while the Disease Model is at the other end, assuming that people's behavior is predetermined for the rest of their lives. My integrative behavioral approach finds itself more in the middle of the spectrum. A behavior is not predetermined for the rest of our life as developmental psychology and neuroscience continues to demonstrate, while at the same time ingrained habits in the brain are not so simple to disregard. Substance use encompasses many individual actions between drug-seeking, preparing, and consuming. This creates a lot of room for flexibility and decision, while neurobiological processes and their adaptations narrow the choice options toward learned goal-seeking to preserve mental energy. Our brain learns to choose the *best option in the moment*. Changing the habit of addiction is almost like learning to drive a car that moves left when we turn the steering wheel right and moves right when we turn the wheel left. We have a strong habitual desire to turn the wheel right when we want to make a right-hand turn from repeated learning ingrained in our neural networks. But we still have room to make a deliberate decision about our behavior and to operate the new wheel function habitually after a period of learning. It comes down to developing motivation for new behaviors that create new habitual networks in the brain, while dampening the substance-use behavioral pattern.

Whether we call addiction a disease or a habit, the importance is grounded in understanding the organic nature of the observable behavior. The path to behavioral health is to utilize an approach that meets the needs of *every* person who uses substances, and provide them with the understanding of what they are actually experiencing. Addiction is no doubt a challenging issue. So not calling it a disease does not excuse the devastation that the behavior can cause, and does not assume total responsibility on the individual. I believe our culture found it to be easier to explain this complex problem by slapping the disease label on it, when what we need is to just flesh out what makes up this whole behavioral process, and lay the components out in a concise framework. The rest of this chapter will tie together my whole Vacuum System of substance-use behavior, to set the tone for the rest of the book.

VACUUM APPROACH

The Vacuum Approach of substance use has **three primary parts** that are interconnected, creating the whole model. These parts include the *Five Factor Development, Dopaminergic System,* and *M.E.R.: Mindfulness, Exposure, Reinforcement.* Earlier, we examined the exclusive depths of each part of the Vacuum Approach. The Five Factors represent the *Development;* the Dopaminergic System represents the *Mechanism;* and M.E.R. represents the *Function* of the model; adding up to the whole behavioral process of substance use. The development answers the "why," the mechanism answers the "how," and the function answers the "what," when it comes to all substance-use behavior. Many models of addiction or substance use are dysfunction-based, where they view and explain substance-use behavior solely from an abnormal standpoint. The Vacuum Approach merely explains the nature of any substance-use behavior, and the individual makes the ruling of their pattern in the context of behavioral health. The following illustration embraces the Vacuum Approach in its entirety.

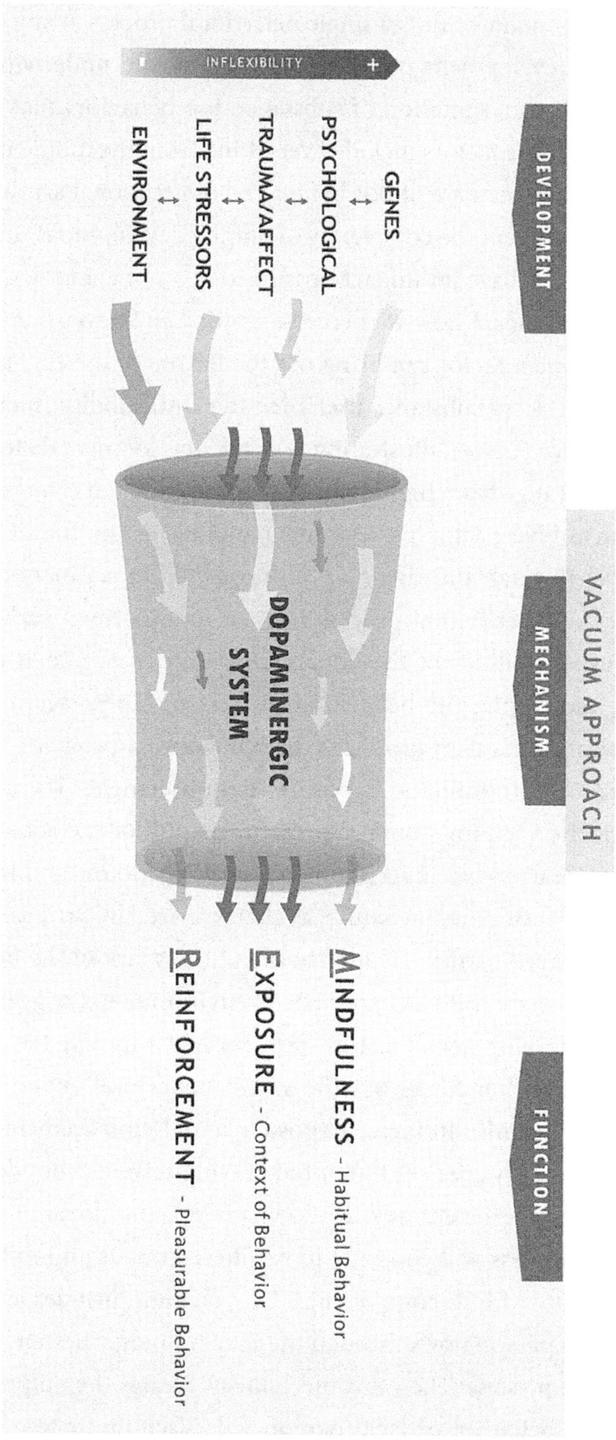
VACUUM APPROACH
DEVELOPMENT
MECHANISM
FUNCTION
INFLEXIBILITY
-
+
GENES
PSYCHOLOGICAL
TRAUMA/AFFECT
LIFE STRESSORS
ENVIRONMENT
DOPAMINERGIC SYSTEM
MINDFULNESS - Habitual Behavior
EXPOSURE - Context of Behavior
REINFORCEMENT - Pleasurable Behavior

This system manufactures a single behavioral process at any given moment of time. The development part encompasses all the underlying factors that contribute to the presentation of substance-use behaviors that we covered in Chapter Two. These factors include everything from the moment we were conceived to the current state of our being. The bidirectional arrows between the Five Factors represent the complexity of human development, and how each of these factors may have an impact or influence on one another. Our *Trauma/ Affect* state can impact how we perceive major *Life Stressors*, or a highly measured *Environment* factor can bring out the flavors of the *Psychological* factor, as seen in adolescent substance use. Then the "Inflexibility" meter simply categorizes the Five Factors, illustrating how the developmental factors of human behavior may range from highly rigid to more flexible to change.

The dense Five Factor Development makes up the totality of a person, which flows through the single vacuum of the Dopaminergic System once a substance-use behavioral process begins. As described earlier, one of the primary responsibilities of the dopamine system is to attach importance to behaviors, motivating the behavioral process to repeat again in the future. This vacuum mechanism produces the whole overt behavior itself, which is illuminated by Mindfulness, Exposure, Reinforcement. The arrows flowing throughout the vacuum system represent the pull of the actual onset of the whole behavioral process. Every human is walking around at this very moment with a varied developmental nature, as characterized by the Five Factor Profile that was portrayed earlier. Then once the initial spark of the behavioral process happens, whether it's an experienced environmental trigger or a thought, the person's developmental nature gets flushed through the dopaminergic vacuum. This further filters out the whole behavioral experience, which is composed of the Mindfulness, Exposure and Reinforcement components. Even if a person experiences the initial craving response but does not act on these internal experiences as they flow through the dopaminergic vacuum, a behavioral process will continue to be filtered out as an inhibited behavior explained by the M.E.R. components. This vacuum includes an input feature when the total person flows through the Dopaminergic System at the onset of the behavioral process. Then this mechanism creates the output of the actual substance-use behavior, or lack thereof. This Vacuum System represents the whole behavioral process, whereas M.E.R. simply represents the finished product of the behavior.

People who use substances at any level cannot be characterized by a single archetype. Substance-use behavior patterns are too complex, individualized, and easy to change over time to be categorized. I barely like using the archetype *social drinker* even though I use it because people generally know that I'm referring to a person who uses alcohol primarily in social settings and does not experience any significant consequences from drinking. Using archetypes can be helpful for understanding and explaining behavioral patterns in a simple manner, as seen in psychopathy and personality dimensions. However, categorizing substance-use behavioral patterns can often be limiting and lazy. After five years in A.A., I started to drink casually and a friend in the program asked me, "Do you think you're an *alcoholic*?" I remember having a difficult time answering his question. To this day, I don't know exactly what features make up the "alcoholic" archetype. I'm not sure if I have fitted this category either way. But as far as answering his question, all I know is there was a time in my life when I needed help for my substance use. My behavioral pattern has changed in various ways throughout my life. This has been reflected by my Five Factor Profile and adjusted Dopaminergic System at each point in time. Instead of limiting behavioral patterns by the use of categorizations and archetypes, the Vacuum Approach views all substance-use behavior like the body of the ocean. The range of behavioral patterns is vast and may greatly alter without any strict archetypal changes between behavioral sequences.

The Five Factor Development will influence the nature of the M.E.R behavior function. The input will correspond to the behavioral output, contingent on the person's dopaminergic mechanism. Everyone's developmental profile presents differently, which is further revealed by the resultant behavior. Take a particular person who abuses substances, for example. The highlights of their Five Factor Profile present with a high level of *Trauma/Affect*, and a moderate to high level of *Life Stressors* and *Environment*. The nature of their M.E.R. function may consist primarily of negative reinforcement to remove affect and stress issues. They may be more exposed to internal emotion-related triggers and environmental circumstances that permit them to misuse substances. Then under the Mindfulness component, this person may experience more cognitive processes of thought content related to the desired outcome of finding relief, elicited by the implicit memory of experiencing the emotion-related triggers. They may experience "expectations" that the substance use will take care of the affect issues or life stress more effectively than other behaviors. These cognitive processes will further motivate the physical actions of substance-seeking, preparing, and then consuming. The frequency of the substance-use behavior will depend on the combination of the Five Factor Profile, its M.E.R. patterns, and the learned implicit reward hierarchy of the Dopaminergic System at each moment in time.

Then we can take a person who measures higher on the *Gene* and *Psychological* factors, but consistently measures low on the *Environment* factor, because they have a healthy social network and stimulating alternative hobbies that fill their time. Their M.E.R. behavior will function differently in this case. Based on their Five Factor Profile, the reinforcement aspects of the substance-use behavior may primarily pertain to the positive reinforcing effects of having fun or experiencing novelty. Then the *Environment* factor may acutely spike if this same person is experiencing boredom or the substance use of others, which is associated with the Exposure component of the behavior as well. One of the chief cognitive processes of this behavioral process may be the attention salience on the immediate external triggers. Then the combination of imagining the desired effect and the reward outweighing the risk thought evaluation may be present. The context and frequency of their substance-use behavior may manifest more in the form of a binge or just infrequent episodic use, rather than daily or regular use, since the *Environment* factor is typically low for this person.

The Vacuum Approach also explains healthy, or more casual, substance-use patterns. *Person Three* from the end of Chapter Two displays how a casual user or "social drinker" may generally measure lower across the five factors. In these particular cases, the nature of M.E.R. will present much differently than in the so-called addictive behavioral patterns. The Reinforcement properties may primarily relate to the positive reinforcement of social enhancement and fun, and be negatively reinforced by relieving the tension from a long workweek, for example. The context of the behavior may be a couple of standard drinks for a few days a week, or several more drinks for only a few drinking occasions in a month. These casual substance-use behaviors may primarily consist of triggers related to the end of the week or having friends over. Then the craving response may be less intense, more at the level of a "consideration" or "desire" response. The cognitive processes may entail more realistic expectations of having a good time, and not expecting that using will be the greatest thing in the world. Attention salience may be less rigid, and the risk-reward evaluation will have a more even balance. These cognitive processes would reflect healthier habitual actions related to substance-use behavior, instead of more impulsive or compulsive actions, as seen in addiction. As these parts of the Vacuum Approach mirror one another, they will also correspond to the person's individualized Dopaminergic System.

People who rarely use substances, perhaps only drinking alcohol on major holidays, may measure significantly lower on the *Gene* factor. This would create a minimal desired effect when the substance is consumed. The Dopaminergic System may be specifically adjusted to motivate substance-use behaviors only under precise circumstances, and not biologically adjusted to be motivated on a regular basis. The Reinforcement nature of this yearly substance-use behavior may be more detailed towards the positive reinforcement of being social harmonious with family members who only visit once a year. These more infrequent patterns of substance use may entail Reinforcement properties that are more indirect, pertaining to social or cultural fulfillment. In contrast, more frequent substance use may directly enhance fulfillment, as seen with boredom or a mental health issue. The Exposure component may be highly narrowed to the external context of the holidays or the special occasion. Then its cognitive processes may comprise the expectations of having a joyous time with the whole family. The attention salience can be more focused on the goal of celebrating or spending time with family, rather than on becoming intoxicated. For the rest of the year, this person's significantly low *Gene* factor for substance use would limit the possibilities for Reinforcement potential. The *Gene* factor only allows so much desired effect, which would only be present under the indirect reward during the holidays. Contexts with substance-related cues or triggers throughout the year might only elicit a "neutral" or "no interest" craving response when exposed. Then the automatic cognition, whether it's the "risk" outweighing the "reward" evaluation, lack of attention salience, or expecting other behaviors to be more satisfying than substance use, will further inhibit the physical actions related to substance use until the annual holiday or other event occurs.

People who do not use any substances could be explained through the Vacuum Approach as well. In cases of nonexistent substance use, the *Gene* factor may be almost absent, where people do not experience any desired effects from substances whatsoever, and possibly experience aversion from substance use. The Dopaminergic System will then be adjusted to avoid substance-use behavior altogether, while choosing alternative behaviors. Even though the overt substance-use behavior is nonexistent for these individuals, M.E.R. still explains this absence, as mentioned earlier. So, the reinforcement elements would be voided, while punishment properties of the behavior keep the behavior inhibited. They may manifest a "no interest" or "disgust"-related craving response when exposed to substance-related cues. Then the cognitive processes when experiencing external substance-related cues would correlate with the inhibited physical actions under the Mindfulness component of the behavioral process. Even my clients give me a puzzled look when I ask them what their substance-use behavior looks like through M.E.R during the moment of our session. Then I explain to them how even identifying their cognitions and contextual features that inhibit substance use during our session is good practice for having awareness of how these different behavioral processes contribute to our behavior or make it absent throughout our life.

Humans are malleable. We constantly change throughout our life, over the course of years, weeks, and even hours. Wherever we are and whenever we come to be, a Five Factor Profile is concurring with our individual substance-use behavior. Many people's substance-use behavioral patterns change throughout their lifespan. Maybe they abuse substances as an adolescent, but then grow out of substance abuse naturally. Some people's substance-use patterns become more severe with time. On the other hand, many people may never experience any significant consequences. But their behavioral pattern still fluctuates, based on the alterations of their Five Factor Profile, due to the natural course of human development. As I'm sitting here writing this in my office, my *Environment* factor is extremely low, in fact, almost nonexistent, because there's no chance of my current environmental nature permitting me to use substances. But once I walk out of work this Friday afternoon, my *Environment* factor will naturally increase. Our brains develop throughout many years, we move in and out of mental health, life throws different kinds of stress at us during different periods of time, our social life will flow like waves, lifestyles will transform, and new behavioral sequences will send tidal waves throughout our developmental nature.

The *development, mechanism,* and *function* parts of the whole Vacuum Approach all work and change together. If the Five Factor Profile changes in any way, this will be reflected in the M.E.R. output and adjustments to the Dopaminergic System. Let's say if a person's M.E.R. addictive pattern results in some depression, then the experienced depression will increase the *Trauma/ Affect* factor simultaneously. This may further enhance the substance abuse behavior revealed by M.E.R. On the other hand, significant substance use consequences that target M.E.R. can have differing implications for the Five Factor Profile. The *Psychological* factor can lower promoting long-term thinking about the future that is favorable for discontinued use. The *Environment* factor can lower due to the cautious circumstances that the addictive consequences created, such as legal issues. Just like the human life renewing a stream of behavioral sequences that stem from the accumulation of developmental processes, substance-related behavioral sequences continue to change the developmental nature of our being as well. So, this feedback loop demonstrates how this Vacuum Model is an autonomous filtering system in and of itself.

This system is also embedded in the encompassing levels of the human experience. The developmental factors incorporate covert genetic expression, our nervous system, and mental health features, with external environmental facets that include our own culture at large. The Dopaminergic System, being an underlying biological mechanism, filters out the overt M.E.R. behavioral experience. Underlying neurobiological processes also feature the components of the M.E.R. behavioral processes. The memory systems of the hippocampus and amygdala become activated when exposed to pertinent contexts, and then the striatum further enhances the craving response. The connected PFC generates the cognitive processes, the motor cortex creates physical action, and then the opioid system and associated neural structures activate during the pleasurable experience.

In politics, the concept of the *power vacuum* is illustrated when a nation loses its central authority and does not have an identifiable government to replace it with. Thus a vacuum is created, where sub-groups flow in, attempting to fill the empty role. This can create chaos and continued instability in a nation if the central government is not properly replaced. This analogy is used for the Vacuum Approach for addiction. Measuring higher across the Five Factor Profile can take away the "central government" of our behavior, resulting in an addictive behavioral pattern explained by M.E.R. The addictive pattern will continue if nothing is replaced. The developmental nature will filter out its corresponding behavior function through the Vacuum System. The goal for overcoming addiction is to take the end of the Vacuum that is filtering out a M.E.R. addictive pattern and hook it up to a healthier M.E.R. attachment. This will filter out a more adaptive behavioral pattern that meets the personal goals of the individual. Instead of leaving the output of the Vacuum filter to the chaos of addiction, the filter should be modified at the very first sign of any instability, to prevent the loss of the whole central government. The next chapter will discuss various strategies that can be used to target the M.E.R. behavioral processes, with a view to further renewing the developmental nature indirectly and directly. Like a cold air intake in a car mechanically helping the efficiency of the engine functioning by maximizing its air and temperature flow, the Vacuum Approach creates a healthy behavioral system that flows and self-corrects within itself as new inputs and outputs are replaced.

The Vacuum Approach of substance-use behavior is Cognitive-Behavioral (CBT) in nature. The model includes learning theory principles of classical and operant conditioning, and the understanding of how cognition influences physical action in regard to the M.E.R. portion. Cognitive-Behavioral Therapy (CBT) does not have a single conceptualization for addiction, and only explains the behavioral process in a two-dimensional fashion. Some believe the reinforcement nature of the behavior is enough to look at, while others only recognize how cognitive distortions lead to vulnerable emotions and the person uses substances in response. While many of these Cognitive-Behavioral Therapy (CBT) formulations explain a slice of substance-use behaviors, they do not explain the whole nature of every behavior. But I think a lot of people may not realize how comprehensive Cognitive-Behavioral Therapy (CBT) is.

The Vacuum Model integrates components of contextual Cognitive-Behavioral Therapy (CBT), neuroscience, and developmental psychology to explain the comprehensive nature of every substance-use behavior on the continuum. Some behavioral health models may create their own lingo or terminology, but I believe it is important to use the same software across already established concepts to maintain understanding and promote integrative approaches.

The Vacuum Approach is considered a Behavioral Model, even though this model is three-dimensional and encompasses multiple levels. The *behavior* is the primary tone of the model because it meets in the middle of the embedded levels. It's easily observed and measured, and it's relatable to everyone in regard to behavioral health. While this model can be used to simply explain substance-use behavior, it can also be used to help people change problematic substance-use patterns. Addiction is a robust force that needs a robust approach that nevertheless delicately addresses its exact nature. This is like the way a black belt in Brazilian Jiu-Jitsu is a robust force: practitioners are able to move like a delicate feather capturing precise detail. Instead of going against the grain of addiction, we need to flow more with the stream of the behavioral pattern and harness its organic processes.

The only thing that the Vacuum Model touches upon is the fundamentals of substance-use behavior. Every person shares the fundamentals of substance-use behavior, but the personal characteristics of our fundamentals will be revealed by the resulting behavioral pattern. We all have genes that impact the effects of substances. We all have psychology, mental health, life stress, and an environment that can enable or disenable substance use. We all have a Dopaminergic System. We all have cognition that assists in "turning on or off" the related physical actions of substance use. All substance-use behavior or its absence is entrenched in a context. We all get exposed to substance-related triggers or cues, which elicit a response somewhere on the "disgust-craving" continuum. Then if any of us have at least considered the use of substances, we have all experienced reinforcement, punishment, or a combination and degree of both. The only differences among people are the characteristics and degree of these various organic processes that make up the individualized behavioral pattern. All substance-use behaviors come from the same fundamental place. Therefore, it's unnecessary to create separation by placing people who uses substances in different boxes, as if people in those boxes are *completely* different from one another in regard to their substance-use behavior. We can learn from healthy substance-use behavioral patterns just as much as we learn from addictive patterns. Plus, focusing on the fundamentals of substance-use behaviors simply informs us what addiction actually *is* without any highly rigid or oversimplified explanations. It truly "is what it is." Treatment will be more attractive with a precise framework that simply unmasks the individualized behavioral processes of problematic substance use.

chapter 5

Tools

How can we change the behavior?

THE NUMBER OF STRATEGIES THAT can be used to change or modify our substance-use behavioral pattern is limitless. I tell my clients all the time: *whatever strategy works for you is the best strategy to use.* The Vacuum Approach is not about using a systematic coping tool recipe to change substance-use behavior; the Vacuum Approach simply extracts the organic processes of the whole substance-use behavioral course in their purest form. Then people have the freedom to choose whatever tools they find effective in targeting the processes of the Vacuum System, to ultimately modify their behavioral pattern.

Earlier in my work life, I facilitated a Stress Management group where I was given a thick binder with hundreds of ways to cope with stress. I found this to be a tad stressful in itself, and a blind way to approach stress management. As I've worked in behavioral health over the years, I've come to realize it's a lot more important to first understand the processes that maintain the behavioral health issue and then provide general strategies that target these processes. Instead of a buckshot approach of providing an overwhelming number of coping strategies, I condensed this thick binder into a concise packet of a couple of pages. It starts out by conceptualizing stress, or explaining what stress *is,* by recognizing all of its components and processes. Then I introduce a common understanding of two broad categories of "cognitive" and "behavioral" strategies that target the processes of stress to effectively manage it. The packet doesn't need to list every single coping tool, but provides an understanding of how many of the things we do in our daily lives to manage stress fit into a Cognitive or Behavioral category of coping. Coping strategies in general either take in the form of doing something, which is behavior, altering our thoughts or perspective, which is cognitive, or a combination of both. People need to primarily understand *how* the coping skill works on the behavioral processes, and not so much of *what* the coping skill is. It's more important to understand the make-up of the behavioral issue, and how coping tools target its processes.

The crucial idea here is to comprehend the Vacuum Model's conceptualization of what all substance use and addiction is, and how strategies target its processes to change the behavioral pattern. I would rather have three coping strategies and know how exactly they modify the behavioral processes, than know a hundred coping skills but not understand these processes at all. During the last three chapters we fleshed out the components and exact nature of substance-use behavior. This chapter will take a look at a general overview of how different strategies or therapeutic interventions address the processes of substance-use behavior in any form. This chapter will not capture every single coping skill that has ever been used to modify substance-use behavior. But you will see *how all* coping strategies target the organic processes that we illustrated in the last three chapters. The goal is to understand how this whole behavioral system works in general, which will lay the foundation for the remainder of this book.

To modify substance-use behavior **directly**, the tools will need to target M.E.R. To modify substance-use behavior **indirectly**, the tools will target the individual's Five Factor Development. If the coping strategies target the M.E.R. properties of the behavior, the underlying factors represented by the Five Factor Profile will adjust accordingly. If the strategies target the Five Factors, then an adjusted M.E.R. behavior will be filtered out. Strategies can target one or a combination of the three aspects of M.E.R., which will alter the whole M.E.R. function. Then the Dopaminergic System will adjust in accordance with developing new behaviors that modify the substance-use behavioral patterns. As the Dopaminergic System adjusts to operate in a healthier manner, the substance-use behavior will move lower on the implicit reward hierarchy. We will look at how some fundamental coping strategies to modify substance-use behavior will target these different processes of the Vacuum Behavioral System in turn.

We will spend more time targeting the M.E.R. processes, since M.E.R. makes up the behavior itself, whereas targeting the Five Factors can be a larger undertaking in regard to making various underlying lifestyle changes. But it's just as important, if not more important, to target these underlying factors of the behavior.

Mindfulness is a process of intentionally paying attention to the experience of the present moment. Mindfulness applies to the habitual aspects of the substance-use behavior. This comprises the actual physical actions, and the cognitive processes that have a bearing on the actions. When we are mindful or "full of mind," we can generally be more aware of our cognition and physical actions, to slow down these processes of the behavior so they can be modified to achieve behavioral health. The tools that target the Mindfulness component of the behavior will ultimately enhance cognitive flexibility. This will further interrupt the rigid patterns of physical actions as seen in problematic use in regard to substance-seeking, preparing, and consuming. Rigid cognitive habits and action habits as seen in addiction like to maintain and stay in comfortable places. The related coping strategies disrupt and unbalance the habitual properties, making the behavior more malleable to change.

The coping strategies that target these processes of the behavior operate by altering the cognitive processes, which will simultaneously reduce or fully inhibit the related physical actions of substance use. We can consider these tools generally as "cognitive strategies." Under this umbrella, straightforward mindfulness can be used as a primary tool to manage these processes. The first step of a mindfulness strategy is to simply notice the automatic cognitive processes occurring that try to motivate the physical actions of substance use. The focus of mindfulness is not to push these thoughts away as "bad," but just to notice them and let them pass through our mind without physically reacting to them. Recognize that a thought is just a thought. When we observe these processes, whether they are the attention biases of the environmental cues or mental images of the desired effects, sometimes a mindful thought can do the trick: "I see how my current cognitions are motivating me to use substances. This is simply manufactured material from the dopamine system in my brain. Minds are wired this way to think about things we like. I don't need to react to it at this time." For some people, simply recognizing how biological mechanisms produce our thoughts can help us attach less importance to our cognition, and then to not react to them as if they are pure reality. It's just an illusion of desire. A simple mindfulness tool can target the attention salience a person may experience during substance misuse, like the person I spoke about earlier with his attention biases while drinking during a wedding. Many other people with problematic use can focus too rigidly on substance-related cues in the environment or on the thought of reaching intoxication. Being mindful of this cognitive experience, the person can first recognize their tunnel vision when it comes to substance use. Then they can begin focusing on other situations in their environment or on other non-relatable thought content. A mindful outlook also shifts the fixed general *attitude* about substance use, from being fanatical to more modest. This will enhance awareness of their total present experience; they will not feel stuck in their experiences, will cultivate cognitive flexibility, and can manage their overall physical actions.

Cognitive Reappraisal or Cognitive Restructuring is another cognitive tool; this one directly changes the cognitive material, unlike mindfulness strategies. Mindfulness tools enhance awareness and cognitive-action flexibility by defusing the power of cognition by creating distance from overactive cognition through simply observing with curiosity. Changing cognitive processes through Cognitive Reappraisal will in turn dictate the corresponding physical actions. Experiencing "romancing the high" cognition or over-expecting the benefits of using substances can motivate extensive substance use, as seen in addiction. A person may reappraise cognition by changing the overly high expectations to more of an attitude of, "The effects of the substance may be fun for a little bit, but it won't be the greatest thing in the world, and the feeling is temporary." This reappraisal may help reduce the compulsive desire to use. I remember the first time I drank after five years of sobriety. I noticed my expectations after a couple beers were, "It was a cool little buzz. But it wasn't as great as I used to think." These expectations after those couple of drinks inhibited the desire to want any more and motivated me to discontinue drinking for the night. Of course, someone in active addiction may not experience these balanced forms of expectations automatically. So intentional Cognitive Reappraisal, in conjunction with a mindful attitude, will create more realistic expectations, further regulating the behavior. For Cognitive Reappraisal to be effective, the importance lies in developing new cognition or thoughts that are realistic and believable to us. The new thoughts should be embedded in facts or interests, and create motivation for healthy forms of substance use or abstinence. One of the downsides of using Positive Affirmations is that people use affirmations that may be too vague or unrealistic. If I'm depressed, simply saying, "I'm great," will not make me feel less depressed. But I can get more specific and say to myself, "I take the initiative to help my colleagues at work, and I try as well in my personal life when I see the need." This new cognitive appraisal could make me feel better, since this statement may be more personal and rooted in fact.

A common Cognitive Reappraisal technique that many people use to inhibit substance use is known as "Playing the Tape Through." The process of this strategy is basically thinking about all of the consequences of frequent substance use when experiencing cognition that motivates continued use. If we "play the tape through" or follow our thoughts all the way through from start to finish, we will be reminded about the ultimate consequences if our habit with substance use continues to increase. Obviously if I think about consequences or the potential consequences of frequent substance use, I will be more motivated to stay sober or use at healthier levels during a given episode. We also need to keep in mind that the consequences of substance use are not inevitable, but thinking about them can help us simply put our foot on the brake pedal of our behavior. On the flip side, a person can use Cognitive Reappraisal by thinking about the positives or *benefits* of being sober or using substances in a healthier form, instead. What are the benefits of having a few drinks tonight rather than having ten? Well, I won't spend as much money, I'll get a relaxing buzz, I'll still have fun, I won't get a hangover, I'll feel good about myself, and I can appreciate drinking at healthier levels rather than feeling consumed by an addiction. Many people who naturally use substances at healthier levels, the so-called social drinkers, may experience this characteristic cognitive process naturally, while a person who has a history of substance misuse needs to intentionally restructure their cognition to this form more consistently to motivate a healthy physical action outcome when it comes to substance use. The nature of Cognitive Reappraisal targets the cognitive processes of: thought content manifested by implicit memories, substance use expectations, the risk-reward cognitive evaluation of using substances, and associated cognitive errors as described from Chapter Three.

A lot of cognitive strategies modify substance-use behavior by creating an adaptive focal point. Many people who are sober from an addiction use the label "addict" or "alcoholic" as a focal point to keep the idea present in their mind that they should not use substances due to the potential addictive outcome. I believe this can be an effective cognitive focal point for many people to help shift their cognitive processes to inhibit substance use. However, I also believe that these labels inform a misconception about substance-use behaviors and maintain shame, and that many people who quit substances do not like this type of a focal point. But if this works effectively for you, keep doing what works. Other focal points can be spiritually based, if we relate well to these types of concepts and ideologies. If we're experiencing cognitive processes that lead us to misuse substances, maybe I can ask myself, "What would my "higher power" or my greater purpose want me to do right now?" Asking this question helps us focus on a concept that we believe in. This will shift cognitive processes, and further dictate overt physical actions related to substance use that aligns with our ideal spiritual outlook. The tool of *praying* has similar mechanisms in altering cognitive processes as well. A Dialectical-Behavior Therapy (DBT) concept of "Wise Mind" has similar focal components of shifting our perspective to our "inner wisdom," which can result in its associated behavior. If we're not into religion or spirituality, then our personal values can simply be our focal points that target our cognition and modify our physical actions of substance abuse. Values can be almost anything, such as family, creativity, nature, career, learning, physical health, recreational activities, friends, and so on. Constructing a hierarchy of our personal values can arrange focal points in our life. Then we engage in daily, weekly, and monthly behaviors that align with our personal values.

People who use substances at healthier levels may do this naturally. After a few drinks on a Thursday night, they could think to themselves, "I'm not going to drink any more tonight because I have my nephew's graduation tomorrow." Or another person who is sober may think, "Well, since I've stopped using I can spend my money on something else I enjoy, or I don't want to start using because I want to spend more time learning how to play the piano." This is known as the "Value Compass" tool or Values-Based Living, which targets our cognitive attention salience and ultimately guides our actions.

Many people with addictive patterns experience a feeling of shame due to the consequences of their substance use. Even cognitive errors, like the Abstinence Violation Effect, can produce feelings of guilt and shame if we use a substance even once after a period of abstinence. Shame can be reappraised as a healthy emotion that motivates a healthy change. But shame oftentimes provides a negative outlook of ourselves and may motivate substance misuse. Cognitive Reappraisal and adaptive focal points can target these cognitive errors that create shame and further perpetuate substance abuse actions. If I have been sober for a year, but I feel guilty and shameful that I had one drink, I can ask myself, "What aligns more with my values; getting drunk today or just having a few drinks?" The answer may be just having a few drinks. This shift in perspective and modifying these cognitive errors will guide my physical actions to only have a couple of drinks or to stop when I think about it. So this action will reinforce more positive beliefs about myself, further reducing shame and improving self-esteem. These are cognitive errors because they could manifest in a healthy context of only having a drink or two, and become counterintuitive if we start abusing substances and using more dangerous drugs in response to the shame. Then engaging in sober actions can target our self-concept and experienced shame as a result of substance misuse in a positive manner. This will simultaneously enhance new cognitive processes that promote ongoing healthy behaviors.

Mindfulness skills can directly target the *consuming* physical actions of our behavior if we have already started to use substances, which will revise our corresponding cognitive processes as well. Mindfully drinking or "using mindfully" should be in every person's toolkit as an extra safety net if we have already passed through the substance-seeking and preparatory actions and started to consume the actual substance. We engage in a stream of behaviors every day and throughout our life without much notice or need to pay attention. Every morning when I get ready for work, I engage in a great number of actions that almost feel like autopilot. The behaviors are not *automatic*, I have just found a routine that works and it turned into a habitual pattern of action. I don't need to pay much attention to the details of laying out my clothes in the morning. But I better turn my mindful switch "on" if I start to use substances, and have had a problematic substance-use pattern in the past! This strategy involves observing our own physical actions when we're using substances as if we're a curious outsider looking in. Notice how much time has passed since you had the first drink. If it seemed like you drank the first one pretty quickly, then casually drink the second one at a more moderate pace, letting a half hour to forty-five minutes pass. Simultaneously shift your cognition onto other non-related aspects of the present situation or onto the long-term future. If you use substances like cannabis, be mindful of how much smoke you inhale to help prevent you from becoming too intoxicated, reaching a satisfying level that is not dictated by acting impulsive. During an episode of substance use, check in with yourself periodically to observe if you have reached the level of intoxication that you desire. If you didn't, continue to mindfully drink or use. But in many cases people realize that they have reached a satisfying intoxication level pretty quickly, and they can at least focus on something else and discontinue the physical actions of consumption once they bring their awareness to it. These mindfulness-related strategies in particular primarily target the physical actions of the M.E.R. behavioral process, while addressing its connected cognition in conjunction.

Various branches of substance abuse intervention utilize many of the strategies that I introduced in this section to target the automatic cognitive processes and associated physical actions. Acceptance Commitment Therapy (ACT), developed by Steven Hayes, is a third-wave Cognitive-Behavioral Therapy (CBT) approach for emotional health issues in general, but also for addictive behaviors. Principles of ACT focus on keeping a mindful distance from the inevitability of thoughts, acceptance of internal experiences, and acting in ways that align with values and an ideal self. These principles help with the ultimate goal of reaching cognitive and behavioral flexibility. Research has demonstrated that ACT has been effective in managing substance abuse behavior and reducing emotional shame.[1,2] Other established branches include Mindfulness-Based Relapse Prevention and Mindfulness-Based Cognitive Therapy, which continue enhancing awareness and modification of thought and associated behavioral processes in substance use. These approaches have also been found to be effective strategies in regulating substance-use behavior, along with overeating behaviors.[3, 4] Whatever techniques are used from these different approaches, the primary principle is that the strategies target and modify the pertinent behavioral processes.

Furthermore, as Cognitive Strategies alter underlying cognitive activity that has bearing on the overt physical actions, covert neurobiological mechanisms are being altered as well. Mindfulness and other skills like Cognitive Reappraisal activate areas of the brain such as the anterior cingulate cortex (ACC) and the dorsal medial prefrontal cortex (dmPFC), which are associated with cognitive and motor control of behavior.[5] This implies that the use of these techniques regulates substance-use behavior by directly targeting these neurobiological areas, and in some cases more effectively than traditional treatment approaches.[6] This may be due to the fact that we are able to manage the behavior more effectively if we use tools that have a direct route throughout these covert and overt processes. While addiction is impacted by the PFC and limbic-striatal connection, cognitive-related strategies activate a more sophisticated part of the PFC and the ACC that further helps downregulate the force of the adjusted Dopaminergic System. Making cognition and the motor actions of substance use more flexible through these practices, neurobiological changes can occur between networks, enhancing the basis for behavioral health.[7]

Since the neuroscience revolution and tech boom, cognitive concepts about powering up our minds have become more popular in various lifestyle areas, such as work and sport performance. A 2016 article in *Business Insider* interviewed a sports psychologist, Kristin Keim, who identified strategies to maximize performance in Olympic athletes under pressure through Cognitive Strategies.[8] Some of the skills include mindfulness meditation, positive self-talk (a form of cognitive reappraisal), and visualizing future performance success before undertaking performance tasks such as doing a presentation at work or a swimming race. For example, if you visualize yourself in your "mind's eye" giving a good speech, this could reduce stress and improve confidence, which can further lead you to perform well and feel in control. Many of these skills will continue to trend, as we continue to better understand the nature of the brain, and as prospering behavioral health in various areas of our life becomes more valued. There are a plethora of ways to make cognition and physical actions more flexible, and this section presents a short list. The main idea is how these strategies target the habitual processes of substance-use behavior within M.E.R. People are encouraged to use whatever is effective for them. As long as they know how it works. Mindfulness is a general state of being, which becomes turned on to produce thought processes and behavioral actions that fulfill what we *really* want with the time we have in our life.

Exposure to substance use-related contexts creates an opportunity for tool implementation to help manage the overall behavior. Strategies that target the Exposure component of M.E.R. will address the contextual aspects of the behavioral process. The two primary targets are contextual triggers and the craving response to use. Triggers encompass multiple levels, such as internal states, the immediate environment, and general life circumstances. Then the "craving response" will be measured along the *disgust-craving* continuum. The tools that target this M.E.R. component will work by shaping the contextual features, which will in turn modify the whole behavior. If a craving sensation occurs, based on a relevant context, it can be managed effectively by defusing its perceived power. The main idea is to be able to observe how context is impacting the function of the substance-use behavior, and alter the contextual processes to produce a behavior that aligns with personal behavioral health.

The first step is to monitor and map out triggers whenever a "consideration" to a "craving" response is experienced. If a person experiences a level of craving, then they can ask themselves the following questions: Where am I? What's going on? What am I doing? Who am I with? What are other people doing? What was I thinking about? How am I feeling? How do I feel about my life right now? Some of these questions can help a person map out the nature of their triggers, which will enhance awareness so that triggers and cravings can be anticipated for when they occur. You can simply identify what the contextual triggers are and rate the craving response on the continuum. Labeling out loud will connect these processes to the linguistic parts of the brain, which will improve insight and diminish the impact of the craving sensation. I even like having clients map out the triggers that elicit a "disgust" or "no interest" response, because this practice will help them better understand how triggers work in general and how they inhibit or motivate substance-use behavior. Also, you can map out the triggers and craving response for caffeine and nicotine use, even if you don't want to change these behaviors. This further translates to other substance-use behaviors that are the actual focus of change, and strengthens the muscle of monitoring and mapping. The skill of monitoring and mapping contextual processes is the foundation for addressing the *Exposure* component when modifying substance-use behavior.

A 2001 article by Vannicelli presents a treatment protocol for individuals who want to learn Moderation Management with alcohol use, on which many of the principles are contextually based.[9] One of the primary strategies of this protocol is to map out "appropriate drinking" situations versus "high-risk drinking" situations. During an initial period of abstinence, the person should look back at their drinking or substance use history and identify the contextual features during problematic substance use versus healthy forms of use. Exploring this and having the data will inform the person of the contextual nature of their substance-use behavior, and what situations may be more likely to create unwanted behaviors. Then the person would abstain more from drinking during the high-risk situations, while permitting themselves to drink in appropriate contexts. Let's say a person looks back in their substance use history and they notice that they typically engage in binge use when they're alone and depressed, but drink at healthier levels during social situations. Then if they reintroduce drinking back into their life and experience a craving to drink when they feel depressed while alone, they should be more mindful of their substance-use behavior. They know from experience that this is a situation where they are more likely to misuse alcohol, compared to being exposed to a different context. Then drinking during other contexts that may have more of a healthy drinking history would be more permissible. A person can continue to log their experiences. The nature of high-risk versus appropriate substance use situations is different for everyone, and they can change throughout the lifespan. But for some people the distinctions of their substance use situational patterns may not be clear. Anyone can benefit from this exercise to better understand the contextual function of their substance-use behavior, and learn to be aware of how particular situations impact their behavioral processes.

These concepts emphasize the strategy of "Stimulus Control" to modify addictive behaviors. Constructing contextual conditions that emits abstinence or more healthy forms of substance use is the function of Stimulus Control.

Residing in a sober living home that administers random breathalyzers and drug tests to the residents is a form of Stimulus Control. A person is less likely to use substances if they live in a context where they have to provide a drug test compared to if they didn't need to. On a smaller scale, if a person wants to begin reducing their cigarette frequency, I will encourage them to use a Stimulus Control strategy. If they smoke on average ten cigarettes a day, I may have them set a condition of only carrying eight cigarettes with them instead of their whole pack when they leave their house. Bringing their whole pack, they may smoke ten, eleven or twelve without thinking about it. But if they carry only eight or less cigarettes with them, then they will have to pace themselves throughout the day while coping with their cravings in between cigarettes. As their tolerance and dependence decreases with nicotine, then they can adapt to fewer cigarettes a day due to Stimulus Control. Then the person can begin carrying only five or six cigarettes with them and so on. If a person wants to reduce their junk food intake, they can make themselves only eat chips out of a small bowl instead of the bag, because they may keep eating until the whole bag is empty versus only eating until the small portion is finished within the bowl. Stimulus Control can also be a strategy to only use substances under specific conditions. So if the person who is quitting smoking is down to two or three cigarettes a day, maybe they will only smoke a cigarette after meals or whenever they go outside. The current Stimulus Control that I place on my substance-use behavior is drinking only one cup of coffee or less a day. I limit myself to one cup of coffee a day to prevent developing a tolerance and dependency to caffeine. Some people may want to drastically reduce their caffeine intake by only drinking it during social situations or when they have a challenging task to complete. So with a lowered tolerance due to that reduction, the person will get more positive effects from the caffeine when they actually need it. Also, Stimulus Control can include selecting *dry days* during the week to not use any substances. You can select Monday through Thursday, or days when you have other activities to attend to during the week.

I've consulted a lot of people who said they have tried various Stimulus Control strategies, such as only drinking beer and not liquor, or only drinking in social situations and not keeping alcohol at home. But they discussed how it did not work and it always led them back to their previous addictive pattern.

One of the biggest reasons why New Year's resolutions don't work is because people set the bar too high or they have unrealistic expectations. The same thing can lead to challenges with Stimulus Control on substance-use behavior. I worked with a client who said that she will only drink on holidays, but I suggested that we should reevaluate this condition and adjust it more sensibly. Only drinking on holidays can be pretty infrequent, which can be problematic in the long run. What can happen is, she drinks on one holiday but the next holiday may not be for a couple months. So in the meantime she may start to justify drinking every other weekend. Then she thinks that wasn't so bad, and it turns into every weekend, and then every weekend turns into every other day, leading to an unwanted habit. So while the initial condition of only drinking on holidays sounds good in theory, this may not be realistic enough for her personally. Once this line is crossed, the condition gets neglected entirely and there is no Stimulus Control in place. I have worked with many people who used Stimulus Control to change their substance-use behavior. But once they violate their conditions, they lose the focus of Stimulus Control and never adjust it. A woman in my group focused on limiting herself to one drink an hour, but found this to be difficult and she would end up drinking impulsively. When she brought this to the group and adjusted it to two drinks an hour, she found more success.

If people use Stimulus Control, they need to develop conditions they can commit to, and that includes a "hardline" with a high priority given to not crossing it. A common hardline is not using previous high-risk substances that the person was addicted to, such as heroin, or never using any alcohol if you're driving. A hardline is a condition that *should never* be crossed under any circumstances, even though other Stimulus Control conditions can be worked on and adjusted. Stimulus Control conditions should be realistic and fit into a person's wanted lifestyle. Instead of only drinking on holidays, maybe allow yourself to drink once a week, but never drink more than two days in a row. If you allow yourself to drink more than once a week, allow yourself a limit on each occasion and never drink when emotionally distressed. If you use substances like cannabis, maybe you can allow yourself to use it as much as you want, but you will never keep a personal supply. This would mean you would use it only in social contexts. Even if a person finds a Stimulus Control that fits into their lifestyle, they can still cross the line of the conditions, which puts them at risk for developing an addictive pattern. But it's important to continue to adjust the conditions realistically, and never neglect Stimulus Control altogether. Also, some people may simply regress back to their addictive pattern because they are not addressing their cognitive-physical action processes under the Mindfulness component when cravings occur in between episodes of substance use. While Stimulus Control can be a helpful tool to shape context, it is not the apex tool to address the Exposure component of the behavior. The most important focus is being able to learn how to manage any level of craving under any situation, circumstance, or context, whether Stimulus Control is in place or not.

A craving response occurs when a person is exposed to pertinent contextual triggers, which can be managed and rested. Next time you experience a desire to use a substance or engage in any other behavior, *time* how long the craving lasts without focusing too much on it. The craving typically escalates, peaks, and then declines, lasting anywhere from twenty seconds to several minutes. In reality, this is not a very long time, and this understanding cuts the power of the craving in half. "Urge Surfing" is a skill that addresses cravings directly by alleviating their power and weight through not acting on the sensation as it escalates and dissolves. Urge Surfing works by first noticing that you are experiencing the craving, and then viewing the craving with your eyes closed as if it were a wave that peaks, and then riding the wave out like a surfer until it breaks down. This tool shares some commonalities with the mindfulness-based approaches that I discussed in the last section. But Urge Surfing directly targets the craving response. The approaches also relate because cognitive processes and craving responses can coincide and influence one another, since all of the M.E.R. properties interconnect. Trying to avoid triggers and cravings can be counterproductive because craving responses are inevitable. Avoidance also supports the attitude that cravings are overly powerful or "dangerous," making the person think they have no control of their behavior. A 2013 study found that many residents of a sober living home viewed that *approach* coping towards substance-related cues in their environment was an opportunity to strengthen their skills to overcome cravings, compared to others who endorsed *avoidance* coping attitudes.[10]

My favorite metaphor about cravings is the paparazzi. If you were a high-profile entertainer in public, what do you think would be the most effective way to deal with the paparazzi? Some may believe that just letting them be and casually talking with them as you go about your daily business can be the most effective. On the other hand, some people may try to fight the paparazzi, try to push them away and yell at them, not knowing that the paparazzi will only come back to you more persistently. Cravings or desires to use substances act the same way as the paparazzi. I hear clients say all the time, "Cravings are so hard to get over. I focus on them, and I try my hardest to push them away, but they're always there and I can't get rid of them." If you try your hardest to push the paparazzi away, they only come back harder. Like when we try to push cravings away, they *seem* to feel more powerful and present. So it's most effective if we treat our cravings like we would with the paparazzi, by simply letting them be there without trying to push them away. You're not avoiding them, but you're also not fighting them and making them your whole world. You're simply accepting their existence. This attitude towards cravings defuses their power, and cravings, like the paparazzi, do not come back as stubbornly if we do not give them any dominance.

Craving responses can occur regularly as we go through our days, especially early on if we're sober from a substance-use pattern. We get bored from time to time, feel stressed, walk past bars, and become exposed to various contexts that elicit a caving response when we're sober. But if a person is not experiencing any cravings naturally, then they are encouraged to intentionally expose themselves to relevant contextual triggers to elicit a craving response so they can strengthen their skills and improve their confidence. Obviously we would not want someone to go visit a drug dealer or put themselves in a situation that can create a risk of physical danger. But there are many forms of healthy exposure exercises, such as having lunch at a bar or watching videos of people consuming drugs, or you can simply close your eyes and imagine a substance use scenario. If a person is experiencing cravings naturally, then there is no need for them to intentionally expose themselves to triggers, since they can practice using their tools in the meantime. Exposure strengthens skills and defuses the perceived power and weight of cravings. So when inevitable cravings occur in the future, the experience will be familiar, and the person will feel a lot more comfortable with it.

If a person has been effectively managing their naturally occurring cravings and they have not experienced any level of craving for some time, then they can start exposure. Before exposure, a person should develop an Exposure Hierarchy, which may start off with easier exposure exercises and then become progressively more challenging. Maybe the first exposure exercise can simply be closing one's eyes and imagining a substance use scenario that produces a craving response. If the person consistently develops a new outcome in their visualization and they feel confident about this exposure, then they can be ready for the next level on the hierarchy. The next exercise can be looking at pictures online of substances, substance use, and then watching videos of people using. Then *in vivo* exercises can include walking through the liquor aisle at the store, going to a bar, and then being around people we know who are using alcohol. How a person progresses through the Exposure Hierarchy is different for every person, depending on their natural craving experiences without exposure, the effectiveness of their tools, and their feelings of confidence in the various exposure exercises. Managing craving responses effectively during exposure is a major prerequisite for a person deciding to reintroduce substance use after a period of abstinence. Thus, the person will be efficient at managing cravings in between substance use episodes so the behavior does not regress back to a problematic pattern.

A client was telling me about an experience he had when he walked past a crowd outside a music festival in downtown Chicago when he was running errands. He experienced a desire to drink when he saw a lot of people walking to the festival, laughing and looking like they were having a good time. He knew that drinking was involved. He said, "They looked like they were having such a good time. After I dropped off the application, I took a different route home because I didn't want to go through that again." Right there, he just gave the craving more power than it deserves! When he told me that, I said to him that if I were with him, I would have encouraged him to actually take the same route back and walk through the crowd again. I pointed out that he effectively managed his desire to drink when he walked through the crowd initially. So taking the same route back would only strengthen his tools to manage the inevitability of cravings for the future. So if he ever wanted to go to a music festival or a similar social situation, he would have already built up the skills to get through any craving that was thrown his way.

I worked at a treatment center that included a sober living component, and I had a client who wanted to move back to an old neighborhood where he used to live, because the rent worked into his budget. However, he was unsure if he wanted to move back there because it used to be his "old stomping grounds." At the time, he had several months sober and was not experiencing any cravings to drink. So we set up a plan for him to go to his old neighborhood every Saturday to have lunch and go to the library. This exposure exercise let him evaluate to see if being in his neighborhood elicited any level of craving. Then he could gain practice in managing cravings if they came up, as he still had the Stimulus Control of living in our facility. So by the time he moved out, the potential cravings that he may face had already become familiar and his skills were strengthened.

There has been considerable research into and emphasis on the use of Cue-Exposure Therapy to effectively manage craving responses with substance use. There's evidence suggesting that exposure exercises with substance-related cues have been effective in reducing craving and enhancing confidence, along with a reduction in brain reactivity in relevant brain networks, as measured by an fMRI when exposed to substance cues after cue-exposure treatment.[11, 12] Cue-Exposure Therapy has also been shown to be effective in reducing cravings in people who are quitting cigarettes after engaging in exposure exercises with images related to smoking.[13] Exposure exercises help people reduce their natural sensitivity to triggers, while improving their confidence to manage cravings for when they do occur. Then being exposed to negative substance-related cues that elicit more of a *disgust* response can help create a realistic outlook for substance use that dampens the craving response in the future. A 2010 study exposed a group of people to alcohol-related pictures paired with negative images. After a series of exposures, they found that they experienced more negative attitudes towards alcohol and drank less compared to other groups.[14] This research demonstrates how implicit associations in the brain in regard to context and craving response are not set in stone, and they can be modified through new experiences with exposure processes.

Context is massive. It's our whole world. But the importance of context shrinks when we simply have the understanding and knowledge of how personal context plays a role in our substance-use behavioral function. Instead of feeling as if context is crowding us like the canopy of a rainforest, we become more like an observant solo climber on a mountaintop, once we implement some of these fundamental tools and tailor them to our own style. Many people with addictive behavioral patterns feel engulfed by the contextual triggers and their associated cravings. But many of the strategies used in this section can make you feel a little more detached from the experience, enabling you to behave more in ways that align with your behavioral health. **Contextual strategies** also provide the opportunity to nudge problematic substance use out of our lives through the enhancement of a fulfilling lifestyle. We will explore this idea as we progress through this book. **Exposure** welcomes the experience of desire or craving to use substances with a more curious attitude. Instead of trying to close the door on an urge, open the door and let the urge come and go as it is, with compassion. It's not about being passive, but mindfully unhooking ourselves from the experience. This sensation, this urge, is merely information that is produced by biological systems in the brain through our present context.

The *Reinforcement* component is primarily addressed by engaging in alternative behaviors that fulfill the reinforcement properties that substance use provides. We need to first understand what substance use does for us, which can vary each time we use substances, as we discussed. Then we engage in alternative behaviors that work in parallel with the reinforcing nature of substance use. If we experience a craving to use a substance, we can observe whether the trigger can be fulfilled through Reinforcement. If so, then we can choose an alternative behavior that addresses the trigger and associated goals in that moment. A simple example would be using substances to temporarily remove stress. We will need to develop and engage in alternative strategies to remove stress, such as exercising, relaxation exercises, and other leisure activities after work. A more complicated situation, such as where a person uses substances to cope with an extensive trauma history, may need more than just choosing alternative coping behaviors. But it is also recommended that they seek out therapy to process the trauma or attend a support group. Regardless, it comes down to developing a stream of *adaptive* behaviors that maximize pleasure while minimizing pain.

The challenge lies in competing with substances that do a great job of mimicking the neural chemicals that maximize temporary pleasure. Substances are predictable and a convenient way to achieve our Reinforcement goals in our lives. It can be challenging to find out what alternative behaviors work. Also, other behaviors may not provide as much immediate pleasure on a biological level as substances can mimic. When discontinuing addictive behavioral patterns, one can quickly discover that, "the highs aren't as high, but the lows aren't as low." A person with an addiction may attempt to maximize their pleasure through their immediate substance-use behavior. But, unfortunately, there can be a high price to pay, one that brings the person to an even lower point after use. If a person wants to modify their substance-use behavior to abstinence or to a healthier form of substance use, developing alternative behaviors is necessary. If I use heroin every single day and I want to cut it out of my life completely, I will need to develop alternative behaviors that override the sole pleasure of substance use. There's no way around it. Let's say I have an addictive pattern with alcohol use, but I want to modify my drinking to healthier levels. I would need to develop alternative behaviors to replace the substance use I want to cut out of my lifestyle. I mean, there needs to be some sacrifice to be able to work towards behavioral health. Our biological systems cannot sustain extensive substance-use pleasure for long without some type of rebound effect.

Actual substance use can still be included in the Reinforcement strategies of modifying substance-misuse patterns, as long it's in conjunction with alternative behaviors. For instance, don't make drinking the only activity in a social setting. Watching a sporting event, playing a board game, or dancing can be included as alternative behaviors that can help bring pleasure, while reducing the drinking behavior to a healthier level. This points out the importance of developing a healthy lifestyle in general. If we're living a healthy lifestyle, we're engaging in a bunch of little alternative behaviors that have either replaced substance use altogether or simply override the wanting to use substances all the time. Some of us need to develop more behaviors that improve our affect regulation, while others may need to develop more hobbies and interests that fulfill the Reinforcement that persistent substance use provided. If we have more alternative behaviors in place that work in parallel with the Reinforcement characteristics of our substance use, then our substance-misuse behavioral patterns are even more malleable to change.

I remember feeling completely liberated when I started drinking after five years of sobriety, and seeing how alcohol was not a major focus in my life. I spent five years of my life being sober, developing thousands of alternative behaviors to be able to deal with stress, loneliness, excitement, and fun without needing to use substances. I had been engaged in a behavioral lifestyle that was adaptive, and did not depend on substances use behaviors. So when I started drinking I felt free that I could enjoy alcohol whenever I desired it, without it having an addictive control over me. It fit well into my lifestyle, in combination with the alternative behaviors that had been developed into habits over the years. I had a moment in college when I was taking acid. I thought to myself at that time, how much I loved drugs and if I had one more day to live, I would just use all of my favorite drugs. Since that time, my attitude towards substance use has completely changed. It was not until I was pushed into developing reinforced alternative behaviors that substance use could eventually fit into my life adaptively.

We typically decide to engage in alternative behaviors when the punishment of substance use exceeds its reward. But humans are fortunate in the sense that we can make this decision at any point. The goal is to make the decision towards alternative behaviors once we start to notice punishment properties with our substance-use behavior. Then we can adjust how substance use can fit adaptively into our lifestyle, or be left out entirely, if that is what we desire. Life is simply a stream of behaviors, and our well-being can be represented by a consistent flowing stream. This is when we choose to use fewer substances, along with engaging in alternative behaviors, since that is what can actually provide us with more pleasure in the long run. Even people who have never had issues with substance use and have no desire to change their behavior could provide insight into how alternative behaviors play a role in their life. This could have prevented substance use ever becoming the central behavior in their lifestyle in the first place. For people who want to modify their substance-use behavior, it may just take more exploring to find behaviors that effectively address emotional health issues, relieve boredom, enhance creativity, support productivity, or whatever a person uses substances for. Reinforcement being the effectual component of the substance-use behavior, it will require a direct behavioral substitute that addresses the goal of substance use.

Many of these strategies can be used to modify substance-use behaviors directly, which modifies its overall M.E.R. functioning. The strategies that were introduced in this chapter are the basic fundamentals of changing substance-use behavior. This is by no means the entire extent of the tools that can be used. Many of you reading this chapter have probably already thought of a bunch of other strategies. That's great, to be thinking about other strategies, and how they relate to the mechanics of the current tools. If you do identify other strategies, think about how those strategies directly target the organic processes of M.E.R., and ultimately shape the whole behavior. The current tools are the general approach to changing substance-use behavioral patterns.

Many of these strategies can be used alone, and have the capability to change the whole M.E.R. function. But it's a good idea to use more of these strategies in combination to modify substance-use behavior more robustly. For instance, a mindfulness technique directly targets the cognition and physical actions of the Mindfulness component, but can also simultaneously manage the contextual processes of craving and alleviate whatever Reinforcement goal that is sought. Engaging in alternative behaviors may primarily address the Reinforcement feature; however, alternative behaviors may also address cravings and shape context indirectly, while simultaneously altering substance-related cognition, further inhibiting substance-use actions. Using strategies in combination, a person can initially use a mindfulness tool to observe the automatic cognitive processes and its contextual cues, while managing the craving by Urge Surfing. The same person could further use Cognitive Reappraisal to think about the benefits of not using, or using at a healthier level. Then choosing an alternative behavior can fulfill the reinforcement goal altogether, or simply reduce the physical actions of consuming substances during an episode. A Stimulus Control strategy and alternative behaviors can be folded into the person's lifestyle, while in conjunction the person is engaging in other Mindfulness and Exposure strategies that address other acute substance-use behavioral processes.

This is how tools impact the whole Vacuum System. Modifying the M.E.R. function directly will then indirectly modify the person's Five Factor Profile, and further adjust the Dopaminergic System accordingly. Then if we target our Five Factor Profile directly, this will in turn filter out a modified M.E.R. behavioral function.

Strategies that may directly address the *Gene* factor include using medication like Naltrexone, which was introduced in Chapter Two. Medications that block the rewarding effect of substances will decrease the Gene factor by altering the gene expression that promotes the euphoric effects of substances. This will predictably impact the filtered M.E.R. behavior. The *Psychological* factor can be addressed in numerous ways. Simply reaching an age where the brain has fully developed will naturally reduce the Psychological factor, and in turn affect the M.E.R. functioning. Other strategies can include strengthening mindfulness skills to reduce general impulsive states, or managing the need for immediate gratification in various areas of one's life. Developing hobbies or other leisure activities will not only target the Reinforcement component directly when substance-use behavioral processes occur, but can also reduce the Psychological factor by addressing personality traits that are geared towards sensation- or novelty-seeking. I worked with a person who discovered that he measured higher on the Psychological factor than the other factors. He had difficulty delaying gratification in various areas of his life. He wanted to drink again in the future. So we made a plan to start working on reducing his Psychological factor by practicing delayed gratification in other areas of his life, such as limiting his sugar intake, delaying checking text messages, or ordering merchandise online instead of going to the store the day of. *Trauma/Affect* and *Life Stressors* factors can be reduced in countless different ways, which goes beyond the scope of this book. But these may include taking psych medication, psychotherapy, coping enhancement, using a support system, and raising self-esteem. The *Environment* factor can be reduced by limiting access to substances through Stimulus Control, by only using substances with people who do not abuse substances, or by placing other activities or commitments in one's life that are valuable. None of these particular strategies that I have mentioned are required or completely necessary. How a person addresses their Five Factor Profile will depend on their individual needs, and how they directly address M.E.R. in combination.

The tools are limitless when it comes to modifying substance-use behavior. The main premise comes down to *how* the different strategies plug into, and impact, the whole Vacuum System. If we observe the Vacuum System of a person with a problematic substance-use pattern, we will be able to see different parts of the system flare out, manifesting the substance misuse. A combination of the Five Factors is disproportionately higher on the profile. Habitual cognitive processes are more rigid and fused, dictating frequent physical actions. The person may feel their contextual triggers and associated craving response are inescapable. The reinforcement properties of their substance use cover more ground in their life, anchoring the behavior's presence. When we can observe these flare-outs in the Vacuum System within ourselves or while helping others, we can begin addressing the individualized areas of the person's system accordingly. It's most recommended to target the Five Factor Profile and all the behavioral processes of M.E.R. holistically to create a smoothly composed system. "The whole is greater than the sum of its parts." It took dissecting all of the individual parts that make up the Vacuum System to be able to really comprehend how different modification tools alter the organic processes of substance-use behaviors.

part 3

The Path

chapter 6

Goals
What do we want?

HUMANS ARE AUTONOMOUS DECISION-MAKERS, and we make decisions based on how we want to conduct our lives. Although we are autonomous, our decisions can be influenced by other circumstances that are not fully in our control. We can decide based on our biology, personality, values, how others act, consequences of past decisions, luck, and even what we perceive as possible. When we want to make a change in our lifestyle, we have an autonomous idea in mind of what we would like our goal to look like. The idea of our goal may not always be conscious. But the idea is present at some level, influencing our decision to ultimately make a lifestyle change. This goal is more valuable than any other goal that another entity could set out for us. Our personal goal is grounded in our autonomous decision-making process that genuinely wants to seek behavioral health.

Our family, public figures, the media, culture, and other institutions give us direct and indirect messages for the idea of what our lifestyle goals ought to look like. While it's helpful to gain all the information we can get from outside resources, we ultimately develop the final perspective ourselves of how our goals in behavioral health should look like. Oftentimes our autonomous goals can be misunderstood by outside resources, and the proper help can be withheld or nonexistent due to our goals not matching the other. As a trained therapist, I've been taught that people already have the answers to the life they want to lead. It just needs to be realized. My practice is to extract this from their unconscious, by pointing out the discrepancies or themes in their narrative to help them paint this picture at a conscious level. I do not define their goals, but I am simply a helpful vehicle towards the goals they seek. A metaphor that I like to use is that therapists or coaches are basically mirrors so that people can learn how to see themselves more clearly. I'm an agent that reflects their path. We all have a path that we are trying to straighten out during our lifetime. Everybody's path will just be paved a little bit differently. We need to walk with people as *they* follow their path. We may draw out various goal interests that the person can narrow down, until they develop adaptive behaviors that fit into the enduring lifestyle they want.

Our addiction industry, and substance abuse treatment in our culture, primarily measures behavioral goals based on abstinence. The success rates and outcomes of the majority of treatment centers focus merely on whether the person has continued staying *sober*. Much of the industry assumes that every person who seeks help for their substance use holds the same universal goal of achieving long-term abstinence. This is assumed, even though they promote "individualized care." Unfortunately, if a person expresses that their goal is not abstinence or they say they don't want to stay sober for the rest of their life, then they may be considered "resistant," "in denial," or "not ready." We need to remember that many of these same people *decide* to get help in the first place, which is driven by a personal goal they have in mind and not imposed by an outside source. A 2005 study with 1,726 participants who were dependent to alcohol found that groups who received twelve sessions of outpatient treatment, received only one session of treatment, and those who dropped out before the first session had *all* already made the majority of their reductions in drinking by the first week of treatment.[1] From another angle, this study also found that only 3% of the reduced drinking outcome could be credited to the outpatient treatment. The dropout group was abstinent 72% of the days. The group who attended all twelve sessions only achieved 4% more improvement after attending the remaining eleven sessions after the first week. These findings support the notion that people are motivated to change their substance-use behavior before they even start treatment, and an autonomous goal already lies within them.

Many professionals in the field don't ask people what their personal goals are for their substance-use behavior, or what they want their lifestyle with substance use to look like. Also, those seeking help do not verbalize what their autonomous goals are, because sobriety is the assumed goal. But then what can happen is these autonomous goals can be expressed in many indirect ways, from trying to sneak alcohol use in a sober living home, switching to a different substance, or just resorting back to their high-risk drug-use pattern. The person's autonomous goals become lost in this process, and their goals are never understood, as they may enter the revolving door of addiction treatment. The appropriate help may never be offered to the person, because their personal goals become misperceived as them being resistant or not ready for help. But as the research shows, I believe people with substance use issues are ready whenever they make the decision to get help or express they want to make some type of change to their behavior. I don't doubt that people who seek help deal with legitimate challenges when it comes to changing their substance-use behavior. But it's important for the person to define what they want their substance-use behavior to look like, so we can provide suitable help that fits their overall lifestyle goals. It's a major misunderstanding on multiple levels if we assume that every single person who wants help with their substance-use behavior needs to consider or even want the same goal of long-term abstinence. During my first six months at a private clinic in 2018 with an intensive outpatient substance abuse program, I kept track of the personal substance use goals of the individuals who were admitted. I found that 63% of the total individuals wanted moderation goals or simply to reduce their substance use intake. Even though it was a small sample size, this finding demonstrates how well over half of the people wanted moderation goals and genuinely wanted to work on changing their substance-use behavioral pattern in a healthy way.

I spent an afternoon one day calling around various substance abuse treatment centers in the U.S., from Illinois to Florida, Texas and Arizona to California. I wanted to see if they could help someone with reducing their alcohol use to healthier levels, or with integrating alcohol use into a healthy lifestyle. I wanted to evaluate to see how various treatment centers would respond to my request if I were an actual client seeking help (or maybe I was just trying to be someone's pain in the ass that day). A few of the places simply stated that they did not offer that kind of help, so I went on to the next one. Some places seemed to dodge it by not saying "yes" or "no," but listed the clinical buzz words they do offer, "stress management, co-occurring disorders, evidence-based treatment," etc. Others seemed more interested in what my insurance plan was, or if they could get me into their residential program without attempting to address my personal goals. Another one recommended that I should consider discontinuing my alcohol use altogether. But I would typically inform them, "Well, I don't think it's necessary to quit using alcohol for the rest of my life. Right now, my consequences of my drinking are relatively mild. I just want to learn new strategies to drink at healthier levels, and let alcohol be part of a healthy lifestyle." For all of the treatment centers I called that afternoon, every single one of them noted that they were unable to help me unless my goal matched their imposed goal of complete abstinence. This didn't surprise me, since I am well versed in the treatment approach in our culture. But at the same time it did feel amazingly discouraging putting myself in the shoes of many people who try to seek help with the goal of using substances at healthier levels, and then being turned away. Many of these places promote having the *best* multidisciplinary staff and using the most advanced treatment approaches. But they could not help me with my personal substance use? If I look at a treatment program for addiction or substance abuse, I should be able to rely on them to help any level of a substance use issue and work with any healthy goal desired. I would even argue that milder substance use issues could be easier for them to treat than more severe cases of addiction.

People are diverse when it comes to the circumstances behind their substance-use behavioral patterns across their lifespan. As we know, this is reflected by the malleable Five Factor Profile of the Vacuum Approach. Also, the substance-use behavioral pattern itself presents in various shapes and sizes, as explained through M.E.R. So without even looking at a person's individualized Vacuum System, we cannot make assumptions as to what their personal goals for their substance-use behavior should be. What do we do with adolescents who come to treatment? The retiree whose substance use changed after their career finished? Or anybody else who decides to get help when they begin to experience the consequences of their substance-use behavior? Most of the traditional approaches will already predetermine the most rigorous treatment from an abstinent orientation without considering the individual. We don't do this with things like depression. If a person were experiencing any level of depression, we wouldn't initially give them the most extreme treatment of Electroconvulsive Therapy (ECT). We may not even start them out with medication. After an assessment, we may start with some minor lifestyle changes, such as exercising, changing their diet, journaling, and actively using a support system. If there is not much of an improvement with these initial strategies, the person can move to regular therapy sessions. Then medication or other rigorous medical interventions can be considered, if necessary. If a person is coming to seek help for their substance-use behavior, using lifetime abstinence protocols may not always be necessary. This is especially the case if this protocol does not align with their autonomous goals.

If a person comes to me with a substance use issue, I ask them what goals they are trying to achieve regarding their behavior and what they would like their substance use to ultimately look like. Many people say they simply want to quit using substances. While I believe abstinence can be one of the safest goals for substance use, I also believe it can be one of the most dangerous, if this goal is not created by the person autonomously. If abstinence is not a personal goal, then the person is at risk for experiencing a polarizing substance use cycle during a good part of their life. They get sober because of the assumed goal, and at some time they may desire to use at healthier levels. Then, due to their misconceptions about substance-use behavior and a feeling of guilt, they end up resorting back to their previous pattern of use, until they get sober again due to its consequences. This cycle can continue because their personal goals were never considered, and the appropriate help was not given. A 2013 study with 1,226 alcohol-dependent individuals showed that a group of people whose goal was "controlled drinking" consistently drank less during drinking days, while the group with the goal of "abstinence" drank the highest number of drinks during drinking days.[2] This study implies that people with an *assumed* goal of abstinence can be more at risk to polarize their substance use if complete abstinence is not their *actual* desired goal. They end up drinking, without any new conscious goal in place. Where people with goals of more controlled drinking can be more mindful of drinking less, if this is a conscious goal that they are actually striving towards. There are many people who do stay sober for the rest of their lives. That is not only one of the safest goals, but can also be the most satisfying if this is truly what they want their substance use goal to be. So if a person declares that their goal is total sobriety, I just make sure that this goal is coming from their autonomous decision-making process and has not been imposed by someone else.

The Vacuum Approach does not make any value judgments about a person's substance-use behavioral pattern either way. The Vacuum System simply explains the whole nature of the behavioral process. Then the person identifies what their autonomous goals with substance use are, and the professional helps them integrate their goals into a lifestyle.

In the field, there are three general categories of goals related to substance use, known as *harm reduction, moderation management,* and *abstinence.* Abstinence is the most traditional approach, while harm reduction and moderation management are more alternative approaches. Harm reduction approaches may typically strive towards abstinence. But they consider that if the person is using in the meantime, they should use certain safeguards to soften the potential "harm" of using substances. An example of this would be needle exchange programs that provide education and clean syringes to prevent medical risks for people who use substances intravenously. More subtle strategies of harm reduction can include drinking water in between alcoholic beverages to prevent hangover impact. Harm reduction assumes that people will use substances regardless, so why not utilize strategies that significantly reduce the potential impact for risk? However, many people warn against harm reduction because they believe this approach enables high-risk substance use. But research has shown that harm reduction has been effective in decreasing high-risk behaviors in many countries, and there's no evidence to support that harm reduction practices increase illicit substance use.[3, 4] Harm reduction embraces a lot of helpful principles that promote safe substance use. But the approach seems to have a negative connotation for those who consider substance use "bad," and the person using is still caught in some dysfunctional cycle. Some attitudes of harm reduction view people who continue to use substances as stubborn, and so people are encouraged to engage in healthy safeguards with substance use until they are "ready" to quit using altogether. The ultimate goal of harm reduction focuses on reducing the harm potential of substance use or any high-risk behavior. This is only a short-term goal. So of course we want to include harm reduction values in all of our approaches, in order to prevent moderate to severe consequences of substance use. This is just good practice and common sense. But we will want to be able to work towards longer-term goals with substance-use behavior.

This leads us more into the long-term focuses of moderation management or moderation-reduction goals. Moderation management was originally set out as an alternative to abstinence-based programs for non-dependent alcohol users who wanted to drink at healthier levels. Through moderation management, people work on achieving their healthy drinking goals by monitoring and logging their alcohol consumption, considering the contexts of their alcohol use, engaging in alternative behaviors, and following other related strategies described in the last chapter. Favorable outcomes show that moderation management has been effective for people with alcohol-related issues, and moderation management is registered in the SAMHSA's (Substance Abuse and Mental Health Services Administration) database as an evidenced-based practice.[5, 6] Whereas harm reduction primarily focuses on lowering the risk of current substance-use patterns, moderation management works on integrating substance use into an already established healthy lifestyle after an initial period of abstinence. For behaviors like sex or food addictions especially, people are forced to learn moderation management, rather than abstinence, because you need to eat to survive and sex can be a necessary mutual value in relationships. We can learn a lot from these other behavioral addictions. When I was talking to those treatment centers that afternoon, one of them said to me, "We treat the underlying cause. So after that, people will find no need to use." Then I was thinking, *okay, but what if we do address the underlying factors of people's addiction, but they just want to drink in social contexts or smoke a doobie on a mountain in Colorado after skiing?* While moderation management was originally developed to help people reduce their alcohol use in a systematic fashion, the idea has become more widespread as a philosophy and general approach to using legal substances more moderately.

If you do consider moderation goals, my recommended golden rule is to develop a lifestyle you can see yourself living for the rest of your life sober. That way, moderate use can be smoothly integrated into your life. There are many people whose substance-use behavior is polarized for years, by either actively abusing substances or being completely abstinent. For many of them, active addiction is not desirable after a while, but total abstinence is not either. Therefore, it can be effective to achieve moderation goals by first living a life that is satisfying enough for long-term sobriety. Then if a substance like alcohol is used, it's just an addition to that life and the behavior can be enjoyed and appreciated. A major tenet of Cognitive Therapy is not developing *positive* thinking as such, but more *realistic* thinking. Not only can positive thinking be ineffective due to not being believable, but *only* thinking "positively" can create unrealistic expectations, and if the expectations are not met, then a person can experience more extreme negative thinking. For many people, abstinence is realistic for them, so it's an effective and believable goal to live by. But if total sobriety is not realistic for a person, they will need to tap into their autonomous goals to figure out if moderation is more of a goal that they want to work towards to prevent polarization. For moderation to be possible, people need to remember that they have to cut some drinking or substance use out of their life. There's no way around this. A realistic perspective about substance use will need to be cultivated, which in turn moderation use will shift an overall perspective about living a healthy lifestyle.

It can be easier to achieve moderation if we understand the exact nature of our Vacuum System. If we can see exactly how the different Vacuum processes influence addictive patterns, then we can use various strategies to precisely target the processes to make the filtered M.E.R. hum at a moderate level. According to the Vacuum Approach, if a person with any severity of addiction can quit using substances at various times of their life or abstain if they experience the most intense cravings, then they can moderate or reduce as much as they want to without substance use becoming a frequent habit again. It's not about being "strong" or having "willpower," just about deliberately targeting the pertinent processes of substance-use behavior within the Vacuum System. That's why it's important to develop a model of addiction that merely lays out the encompassing processes of all substance-use behaviors from start to finish.

The one thing I do not like about the approach of moderation management is that it seems to emphasize categories and the separation between *types* of people who use substances. If a person is drinking at healthier levels, are we always going to view them as a person who "moderates"? This is as if they are still tied to their previous problematic use. Can we just view their present behavior in context, as we would for any ones else's behavior? Another situation we need to consider is a person who may have a drink spontaneously in the future, while they have a general goal of sobriety. This person would technically be abstinent for the majority of their life, but may not drink *enough* to be considered "moderating." They cannot be placed into a goal category. But they are simply working towards healthy substance-use behavioral goals, if they're abstinent for weeks or months at a time and then have a drink every so often. A person like this can be misled in the categorical goal process if their individualized goals are not considered. Another issue that needs to be dissected is this: if a person has an issue in their life, it doesn't always mean that their substance use is causing it. If substance use is impacting the issue, then the person needs to explore at what magnitude, and address the substance-use behavior and lifestyle issue accordingly. At the end of the day it doesn't matter if we are abstinent or moderating, but if we live in the context of personal behavioral health.

Harm reduction, moderation management, and abstinence are the three pillars of substance-use behavioral goals. Each one of these modes carries a larger underlying value. The core idea of harm reduction is to make substance use as safe as possible, and minimize its consequences however we can. Moderation management mainly focuses on reducing substance use to healthier long-term levels, and integrating it into a healthy lifestyle. The primary value of abstinence is to be able to tolerate and enjoy life without the use of and dependency on substances. The Vacuum Approach combines these three pillars of substance use goals into a single philosophy that creates more flexible behavioral experiences. The key interest is living a lifestyle of wellness, which will look different for every person. Using these three categories *separately* only creates more division and puts unnecessary expectations on people. The most important idea of the Vacuum Approach is to incorporate these three primary values of substance-use behavior into whatever the individual's behavioral goals are. *Every* goal of substance-use behavior includes sobriety being a large portion of a person's lifestyle. Healthy moderation principles lie dormant until they become activated if a person decides to use substances. Then, reducing the risk potential of substance use is the most immediate importance if the behavior is engaged. The foundation of a person with an addiction is "substance use," while the goal is to flip this, making sobriety the foundation through the implementation of the *tools*. It's not until we create a sober foundation that complete abstinence can continue as a successful goal, or healthy substance-use patterns can be included on this foundation, if desired. Behavioral patterns and their goals can be fluid and achievable as long as they originate from the autonomous decision-making process, and merge the three pillars of substance use goal orientations.

If a person's goal is to discontinue substance use altogether, then they make the decision to get sober and address their Vacuum System accordingly, to maintain their lifestyle. But if a person has a goal to use substances at healthier levels, the question arises as to whether the person should initiate abstinence first or if they could just start reducing their use to moderation. If people have a high tolerance and are actually chemically dependent to substances, as seen in more severe addictions, it's recommended that they receive medical detox to get back to their physiological baseline with substances. It's especially important to receive medically monitored detox for substances like alcohol and sedative-hypnotic drugs like Clonazepam or Xanax if a person is chemically dependent, since withdrawal from these classes of substances can cause acute health risks. One of the benefits of getting back to a chemical baseline after detoxing is that a person will be able to experience the full effect of a single dose of a substance if the behavior is reintroduced. Experiencing the full effect of a dose can help a person envision how their substance-use behavior will unfold in the lifestyle they want. If a person has a chemically dependent habit, their substance-use pattern can be blurry and they may lose touch with what their substance-use behavior did for them initially. So after detoxing, a person having a single alcoholic beverage may experience some intoxicating effects from just one drink. Then they will be able to envision, "Oh, I feel pretty good just from one or two drinks. So if I go out with friends during a long night out, I won't have to drink more than four." Similarly, if we reintroduce coffee or caffeine use back into our lives, we will be able to observe how much a single dose does for us. Then we can engage in our coffee use to increase our energy when it matters most. Thinking ahead about this after resetting our body with substance use, we will be able to be more mindful of how fewer doses provide us the desired effect quicker than we thought. This would help keep us using substances at healthier levels, and our tolerance would then stay at a lower level. We would be able to see how substance use could fit into our lifestyle, and then start to appreciate substances more once we re-engage at our baseline.

Other situations where it is recommended that people initiate a period of abstinence before reintroducing substance use include addressing issues that may need more attention in a sober context. A person with problematic substance use who measures high on the Trauma/Affect factor of their profile may engage in substance use to cope with the manifestation of traumatic memories. So the person may need to be sober to process their trauma effectively, since substance abuse would only hinder the processing of trauma. This is similar to grief and loss issues, under the Life Stressors factor. A person may need to engage in alternative behaviors to process personal issues, and not engage in behaviors like substance abuse that only avoid working towards other goals that pertain to mental health. According to a person's Five Factor Profile, they may just have more long-standing issues that need more focus and need to use alternative behaviors before integrating substance use into their lifestyle after an addictive pattern.

An initial period of abstinence can also just be good general practice if healthy substance use is a desired long-term goal. As discussed earlier, the protocol of *moderation management* recommends at least an initial period of thirty days' abstinence to map out contextual triggers, practice managing cravings, and understand high-risk drinking situations. While sober, we can better understand our substance-use behavior in general, explore how it functions in our life, and develop alternative behaviors that help put a wedge between substance use sequences. When I say we need to learn how to *tolerate* sobriety, we need to be able to tolerate any kind of discomfort that life throws at us without using substances. This includes stress and grief, as well as other emotional discomfort. Learning to *enjoy* life sober pertains to lifestyle situations like not using a substance every time we're bored, when we go out with friends, or attend special events. The recommended initial period of abstinence can last anywhere from completing detox to years of sobriety. Some people may find that detoxing was enough, while other people may desire longer initial stretches of sobriety of thirty days to six months or a year to work on the underlying factors of their previous addictive behavior. I spent five years sober with the intention of being sober for the rest of my life. Through this long-term period of abstinence, I inadvertently lowered the Five Factors in my profile pretty drastically. So when I decided to drink, a healthy substance-use pattern was filtered out with more ease. The length of initial abstinence will vary for each person. The process of this period of abstinence will serve different needs in regard to the person's substance-use behavioral goals.

Then there are people with less severe problematic use who may not necessarily need to "get sober" or engage in an initial period of abstinence to incorporate healthy substance use in their life. They may not be chemically dependent or need to work on a personal issue that any substance use blatantly interferes with. They can just start using fewer substances until they get to an amount that they believe is healthy and causes minimal consequences. This can occur within one night of drinking when we catch ourselves drinking a little more than we intended. So we just discontinue our use for the night. Other situations may stretch across a longer period of time, where we binge use or use a larger amount every other day. Within these scenarios we can tweak the behavioral patterns by re-engaging in other hobbies or activities for the days following use. Then we would consider using substances again during the next weekend or however long we believe is an appropriate amount of time for our desired healthy lifestyle. However we tweak the behavioral pattern from misuse to healthy use will, again, depend on the nature of the Vacuum System. For special cases of people addicted to their opioid medication for pain management, they may need to consult with their physician to change medication or find an alternative for their pain issue. It does not matter so much about *how* the person gets to their goal; what does matter is if they achieve their personal goal for substance-use behavior. A person may want complete sobriety, regular healthy substance use, or more intermittent use. If substance use *is* involved in their goals, they may find the need to experience an initial period of abstinence to meet their long-term goal, while others may simply just reduce their use. Then we will all vary as to what tools we will use to reach our substance-use behavioral goals. Over time, if our behaviors become well conditioned to our lifestyle, then our substance use would become almost second nature without much conscious tool implementation. This is when substance-use behavior, like any other behavior in our lives, simply becomes part of the stream of our experiences.

I worked with a twenty-six-year-old man who had a mild to moderate problematic alcohol use pattern. His initial goal was moderation. As he attended our groups and learned about the behavioral processes and skills to manage his behavior, he was having success with moderation. He would have one to five drinks, depending on the social occasion, and he stopped drinking at work and during the day. He expressed satisfaction with his behavioral pattern. But during the latter part of treatment he switched his substance use goal from moderation to abstinence. Even though his substance-use behavioral pattern was healthier and he was satisfied with his use for the most part, he decided on abstinence. What he was not enjoying was after having only a couple of drinks, he would feel agitated when focusing on drinking more. So he chose to completely close the door on alcohol, so he didn't have to think about it. He realized that maybe he measured higher on the Gene factor than he had thought, where his biology *only* liked the feeling of being drunk, and this primary factor drove his problematic pattern in the past more than the other factors. So in that case, his particular interest in feeling excessive intoxication is simply a *preference* based on his very high Gene factor, and he decided abstinence was the best route for him to take.

The best part of this was that he was sensitive to the mild consequences of the discomfort of thinking about alcohol too much, and he discovered this behavioral goal on his own as treatment progressed. Nobody else chose this goal for him. This is what it's all about: exploring our autonomous goals with substance use. For many people, abstinence may be the best solution, to shut the door on substances for good. But people have many options about how they want to conduct their behavioral pattern moving forward.

"Motivational Interviewing" is a method developed by William Miller and Stephen Rollnick to help individuals build intrinsic motivation to change their behavior. Studies have demonstrated over the years that Motivational Interviewing (MI) has been effective in helping people change many behaviors that can cause unwanted consequences and long-term health risks.[7] Since its development, Motivational Interviewing has been popular in empowering people to increase their motivation to work towards substance use goals. The method works by extracting people's internal motivations by bringing attention to the discrepancy between their expressed desires to change and current behavior status. Then behavioral goals can be further explored and identified. Let's say a person states, "My drinking has caused my family to be upset with me, and I hate waking up the next day with that guilt and feeling hung over. But it's not like I ever lost a job or got arrested for my drinking." An ineffective response to this person would be to say that they are in denial and minimizing their drinking. An effective Motivational Interviewing response would fully capture what the person truly wants and what they're really trying to say. Our response can be, "It sounds like your drinking has created some consequences in your life that you're concerned about. While there is a part of you that enjoys drinking, you would like to be able to continue to enjoy it without it interfering with other things you value in your life." This process can specify personal goals, and then the person will take the proper actions that align with their combined values and goals. The idea of Motivational Interviewing is to help people tap into their autonomous goals and foster their autonomous decision-making process.

Unwanted consequences are generally the motivation for people's initial decision to change their substance-use behavior. We hear it all the time when they talk about their substance use, once they stop or begin the process of coming to treatment. They talk about their legal issues, health complications, how much money they lost, the people they hurt, the guilt they feel, and the job they lost. These consequences stay fresh for some time, and can be an effective short-term motivator for behavior change. They may quit using substances at the onset of treatment, or disengage their substance use on their own. While this is an effective internal motivator to change the behavior initially, it may not effectively last for long-term behavioral goals. We will have to eventually switch from being motivated by the consequences of our addiction to focusing on the benefits of healthy levels of substance use or complete abstinence as the long-term motivator for behavioral change. After the consequences become more distant in a person's life, Motivational Interviewing will be used more thoroughly to help people see the overall impact of their previous substance-use pattern. Then they can cultivate how either abstinence or healthier substance use can be more beneficial to their life. People typically experience the accumulation of their consequences as a result of their substance-use behavioral *pattern*, rather than individual behaviors of substance use. So when helping a person change their behavior, it's the pattern of their substance use that should be explored for change and not so much using substances in general.

The use of Motivational Interviewing has been important in the field of addiction because it can be challenging to motivate people towards the traditional idea of complete abstinence. It's a tall order to get someone motivated to never use substances again, no matter who they are. Nobody enjoys the consequences of their substance-use behavior. So this can be initial starting point to create some momentum towards whatever their substance use goals are. But expecting a person to live a totally sober lifestyle can be very difficult if this does not originate from their autonomous goals. Of course they want to make a change and achieve some goal, due to experiencing consequences from their current pattern. But Motivational Interviewing will have a minimal effect if the goal is imposed by some external source. So if we build a new goal-oriented approach to addiction and problematic substance use, people will be more drawn to receive help for their behavior. Like in the movie *Field of Dreams*, "If you build it, they will come."

As I mentioned in Chapter One, 87% of people who have issues with substance use in the U.S. do *not* seek treatment or some type of help. A percentage of this population may resolve their substance use issues on their own, without any formal help. Another percentage may avoid help because they are not motivated by an assumed goal that would be imposed onto them. Also, people may believe that they need to reach some type of "rock bottom" in order to strive toward the traditional approach of complete abstinence. For those reasons, and others, people don't seek help. They continue their substance-use pattern, and experience more severe consequences. *Then* they are motivated to seek treatment, once they believe they fit the traditional description of a problematic substance user depicted by our treatment culture. People should be able to feel motivated to seek help a lot earlier in their substance misuse pattern. But they don't, because the treatment industry highly pathologizes *any* case of substance misuse. Nobody would seek treatment for his or her depression until it becomes absolutely severe, if the only treatment approach that we provided was ECT. But with more options, people can seek help to alleviate their depressive symptoms a lot earlier on, through approaches that meet their individual needs and autonomous goals.

Motivational Interviewing can be a much easier process if we're able to choose any goal that we desire for our substance use. If I start to notice some mild consequences with my substance use, I will not go to a program where they will tell me that I need to succumb to a universal goal of abstinence for the rest of my life. But if I went somewhere that people would help me tap into my autonomous goals, I would most likely be more honest about my substance use and motivated to work collaboratively anyway I could to modify my behavior. Regardless of a person's substance use severity, anyone should be able to benefit from treatment or some type of help, as long as we work with the person's autonomous goals and address the exact nature of their Vacuum System. Just as how anyone can be psychoanalyzed to have better insight into themselves, or how everyone is working towards some type of behavioral health in their life. Every person can benefit from learning about the processes of their substance-use behavior to optimize their goals with it. This approach can be appealing to many people with mild to moderate substance use issues. Therefore, more people will seek out treatment that is appropriate for them individually. We may start to see fewer cases of severe substance misuse, while seeing more cases of mild to moderate substance use, since people will be more motivated to seek treatment earlier, once they start noticing consequences and knowing that they can work with any goal they wish.

Shame and addiction are oftentimes linked due to people feeling ashamed of their continuous substance use and the consequences that result. People can experience reduced shame for their substance misuse if they seek help earlier for milder consequences rather than waiting for more severe consequences. So by building an approach that can be more attractive to a wider audience who misuse use substances, the progression of shame can be prevented and, when it occurs, then dissolved more rapidly. Guilt and shame can be a healthy motivation to start a change. Then modifying the behavior to align with our personal goals will result in more favorable emotions. We hear a lot about the "war stories" of substance use, and the devastating experiences that the behavior created, from people in treatment or who are sober. This may only perpetuate shame. But we never hear or talk about the times of healthy substance use. Sure, talking about war stories will motivate me not to engage in my previous pattern of use. But it won't necessarily motivate me to engage in healthy substance use if this is my goal. If that's the goal, I want to hear about people's past healthy substance use, or when they were sober and started to use at healthy levels. I want to know how they do it, and hear less about war stories. People will continue to engage in addictive patterns, despite the devastating war stories. So thinking and talking about the benefits for alternative options can be more motivating. Motivational Interviewing will surely be more of an automatic process once we start to shift the values of substance-use behavioral goals to a more sensible approach.

Furthermore, the dynamics of the "Stages of Change" developed by James Prochaska and Carlo Di Clemente will also change if the values of substance use goals transform. The five Stages of Change is a model that is used to monitor and understand where a person is in the process of changing problematic behaviors.

1. The first stage of change is **precontemplation**. During this initial stage, the person has no present thought about changing their behavior, and believes that the behavior is not creating any significant issues in their life.

2. In the **contemplation** stage, the person begins to consider the problems that their substance use has created, and they are on the fence about making a decision.

3. The **preparation** stage occurs when the person is beginning the initial steps of behavior change by gathering information or developing a plan that they believe will guide their path for change.

4. The **action** stage is when the person is actually engaging in new behaviors and trying out new strategies to modify their behavior, or simply not engaging in the behavior or its previous pattern.

5. The last stage of *maintenance* has been reached when the person is living a lifestyle that is aligned with their autonomous goals, and feels confident in their developed behavior to get through any challenges that may come up.

When people don't believe in the universal goal of complete abstinence, they are considered to be in the *precontemplation* stage of change by the standards of the traditional approach. But the person may be a lot more motivated than they appear. They are actually at the *contemplation* or *preparation* stage of change if they are recognizing the consequences and express a desire to work towards their personal goals of substance use. People are already at the *action* stage of change if they have quit using substances before they receive help and their goal is abstinence. They will just need to further develop behaviors and a lifestyle that pushes them into the *maintenance* stage of change for lasting goal maintenance. If someone is at the precontemplation stage of change, they're not even at the door of getting any type of help. Plus, in that moment of substance use, they believe it's their best behavioral option. Once a person comes to treatment or talks about changing their behavior, then they should automatically be considered in the contemplation or preparation stage. Making this effort presents how the person intrinsically wants their behavior to be different in some way. Then it's the helper's job to elicit their autonomous goals in order to progress further through the stages of change. By the end of the preparation stage, the person should have a clear picture of their long-term substance-use behavioral goals. Then the action stage will involve trying out various behaviors and tools that promote healthy substance-use patterns or maintain total sobriety. Then the maintenance stage will involve actively living the autonomous goals, as the wanted behavioral patterns are well integrated into a lifestyle. Maintenance functioning has not much to do with whether substances are used or not, and has nothing to do with how many consecutive days sober a person has. But it has all to do with living the overall long-term goals.

Self-efficacy is a concept that has been used to explain how the nature of personal beliefs about the motivation and execution of challenging tasks impact behavior. If a person measures higher on self-efficacy, then they will carry more beliefs that they have greater influence and capabilities to overcome behavioral challenges. This could motivate them to take more actions that lead to success. While people who measure lower on self-efficacy will hold more beliefs that they don't have the capacities to influence situations or execute challenges effectively. So this can lead to more behaviors like procrastination or self-sabotage that create less successful outcomes. Self-efficacy is an important concept in behavioral health for gauging how personal beliefs about our confidence to overcome challenges impact the achievement of our behavioral health goals. The level of self-efficacy can be derived from various avenues, such as personality, external experiences, and our knowledge of the subject. While personal faculties like self-esteem can impact our general level of self-efficacy, just having the right information can help increase it as well. My self-efficacy for getting my first mortgage was very low, simply because I was inexperienced with this subject and did not have the right information going into it. I felt timid. I didn't know what questions to ask, what language to use in my emails, and felt uncertain requesting different things. But my self-efficacy increased as I progressed through the closing process, and learned more about loan borrower rights. I became more assertive, and took more deliberate action in the process to create the outcomes that I knew I had control over. The goal of this book is to provide the information about the exact nature of substance-use behavior, so people's self-efficacy can increase to achieve whatever their goals are with substance use.

It has been found that people's level of self-efficacy can predict the achievement of their personal abstinence or substance use moderation goals, along with their sense of control over their behavior.[8, 9] I will have an increased self-efficacy to alter my behavioral pattern for however I would like, if I have a full understanding of how the substance-use behavioral process works through the Vacuum System. Imposing a universal goal of complete abstinence and routinely expecting an addictive pattern to occur if a single substance is used, will seriously undermine a person's self-efficacy. This message tells the person that they have absolutely zero control over their behavior, even though this idea has been refuted by research and by the anecdotal experiences of people who have already quit using substances before beginning treatment, who don't use every time they crave, or who engage in healthier substance-use patterns after an addiction. Where people have their own goals concerning their substance use, the helper's primary goal for the person is helping them enhance their self-efficacy over their behavior, so they would never have to go to treatment again, and they can adjust their behavior as needed.

Sober counts or consecutive days sober will soon be withdrawn as the gold standard for success outcomes with addiction. Success outcomes should be more focused on general quality of life, and not so much about substance use itself. Addressing the underlying Five Factor Profile will improve the person's quality of life, which in turn filters out a new M.E.R. pattern. Whether it's a healthy level of substance use, total abstinence, or somewhere in between. Then the wiring of the Dopaminergic System within the Vacuum will adjust simultaneously to the updated behavioral experiences. I imagine that the amount of substance use has some correlation with quality of life. Using substances all day, every day, -can create many unwanted consequences, which can impair quality of life and maintain an addictive cycle in the Vacuum System. A person working toward a quality life will generally reduce their substance use. But there is a margin where the amount of substance use, from abstinence to healthier use, ultimately doesn't matter: the person feeling satisfied with their life in the long run is what matters, and not where they fall along this margin of use. So a person should not worry as much about whether they will ever use again or not. If it happens, it happens. But if it does happen, then just make sure that the behavior incorporates the three pillars of substance-use goals. Instead of focusing primarily on sobriety, treatment needs to place more emphasis on quality of life, fulfillment, self-efficacy, and other mental health measures. If a person initially wants to make a change to their problematic substance use, they actually just want to improve their overall quality of life, regardless of the goal. I worked with an intensive outpatient program that included groups with mixed substance-use behavioral goals. But the common thread that tied everyone together was that they were all there due to experiencing some level of consequences from their substance use, and they wanted to make some type of behavioral change to achieve wellness.

chapter 7

Language
How does culture influence our idea of behavior?

JUST AS OUR BEHAVIORAL EXPERIENCES are fluid and ever-changing like a stream, culture will continue to change like the stream throughout human history. One of the biggest windows into culture is language. Many cultures have their own written and verbal language, including various dialects for specific geographical regions. Language helps people connect socially and convey understanding of cultural ideas and practices, and it provides experiential meaning. Language has enabled humans to join on a global level to create the largest social networks of any species, to engage in exploration, and to pursue goals that continue to innovate and transform the world. There have been many major advances in human history, from the discovery of fire to the printing press, and from the internal combustion engine to the Internet. We will continue to come across major discoveries, including ones that will occur many years from now that we cannot even fathom. Language and its function of sharing information have made it continually possible to grow existing ideas exponentially to evolve culture. Take a "Biology 101" course in college. How many years do you think it took to acquire all the information in this single introductory course?

While language is a robust instrument of our existence, language and the ideas that it conceals can also be pretty limiting. *Knowing* is never fully known. We are restricted within the bounds of things that have already happened within history, the present experiences of our senses, and our imagination of the future. Our imagination is still limited by existing ideas we already know. Language represents these bounded places in time, and restricts our understanding of the objective world. For instance, the different words used to describe color by various cultures will influence the actual perception of color for people in those cultures. There is a single word for the color *blue* that can represent "lighter" or "darker" shades of the color in the English language, while *lighter blue* and *darker blue* in Russian are represented by two completely distinct words, *goluboy* and *siniy*. A study showed that Russian speakers were quicker at identifying varying shades of blue than English speakers.[1] This is due to the fact that Russian speakers have more of a distinct language to describe different kinds of blue than English speakers, who use the same term for different shades. This small finding reinforces the idea that cultural language can limit our understanding of the world. But our understanding will continue to update, as ideas change in relationship to culture.

If we home in on behavioral health, we will be able to observe how our attitude and understanding about various mental health issues has changed over time. During the World War II era, for instance, "shell shock" and "battle fatigue" were terms commonly used to describe the psychosomatic symptoms of what is currently known as PTSD. These are terms that have changed throughout history, representing the same exact experiences. The terms have been refined to depict our better understanding of the condition. Therefore, an updated understanding will not only influence how we help treat the symptoms, but also how we view and approach people who have them. Another classic example is the use of the term *mentally insane*, for people experiencing severe presentations of auditory hallucinations and holding delusional beliefs, as seen with Schizophrenia-related conditions. If we view someone as "mentally insane," we may start to see them as dangerous and grotesque. Then in turn we may treat them that way. But people with these related issues have organic brain conditions that alter processes in the brain and manifest these symptoms. They appear as bizarre or unusual, but less so once we understand how the brain works. With this updated understanding, we are able to view and treat people with these conditions with more patience and humanity. I don't even like the more modern use of the term *psychotic disorders* for this precise reason. Then we can have a full discussion just about how various cultures have viewed substances differently throughout human history. This is seen from the use of small doses of opium to relieve the distress of babies in ancient cultures, to modern alcohol and cannabis prohibition, and the view of prescription narcotics, to the use of psychedelics for processing trauma. How or why have views changed throughout history? The field of behavioral health and substance use has its own history about how language and its relationship with culture influence its understanding and meaning about *its* objective reality. This in turn will impact our approaches and practices.

This chapter is about examining how culturally limiting beliefs, and language about substance-misuse behavior, create unnecessary barriers. As history demonstrates, language and ideas in behavioral health will continue to change throughout time as our understanding updates. Culture is not *real,* in the sense of not existing as a fixed objective aspect of nature. Culture is a hypothetical construct that keeps on updating. This can influence a false sense of direction through the creation of fictional ideas about the world, although cultural ideas and the use of language can be a good thing to *help* provide understanding and meaning for different concepts in human practices. While fixed universal aspects of nature are valuable as well for understanding the world and our experiences. This outlook recognizes the importance of how the purity of things in nature will always stay constant and *true,* no matter how much time in history has passed or what cultural perspective describes the idea. Like the symptoms of "shell shock" or PTSD have always been the same in nature. Just culture and bounded time have shaped what we named it and how we approached it. Too much of one thing can create misdirection. Too much focus on cultural narratives will only create rigidity and stagnation, while too much focus on fixed universal nature will leave us lost in time and cause us to lose our footing with our sense of reality. To understand a concept in a timeless and objective fashion, a virtuous balance between cultural ideas and principles of universal nature will need to be aimed for. This is why I developed the *organic* processes of substance behavior and its Vacuum System. I simply lay out the universal components of every single substance-use behavior that occurred in any form in nature. I try to use just enough cultural language to describe it with objectivity, without creating too many expectations about the behavior. We will work towards quashing some of the addiction-related language that only creates limitations, while lighting up our view of what substance-use behavior is in its purest sense.

I cringe every time I hear "addict," or its close neighbor "alcoholic." Many people don't mind these labels and often find them useful, while many others find them demeaning. If there was only one person in this world who did not like this form of identity and it created shame only for them, then I'd be perfectly fine with throwing away the use of these labels altogether. In the broader scope of behavioral health, many people avoid seeking help or discontinue services for their mental health needs because of the stigma of being labeled with a *mental illness*.[2] Furthermore, labels in mental health care can lower people's self-esteem and self-efficacy, which can lead to poorer coping responses.[3] The label of "food addict" can be associated with the stigma of obesity.[4] Then the stigma of addiction labels for substance use can continue to negatively impact a person's well-being even if treatment is effective.[5] If all we have to do is eliminate the use of the labels *addict* and *alcoholic* to improve treatment initiation, increase self-efficacy and reduce shame over substance abuse behavior, then this should be a routine practice in the culture of substance use and addiction. What more is being explained by using these labels, and what more could we be gaining if we stopped using them? Calling a person an addict does not help them understand their addictive pattern more. Labels don't have to be necessary if the person understands the exact nature of their substance-use behavioral process.

The use of the term *addict* or *alcoholic* to identify a person who has engaged in a substance abuse behavioral pattern was derived from the time of the origination of the 12-Step era and the perpetuated outlook of addiction in our culture for the last century. Since 12-Step approaches have been the dominant model of many addiction treatment programs, 12-Step ideas have been woven into the fabric of professional settings in the field, producing language that creates many negative consequences. There are many clinicians and professionals in the field who continue to call their own clients and the population they work with "addicts" or "alcoholics." Even if a person comes in to address their mild issue with alcohol use, they may be automatically labeled an *alcoholic*. How is this helpful, and what kind of message are we sending to the person? Many people with mild issues with substance use may never initiate help to adjust their behavior because they may not believe they're *really* an "alcoholic" or "addict." While they may have a desire to address their behavior, they don't do so to prevent being labeled, or they don't believe they fit the identity of those labels. But a person who has had prior treatment can experience a Self-fulfilling Prophecy if they were to ever use again, due to being labeled an addict by their therapist, peers, and society. If we believe we are something, based on what others or our culture tells us, then we can start seeking out things that confirm these beliefs and act out those labels without realizing it. If I had been to treatment more than once because I never received the proper help in regard to my autonomous goals, I would start to believe that I was an *addict* based on what everyone is telling me and on the evidence of going back to treatment multiple times. So if I believe I'm an addict and I have a single drink or joint, then like a Self-fulfilling Prophecy, I would think to myself that I had completely lost control. Then at a subconscious level, I may think, *might as well just keep using more*, until that self-image becomes prophesized into an actual addictive behavioral cycle. These labels create a fragmented self-concept that is derived from cultural narratives, and not based in objective reality.

The actual behavior is the objective reality. If a person has been living an abstinent lifestyle for some time, there is no way they can be an addict or alcoholic because they're not "addicted" to a substance or misusing alcohol at this very moment. Our identity and self-concept are fluid and always changing throughout our lives. We like certain types of music, learn to like new activities, or prefer different kinds of food. But these various things do not bring about fixed labels that are cemented into our self-concept. Sure, there are times in our life when we misuse substances or engage in addictive behaviors, but these are just behaviors, and not who we are, necessarily. A person didn't have a drink or even engage in a cocaine binge during a weekend after a period of abstinence because they're an "addict" or "alcoholic"; these behaviors occurred based on the manifestation of their Vacuum System in objective reality. Then the person can adjust their system however is needed.

It's very lazy for professionals and others in our culture to call people who have associated behavioral patterns *addicts* or *alcoholics*. It's a quick and easy way to identify people. But it has a cost. We need to take responsibility to not fall into the convenience of using these labels. We can take a little more time to say, "people with substance abuse issues" or "has a history of addictive patterns" when needed. Someday we may even see a change in the cultural usage of *substance abuse*. But again, we need some cultural language to maintain our footing, while aiming towards fixed universal nature. Many people in the industry emphasize the importance of reducing the stigma of addiction, but they continue using culturally driven labels that do more harm than good. Also, the use of these labels continues to create separation between people who are labeled as *addicts* versus *non-addicts* (or "normies"), as if there is a strict categorical line. This does not align with the objective reality of behavioral fluidity and how the processes of substance-use behaviors work. The Vacuum System recognizes that behavioral patterns can fluctuate pretty widely over time, and stresses the difficulty in drawing any categorical lines between people's behavioral patterns.

The larger concept of *Recovery* should also be deliberated in this discussion. The term is used in our culture to identify oneself as, "I'm a recovering…" or to identify the process of changing the substance-use behavior, such as "a person in recovery" or "being in recovery." I've facilitated groups where people would actually argue and get pissed off about using "recover*ed*" versus "recover*ing*" as identifiers. But I sit here now with the outlook that these terms should be dissolved over time. A 700-participant survey found that people who identified as being "recovered" or an "ex-addict" reported higher rates of psychological health and slightly better lifestyle functioning than people who identified as being an "addict" or "in recovery."[6] However, I do like Recovery more than the use of alcoholic or addict. But Recovery is still a medical term that continues to attach people to a "dysfunction." It implies that they are dealing with something they will never get over, despite the addictive behavioral pattern not being present any longer. Even when I started to drink after five years in A.A., I rebranded the definition of being *in Recovery* by identifying as a person in Recovery from an "addictive behavioral pattern." I continue to encourage this outlook for anyone who may be sober from an addiction, but want to reintegrate substance use into his or her life. This can help them maintain focus to continue working towards the behavioral goals they desire. But with this personal outlook, I don't consider myself to be in "Recovery" necessarily. My behavior just *is*, and I would modify my behavior accordingly in my Vacuum

System if it were to change. A self-image of being in recovery is not necessary for me anymore. If my addictive behavioral pattern is not currently existent, then I'm not "recovering" from anything anymore. But some people will add that a person is still in Recovery because they are continuing to address the underlying issues that motivated the prior substance abuse. I would then point out that those other underlying issues are not motivating any substance misuse at the present moment. So it has no connection to a substance-use behavior currently. We just have these other things to address, like anyone else in the world. So that would mean, as humans, we're all *Recovering* from something. This may be precisely true, but it is not necessary to conceptualize people as a whole in this way. It is especially not exclusively attributable to people with current or previous substance use issues, which only creates division among people and prolongs a fixed self-concept for a lifetime.

The use of "sobriety dates" reinforces these labels, and our addiction culture tries to fix this little time capsule into our self-identity. Sobriety dates can be rewarding and activate our motivational system to continue living a healthy lifestyle. But on the other hand, sobriety dates can create unnecessary pressure. If a person uses a single substance, then they can feel like a failure due to violating their "continuous sobriety identity." Then they may succumb to the Self-fulfilling Prophecy of engaging in the previous addictive pattern. I had a client discussing in group how she "finally" got her longest period of sobriety because prior to her current abstinence, she drank every once in a while when she had six months clean from her illicit substance abuse. If we were in an individual session, I would have explored the true nature of her behavior and quality of life at the time, and not so much about the alcohol use in itself or being abstinent or not. Sobriety dates or days of consecutive substance use do not explain a whole lot. I can use substances every single day, but what if it's only one beer? I can be sober every day, but I can still be miserable.

What's the mechanism behind using sobriety dates? It can be a motivator for progress, or it can be a reminder of previous behavioral patterns that we do not want to re-engage in. This is all good stuff. But my motivator should not be a "date" that is an artificial sense of reality, but the motivation to live the life that I actually want that is tangible in the present moment. I can remember my previous addictive pattern without having an exclusive sobriety date or having consecutive days sober. I will never forget September 2011, even though I haven't maintained continuous "sobriety" since. This was the last time I engaged in an addictive or high-risk substance-use behavioral pattern. I can reflect on that time in my life at any point to remember where I have been, and where I want to continue going. It's a pertinent part of my story, but "sober time" is an illusion that is not attached to a current identity. If I were to engage in a substance-abuse behavioral pattern after this period, I wouldn't have to feel like I "lost all of this *time*." Instead, with an increased self-efficacy about substance-use behaviors, I would have been able to modify the substance-misuse pattern a lot earlier on, before it got to the level of September 2011. Other people in our culture also point out the use of sobriety dates to demonstrate hope to others that "it works." Many people find ways to grow out of their addiction without the use of any program, and we always knew stories existed of people leaving their addiction behind. It's a common theme whenever people talk about addiction. People are overcoming their addictions every day! If we need to actually see people representing long sobriety dates to help maintain our modified behavior, then that could mean we don't believe in ourselves enough to continue. But your self-efficacy has increased dramatically if you have read this far. You have enhanced your understanding of the exact nature of all substance use-behavior, how tools shape the behavior, and are now exploring the misconceptions about the behavior.

There is an abundance of secondary language that perpetuates the misconceptions of substance use-behavior, and also maintains divisions among people who use substances. A common overgeneralization that I have read from treatment centers and observe in society is that people are "suffering" from addiction. Yes, there are people who find themselves in horrible conditions with an addiction, and may feel like they're in a hopeless state. But not every person who misuses substances is *suffering* necessarily, although some are. This generalization implies that every person who has a substance use issue is in a *severe* state of addiction. This attitude only keeps people with mild to moderate cases from seeking out help, because they may think they're not "suffering" enough. "Suffering" language goes along with the situation where a person in treatment says, "I wasn't like them" or "I wasn't that bad." But then we as professionals tell them that they are in denial, or they need to "look at the similarities versus the differences." They're not in denial, nor do they need to look at the similarities. What they said is actually a true statement, and they may just be saying it out of defense because society is telling them that they're no different than any other "addict." It can be true that someone else's alcohol use pattern is a lot milder issue than mine, or that others faced a lot more devastation related to their behavioral habit. People's behavioral patterns with substance use are individual, and will be different from one another. Many addictive patterns may appear to look the same as our culture tries to generalize, but they are pretty original if you look closely at the Vacuum System. The patterns can be very different, based on the person's Five Factor Profile, and how it fluctuates throughout the lifespan trajectory. The Five Factors will filter through the Dopaminergic System, which has a personalized reward hierarchy. Then the individualized M.E.R. characteristics illuminate various habitual cognitive-action frequencies, embedded in personal contexts, manifesting varying levels of craving responses, and encompassing a countless number of reinforcement properties. It's like if we take a glance at multiple mandalas that depict the sun. We can generalize that these are creative pictures of the sun. But if we look closer at each mandala, we will see individual uniqueness and originality.

Other secondary language includes the concept of being a *dry drunk*. This label describes a person who is physically sober from substance use. But they may lie, seem irritated all the time, or basically not be addressing other areas in their life, even as they are sober from an addiction. I call the label of "dry drunk" into question, to explore how conducive it is for people's self-esteem. If a person is sober from substance use, any other "issue" in their life is a separate entity from their substance-use behavior. This concept is still tying a person to an addict identity and an addictive behavioral pattern when one does not exist. If you were to look at their Vacuum System, M.E.R. would explain that the behavior is absent. In objective reality, the person's substance-use behavior is managed, while they may have other things that they want to work on to maintain behavioral health, as reflected by their Five Factor Profile. It does not always have to be associated with a previous addiction. There can be people who seem grumpy all of the time because *society* wants them to stay abstinent due to their alcohol misuse in the past, but calling them a "dry drunk" does not help them; it only shames them. So the goal would be to explore with the person whether they want to include alcohol into the lifestyle they want, or simply find various alternative behavioral options that can make them happier and more fulfilled.

This leads us into other language, such as "addicts lie, cheat and steal," which is a huge and expensive stereotype. Not every person who is engaging or has engaged in substance misuse in the past, has "lied, cheated or stolen." I heard a person facilitating a training on support groups say, "How can you tell if an alcoholic is lying? … See if their lips are moving." As witty as it was, this statement is not helpful and does not capture the majority of people with substance-use issues. Stereotypes and attitudes like this keep many people with substance-misuse behaviors from seeking help. This does not capture *person-centered* care. If professionals carry attitudes like this, then their sentiments will be shown in their practices by expressing agitation and suspicion towards clients. Then they'll provide rigid directives, as if we know what is best for everyone. The person will feel more shame, and may feel the need to always have to *prove* themselves to their therapist and everybody else in their life. Hence, the reason for the pressure of maintaining sobriety dates, and getting rid of any ounce of imperfection, to prevent being called a "dry drunk." At the end of the day, sometimes we just have to not give a shit about what others think.

Then we can observe how some of the language that many people use when modifying their substance-use behavior creates a set of its own barriers. I hear people in group and individual sessions say things like, "I'm *fighting* my addiction" or "I've got to beat this thing!" I point out to them, "You are beating it! You're sober in this very moment, and have been for some time now." All they seem to think about is how many times they have been to treatment, or the years when they wish they had addressed their behavior. I worked with a person who always used this type of self-defeating language about needing to beat their addiction, even though I would always point out that their addiction was beaten, and he didn't have to go back to his addiction. It took me pointing it out many times before he was able to catch himself on his own. I reminded him how his current behavior did not reflect substance abuse, and how he was putting too much pressure on himself believing that some imaginary addiction was more powerful than him. He didn't even realize that he would engage in these habitual thought processes when he was sober. For a long time, he seemed to always believe that he needed to work the program harder, and think he was missing something, out of fear of an addictive behavior that was not present.

The idea of *fighting* an addiction is a false belief, not objective reality, if people have already made the decision to discontinue their addiction, whether they're moderating or abstinent. Now imagine if a person with these kinds of beliefs actually had a single substance. The Abstinence Violation Effect-*cognitive error* may manifest guilt and shame. This will further activate the belief that "powerful addiction needs to be fought," making the person submit to the addict identity, leading to a Self-fulfilling Prophecy. This sequence of cognitive experiences after a single use of a substance can coincide with the physical actions of substance misuse. But now with the knowledge we have about substance-use behaviors and utilizing the *tools* from Chapter Five, we can modify these cognitive processes and the corresponding physical actions of the behavior. These beliefs and the use of unhelpful language also relate to why people may have difficulty managing cravings to use substances, as discussed earlier. If we view cravings as being like the paparazzi, we can be more tolerant of the experience and realize that we have more power over our response to it. If we *believe* it to be a struggle, we will *experience* it that way. It's important to be aware of this use of language, since this language can be embedded in the cognitive processes of M.E.R. and have a direct impact on the behavior.

This brings us all the way back to the disease concept. We spoke earlier about how neuroscience refutes the *disease* model by recognizing that the plastic brain changes are a natural phenomenon when a behavior is learned, and how there is no single gene that *predetermines* a person will develop an addiction. Furthermore, we discussed how this disease label is not needed to explain substance-use behavioral processes. The term creates more stigma, which aligns with the generalized use of the labels "alcoholic" and "addict." I believe a reason why the disease concept came about was to alleviate the misrepresented *moral failing* outlook, and to take addiction more seriously by grouping it with the medical model for insurance purposes. This reasoning may have had good intentions. But this view maintains lifelong stigma, and neglects a large population who would never initiate treatment due to the misrepresentation of their behavior.

Also, who is able to, or has the authority to, label a person coming to treatment as having the disease? Does everyone who attends treatment, and has varying levels of substance use, have the disease? I don't understand how this can be a general practice in behavioral health.

How would we use this term for adolescents? The majority of treatment centers and our culture as a whole generalize adults with any form of substance abuse as having the disease, but I see a less use of the disease term for adolescents with substance-use issues. It can be detrimental to label an adolescent or an emerging adult as having a disease, since they are still developing their identity. But let's say a seventeen-year-old has been abusing substances since he or she was twelve. Wouldn't this be enough time for them to have abused substances and developed the disease? But we won't label them as having the disease due to the stigma behind it, and rightly so! However, we may use scare tactics and tell the adolescent that if they continue to use or abuse substances they will develop the disease. Even though they have already been engaging in the problematic use. Also, the data shows that the majority of people quit using illegal substances by the age of thirty without any intervention,[7] which invalidates the universal idea of the *progressive brain disease* of addiction. So then, when would the cut-off age to get the disease be? Will they be labeled as having a disease on their eighteenth birthday, or after they turn thirty if they continue to misuse substances? People decreasing or increasing in their substance use with age will depend on tolerance-dependency, life developments, and other circumstances occurring within their Five Factor Profile, and not some progressive disease. We also seem to automatically label an *adult* with the disease, without giving *them* a grace period of not being labeled with the disease, such as if they were misusing substances as an adolescent. It's difficult to have a categorical line, especially one with such a severe description as a disease, when in reality, behavior is a lot more of a fluid experience.

The transmission of addiction being a disease in our culture creates rigid beliefs within individuals, which can further influence their behavioral experiences. Some research has shown that people who held more beliefs that addiction was a "disease" or that they were "powerless" over their behavior, experienced more relapse and binge use than those who held more "choice" views of substance-use behavior.[8, 9] Much of these personal belief systems were developed through treatment approaches like the Minnesota Model and the old-school view of "alcohol*ism*" being a stark medical condition in the last century. These beliefs about the diseased nature of addictive behaviors has led many to believe, "My best thinking got me here," or "My thinking is messed up. I can't stay in my mind too long or bad things happen." I have heard these statements used a lot in treatment settings, implying that *all* of their thinking is "bad," and even their best thinking got them continuing their addiction. This is simply not true. When a person makes the decision to get sober, their thinking may go something like this, "I don't want to continue this. I don't want to hurt myself or upset my family anymore. I have so much to live for." This is great thinking! This thought process modified their substance-use behavior and led to them getting sober or reducing their consumption. As they stay sober, I hear many continuing to use this language even though they are living a healthy lifestyle in objective reality. So no, their best thinking did not keep them stuck in their addiction, and they produced a lot of healthy thinking patterns that dictate their behavioral health. Sure, we can experience thinking from time to time that may be impulsive in nature, or desire immediate gratification. But we also experience a tide of healthy thought processes that washes over that thinking. Remember, our thinking or cognitive processes have a bearing on our overt physical actions, as explained by M.E.R. Many of the beliefs related to the disease concept and powerlessness of the behavior fall under the *cognitive errors* category of the cognitive processes within the Mindfulness component of M.E.R. This will only coincide with the physical actions of substance use as demonstrated by research and clinical data.

The Canadian Centre on Substance Use and Addiction (CCSA) facilitated a very insightful survey in 2016 of 855 people in Canada who identified as being *in recovery* from addiction.[10] Eighty-three percent of the people who completed the survey had one or more barriers that kept them from initiating "recovery." The top barrier, reported by 55% of people was, "not being ready, not believing you had a problem, or not believing problem was serious enough." This is a big finding, that in more than half of people who had challenges seeking help initially, the challenges were due to believing their substance use was not serious enough or they were not ready. The implication here is that these people know that our addiction culture will tell them that they have a incurable disease, and that they will need to quit using substances for the rest of their life. The person will believe that their substance-use behavior is not as severe as this cultural description. Then they will continue their substance abuse pattern until more severe consequences occur, and they become *ready*. The second-largest barrier to initiating recovery was worrying about what other people would think of them, which 50% of the people identified. This is associated with the first barrier of the apprehension to address their behavior, because the person knows that they may need to surrender to an addict identity, and need to alter their life to meet the expectation of total abstinence. These findings and implications align with the result, that 92% of the whole sample has used 12-Step support to address their behavior. As we know, 12-Step models view any level of addiction as highly pathological, with the disease concept and lifetime abstinence at its forefront. So it appears that many of these people who took the survey did not begin to modify their substance-use behavior until they perceived their behavior as more severe, fitting the cultural view of an "addict." So then it became more permissible for them to utilize the widespread 12-Step approach that centralizes this level of severity.

The CCSA's survey explored other views related to reasons for starting and sustaining recovery, and what it means to be in recovery. Sixty-nine percent of the people identified that a "quality life" was the primary reason to *start* their recovery, while 85% of the people identified "quality of life" as a reason to *maintain* recovery. But when identifying the definition of recovery, only 14% believed the definition of recovery pertained to a "quality life," while 52% believed that "abstinence" was the definition of recovery. "Abstinence" was the top definition of what it means to be in recovery, whereas "quality of life" came second, all the way down at 14%, even though "quality of life" was the chief reason people started and maintained their recovery. This discrepancy demonstrates how the cultural language and behavioral health outlook used with addictive behaviors are embedded into people's beliefs about their behavioral goals in their personal lives. Additionally, a third (33%) of the people in this survey perceived that they experienced stigma and discrimination even as they maintained their recovery, and 14% continued to worry about what others would think of them as a barrier to maintaining recovery. The cultural language and view on addiction are largely responsible for these findings, and

not so much whether people are "ready." People want a quality life a lot earlier in the trajectory of their problematic pattern than we assume. We have all
these expectations about others who experience any substance abuse patterns
in their life. Then our expectations cause more harm by isolating them in a
group, as if they all use substances the same way and that is different from the
rest of society.

We have to remember that this survey exclusively targeted people who identified as being "in recovery;" the participants were required to identify as such,
to be permitted to complete the survey. Having this identifier as a criterion for
inclusion of the survey targets a limited sub-set of people who have a previous
history of substance-abuse patterns. Many people with prior substance-use
issues could have resolved their addiction naturally during the life trajectory,
or overcome their addiction through alternative approaches where they may
never have considered the term *recovery*. Therefore, they would not find themselves taking this survey, even though they had a previous addictive behavioral
pattern like the others in the survey. The population in the survey is just a slice
of people who have resolved their addiction, and does not fully represent every
person who has done so. The problem is that treatment for substance use issues
in our culture only represents a more severe sub-set of people, and does not
represent or have a platform that welcomes every person with any level of a
substance-use concern.

A co-author of *The Freedom Model for Addictions*, Steven Slate, made the
following connection. An associate of Stanford's Behavioral Science Center and
sociology professor at Princeton, Robert A. Scott conducted a relevant study
over fifty years ago, outlined in his *The Making of Blind Men*.[11] Scott interviewed
about a hundred people who met the standard threshold of blindness, and a
hundred workers from various agencies that aid people with visual impairments. He categorized two types of agencies. One type was called an *accommodative* approach, where the agency creates an environment for blind people
where they are required to learn Braille, operate highly restricted mobility
aids, trained for low competitive employment, and receive rewards for trivial
achievements. Also, many of the people's personal goals are subtly ignored,
and the person is only able to receive services if they are willing to "accept"
their permanent blindness. Starting to sound familiar? On the other hand, the

restorative approach agencies focus on teaching the individual various skills to be able to function in a regular life in their communities and society at large. They train the utilization of other senses, learn the use of various mechanical devices, train in more competitive employment, get visual wear that help them read bolder print, and are instilled with psychological security. Scott's major finding was that people with visual impairments who participated in the *restorative* type agencies generally functioned better, independently in their community by working more competitive jobs and were more socially involved, compared to people who went through the *accommodative* approach, who believed that they needed to depend on the highly restricted environmental accommodations.

Despite the people in both groups having an actual medical condition of mixed level of visual impairment, he found that people from the *accommodative* agencies took on the stereotypical role of a "blind person." They acted out the attitudes and characteristics that they're forever helpless individuals, in which this rigid cultural narrative socialized their identity and behavioral autonomy. Meanwhile, people from the *restorative* agencies did not succumb to a "blind person" identity, and engaged in practices that met their individualized needs so they could lead a fully functioning life. All of the people from the *accommodative* approach are assumed to have the same goals and practices as the most severely blind population, even though the majority of them have enough vision to be able to utilize practices that would help them live independent lives. Unfortunately, these people take on a role that disrupts their behavioral potential, and keeps them stuck in a role that does not capture the objective reality of their condition.

Our addiction culture reflects these findings. People who go through traditional substance abuse treatment, or are generally exposed to the cultural narratives about addiction, can start to take on the "addict" role. They may begin to carry the attitude that they have absolutely no influence over their substance-use behavior. So they feel the need to rely on a program daily because of their "flawed" thinking, and the belief that they need to fight a lifelong battle with a disease. They will learn to play this social role as a diseased person in recovery. The attitude of needing to fulfill every recovery expectation will be exhibited, and they will experience fear and a sense of struggle when exposed to substance use contexts. Then if a person uses a single substance, they can feel a sense of chaos and act out the behavioral pattern until the addict role becomes actualized. I have interacted with many people who carry similar attitudes to the diseased addicted role, even though they don't have an active addiction. But they don't realize how their socialized identity and beliefs about their behavior in many cases can actually contribute to an addiction. So if we drop all of the unnecessary cultural attitudes and labels, but provide the proper skills about the direct substance-use behavioral process, then a person can take on the role as the executive of their behavioral health. The famous Stanford Prison Experiment demonstrated the power of these social role processes, and how they impact attitudes and behavior. When the Stanford students took on the role as a prisoner or guard, they exhibited real-life behaviors and attitudes of these roles. This led to the experiment ending prematurely. We don't need to assign people an identity role when they already want to change their substance misuse behavior. Let's just address their behavior as it comes along.

Language is a powerful instrument that influences our behavior and perspective on substance-use behaviors within a cultural context. Applications within the field of addiction can be a lot more efficient if cultural language barriers can be transformed to represent the objective reality of the behavior. I see many arguments on social media about what addiction is and how to best approach it. While each argument has a kernel of truth or reality to it, it seems to be difficult for people to find common ground to simply capture the nature of the behavior. We need to all get on the same page. So what is it that we can all agree on when it comes to addiction, and how to approach treatment? Can we all agree that substance use or abuse is a *behavior*, or a pattern of behavior? We can agree that there are multiple etiologies for the development of addiction, and there is not a single route to develop the behavioral pattern. We can agree that neural changes in the brain occur as the behavior sequence is learned and engaged in. Based on the data, can we agree that there are many people who can learn to reduce their substance use to healthier levels, while others may find it more difficult to do so? Then people may follow up and say, "the people who can are not *real* 'alcoholics' or 'addicts.'" But this idea misses the point. Whether a person with an addiction has the potential to use substances at healthier levels with more ease or not, the treatment and "helping" culture of addiction should be able to accommodate any level of a substance use issue and healthy goals that are desired. Whether they fit the cultural description of an alcoholic or not, they can benefit from some type of intervention. We can agree that there is not a single route to achieving a healthy lifestyle, where addictive patterns are not present. Humans are pretty creative about finding personal ways to achieve behavioral health that are unique to their needs. Even if you look closely at a group of people who are engaged in 12-Step programs, their lifestyles and what works for them can be extremely different from one another. Plus we know that many people who had previous addictions are not involved in any self-help programs. Then can we agree that not every person who has a prior addiction or wants to seek help for his or her behavior wants to succumb to an *addict* identity, or identify as a person in *recovery*? People may follow up with, "Well that's what they are, and they need to be in recovery." Okay, I get what you're saying and I see the objectivity that they did have an "addictive" pattern at some time of their life, and making some lifestyle changes is recommended. But not every person is going to believe in the addict identity or identify as being in recovery. This may only prolong shame for them personally, and they'll continue to achieve a healthy lifestyle without the use of these labels and identities.

We need a common ground for the use of addiction language to help us move forward. If the language barriers of our cultural view on addiction shift, then people with any problematic substance use can find treatment more comprehensive and appealing. We don't need to get rid of treatment, but rebrand it and encompass the reality of every person with a substance abuse behavioral pattern. Less descriptive language on addiction can actually mean more for us. Much of the "disease recovery" language was also developed in attempts to slow down the behavior. But it can create more harm for many people, furthering severe substance use. It's a bit like the way the sport of football has developed more rule restrictions, and enhanced equipment protocols for players to sustain forceful physical contact, in order to minimize concussions. While these practices could perhaps reduce potential harm, does it really reduce the aggressive tackling behavior that can lead to concussions? A player with full body and head protection may think that they can hit another player as hard as they want because of all the equipment, even though they don't realize how the forceful motion can move the brain over time, influencing the potential for a traumatic brain injury (TBI). But what if we went back to less equipment restrictions and players didn't wear any helmets? People may immediately react that the problem will get worse. But without helmets and with less equipment, players will think twice about using their whole body to hit the other player as hard as they can. This will change the behavioral dynamic. The players will go after each other's head less, and more after the ball. This is the primary goal. So with fewer restrictions, the behavior of aggressive tackling may reduce, while more strategic behaviors will increase to achieve the wanted goals of the game. Using less *restrictive* language with addiction, will lead people to address their behavior and lifestyle for exactly what it is. Pure language to merely explain the whole behavioral process and utilizing tools to target these individualized processes will suffice, without the unnecessary language that only creates pre-determined expectations on the behavior. We cannot *bowl* with precision until we get rid of the bumpers, and learn the direct technique to get the bowling ball down the lane without it going into the gutter.

So if we strip away all the language of disease — addict, alcoholic, alcoholism, recovery and the secondary language that goes along with it — what will this leave us with? This would force us to not use generalized *bumpers* that attempt to restrict the behavior. But it will make us simply look at the exact nature of the behavioral process, and use tools that plug into these processes to modify the behavioral pattern with precision. A person will be forced to think twice about their behavior once they're left with just the fundamental understanding of all substance-use behaviors. Underneath the addiction, are people as they truly want to be. They just have these behavioral patterns that do not align with their ideal self. Humans are autonomous agents who appear in the fabric of culture, in which our identity can be highly influenced by cultural narratives. Our identity is not fixed in time. Our identity would appear a bit different if our self and its behaviors were placed in a different period of time. Many people like the associated recovery identities. But many other people do not find these identities helpful, and find the need to move on from their addiction. Therefore, there's nothing wrong with individual usage of identity descriptors. But these labels and excessive language should be taken down as a general practice due to the creation of false assumptions about the behavior at a cultural and personal level.

What will our addiction language look like a thousand years from now, or even two hundred years from now? We can see how cultural language and ideas change drastically with time. Our understanding is always updating with the acceleration of information. I hope the addict identity gets lost with time. That way, people can seek treatment a lot earlier when their behavior is less severe, and tweak their behavioral pattern as if they were just going to see a nutritionist to change their diet. Therefore, a lot more people will be addressing their substance-use behavior without putting their life on pause, and treatment can be a lot cheaper due to its widespread application. But to get to this point, we need to view the approach of problematic substance use more pragmatically, and without the worry of a lifelong identity fixation. We are who we are, as we appear in objective reality, and our ever-changing behaviors incorporate processes that have a fixed universal nature that is timeless.

chapter 8

Support

Why are other people considered?

WHEN COLLEGE FOOTBALL SETS IN and the brisk late afternoon sun touches the colorful trees in the Midwest, I get a nostalgic feeling for where I have been since concluding my addiction in September 2011. When I woke up sober, I felt a sense of relief that I was making the decision to end my addiction. But at the same time I felt drained knowing that I was out on bond, and I had my work cut out for me to get my life back on track. I primarily wanted to go to rehab to make a better case for my felony drug possession. Plus I knew they were going to court mandate me since it was my second charge in two years. But I was pretty motivated to live a healthy lifestyle regardless, so that I discontinued my substance use fourteen days prior to being admitted to rehab. As long as I was engaged in A.A. at the time, I knew I didn't need rehab to stay sober *per se*. I don't retain any pertinent information or skills from rehab in particular. All rehab did was show me that I was not the only person my age dealing with this behavior, and the clinical authority at the time reinforced my 12-Step involvement.

I was discharged from my 28-day treatment just in time for Game 5 of the World Series. I remember sitting there watching some great baseball between the St. Louis Cardinals and the Texas Rangers in my mother's darkened living room. I was feeling lonely because my girlfriend had left me, while feeling unfulfilled because I was supposed to be in college two states away. But all I knew at the time was that my addictive behavioral pattern was now absent. I just wanted my life to be the way it had been. But now I was back home sitting on my mother's couch, and it was the first fall that I wasn't in school since I was a toddler. A couple weeks later, I was sitting in the courtroom waiting for my name to be called as I watched others go by, one by one, to get their next court date. I suddenly noticed the father of one of my high school buddies walking toward a seat in the row in front of me. I've personally experienced his funny, but belligerent, drunken nights. When he saw me that day, he had a look of shame and embarrassment for sitting in a "criminal" courtroom with one of his son's friends. Knowing that he watched the Cardinals play every night, I congratulated him on winning the World Series. Still noticing some discomfort, I broke the ice by whispering to him, "They just want to ruin the fucking fun, huh?" For that moment, we were able to bond over not feeling shame for being where we were at in our lives.

One afternoon, I was longboarding home from an A.A. meeting when an older man in a car stopped me, saying that he was coming from the meeting and asked if we lived in the same neighborhood. He suggested that he would pick me up every day to go to the meeting. For the next seven months, Vic picked me up twice a day for the afternoon and evening meetings at the local club as I ironed out my life. Vic probably stood at five foot three, with a goatee, a cane, and a country accent. He was Texas raised, retired from working at O'Hare airport, had served two tours in Vietnam, and you would see him chain smoke his Pall Malls laughing. When he picked me up, we would discuss the *Seinfeld* episode had TBS aired that evening. Then we would switch between listening to Chicago Blackhawks hockey on the radio and his Led Zeppelin CDs before going into the meeting. Before the afternoon meetings, we would laugh about the different characters we attended the meetings with. I would carol Van Morrison's rendition of "Baby, Please Don't Go," while Vic mocked my verbal melody as he tried to guess what it was. On our way to the meetings, he would often point out my apparent loneliness and despair, which I was trying to conceal from the rest of the world as I lived in my fantasies. Vic really cared about my well-being, and would even stop in my driveway just to express it to my mother if she was doing yard work. Vic wanted nothing more from me than to be healthy and share a laugh. Here was a man spending the last years of his life with me, sharing joyful little moments that can be as valuable as anything in this world. I will surely never forget Vic, and how supportive he was after my addiction.

Alcoholics Anonymous was a springboard into the lifestyle that I ultimately wanted, which included to be able to use alcohol at healthier levels, believe it or not. My 12-Step involvement provided me a template for how people live life after an addiction. My sponsor didn't emphasize the 12 Steps so much, but demonstrated the fun in sobriety and taking an initiative in your life. "Suit up and show up," he always said. By the time I was eight months sober, I was ready to serve my five weeks in county jail in central Minnesota. I was probably one of the cheerier fellows in that jail, since I had been already immersed into a healthy lifestyle and had been getting my life back in order for some time prior to sentencing. I was keen to pass the time by plowing the jail's pepper and tomato patch, helping build a "Schoolhouse Rock!" theatre set, and painting yellow street curbs in modest surrounding towns. When I moved to my father's home in Chicago for school, I met a lot of people my age in A.A. We went to sporting events, attended live music, and stayed out all morning at nightclubs, while sober as judges. Some of the old timers in the meetings didn't approve of our lifestyle, but we used A.A. as a launching pad to learn to enjoy life without needing to be intoxicated.

Here we are going to explore and critique 12-Step self-help support groups, such as Alcoholics Anonymous. There are many benefits to 12-Step involvement, while we are coming to see that there are many deficits to these programs, as our understanding about addictive behaviors become more updated. I hope to objectively analyze how the various components of these support groups work, and recognize the reality of people who do not find these programs beneficial for them. I will spend most of the time exploring the use of 12-Step programs, since the majority of treatment centers in our culture facilitate the involvement of this style of support. Then you will be better able to understand how the components of other support groups, such as S.M.A.R.T. Recovery, Moderation Management, Celebrate Recovery, and Refuge Recovery, are applied. Just as the whole substance-use behavior process should be understood in its purest form to best modify it, support groups can be utilized more efficiently if we understand the exact nature of how they work as well.

It's no surprise that 12-Step programs have helped many people over the years. People get into silly arguments whether 12-Step programs are effective or not. Of course they can be effective, since we know many people involved in 12-Step programs living a healthy lifestyle. However, 12-Step involvement is not a *requirement* to stop an addiction or live a healthy lifestyle. Also, not every person with an addictive behavioral pattern will choose to use these programs to change their behavior. We even know that people can overcome their addiction and live a healthy life without any type of program. But we know that the utilization of 12-Step programs is highly prevalent in our addiction culture, and widespread in many countries with various languages. Fleshing out the behavioral health processes behind the different aspects of 12-Step programs can help us better understand what exactly makes these programs effective for individuals. Plus how they modify the substance-use behavior when applied to a person's Vacuum System.

One of the major and most effective vehicles of 12-Step programs is the social component. There are many facets to these related support programs that incorporate a social aspect. We can first consider the many social faculties of the human brain. This can help enable people to change their substance-use behavior indirectly through social support programs, such as Alcoholics Anonymous. We experience many positive social emotions, such as pride, compassion, love, and empathy. We have localized *mirror neurons* that light up in various parts of the cerebral cortex when we observe the actions or emotional experiences of others, as if we're taking the same actions or feeling the same emotions. This is when emotions like compassion and empathy can manifest. When the mind is at a wakeful resting state and not attentive to an external task, a set of different areas of the brain known as the Default Mode Network (DMN) is turned on. When this network is turned on, we're thinking about different aspects about ourselves, thinking about the past or future, and then thinking about others in regard to what they are thinking or feeling while making other social evaluations. Our sophisticated social brains may explain why humans are so good at gossip, and why we're attracted to reality television. So, 12-Step programs and other recovery-based groups effectively take advantage of our social brain to ultimately modify our substance-use behavior through support and social connection.

One of the major components of 12-Step programs is the meeting, which encompasses a group of people. The group can be as small as two people, or as large as thousands of people in a single room. I've been to a conference in Phoenix, Arizona, where the Saturday night speaker meeting included 4,000 people. What makes any group effective is the members in the group sharing a common goal. So obviously the goal of the people in Alcoholics Anonymous or Narcotics Anonymous would be to maintain discontinued substance abuse. If you want any group to get along, give them a common goal. In science fiction, the only way that all the countries in world can be unified is if there is a significant threat from another planet and we need to work together to defeat it. The groups in 12-Step programs work together to defeat addiction. If you put all the language and concepts of 12-Step programs aside, you will still have the purity of a group of people sharing a common goal helping each other in dynamic ways.

The psychiatrist, Irvin D. Yalom, revolutionized psychotherapeutic groups through his life's work in the twentieth century. He identified eleven factors that help people change in groups, which are found in his book, *The Theory and Practice of Group Psychotherapy*.[1] This book is a staple in any graduate program in clinical psychology. Yalom's group factors are highly applicable to 12-Step meetings for individual behavioral change, and pure in the sense that humans access these factors in any therapeutic social setting.

The first factor, *instillation of hope,* occurs when social processes in the meeting create a sense of hope and optimism for individuals. A person can experience a sense of hope after hearing another member's story about their early challenges of changing their substance-use behavior, and how it became easier to live the life they want. This can further motivate behavior change implementation.

Universality was what I experienced when I went to treatment, by observing and being around others who had the same problem as me. I felt less alone, and not ashamed of my behavior. This factor is easily recognized in all 12-Step meetings. The presence of the *cohesiveness* factor may depend on the format of the meeting, the flow of it, and the content of the sharing. If group cohesion is high, members will feel a sense of acceptance and closeness with one another in the meeting.

Socializing techniques and *interpersonal learning* involve enhancing social skills, and developing supportive relationships in a sober context. Many people may use substances as a social lubricant, or have been isolated due to their addiction. So these factors in the group or meeting can cultivate the learning of social skills without the need for substance use. They will further reintegrate individuals back into healthy relationships, which reinforce overall healthy living.

Altruism can allow people to have a sense of purpose and find meaning in helping others with their substance-use behavior by sharing their own experiences in a meeting.

This factor goes hand-in-hand with *imparting information*, which is the mere sharing of information and skills in a meeting to enhance knowledge to modify the behavior.

Imitating behavior is part of this cluster, enabling people to practice coping strategies and utilize perspectives that others express in the group.

Then *cathartic* expression may commonly present in many therapeutic self-help groups. People may share a wide array of emotional experiences and other stressful life transitions that could be driving their addiction. This sharing can help people find a sense of relief or resolution through the cathartic processing experience in a group setting.

As a result, some people may benefit from the *corrective recapitulation* factor. This is where they learn to express themselves openly in a vulnerable social setting by receiving the proper emotional support and connection that they may never have experienced with their family of origin. Corrective recapitulation may pertain more to psychotherapy groups. But 12-Step meetings provide the opportunity to resolve early childhood and family experiences in indirect ways.

Lastly, the *existential* factor becomes activated when members in the meeting discuss about the concept of "acceptance." The idea of acceptance is often used in 12-Step programs to acknowledge the inevitabilities in life, and working through any circumstance without the absolute need to use substances.

These group factors do not modify substance-use behaviors directly, since they don't directly target the M.E.R. processes. But these factors are purely what make 12-Step meetings empowering in themselves. The *effects* of Yalom's factors, through the meetings, work by motivating people to take the direct actions to change their behavioral patterns and maintain the changes. People leaving the meeting can feel empowered, optimistic, and psychologically flexible, able to implement the tools to modify their unwanted habits. If you go to any 12-Step meeting in the world, you can automatically feel understood and accepted through the activation of these group factors. All of these effects of the group will help lower the factors of a person's Five Factor Profile in a variety of ways. Then this ultimately filters out a new substance-use behavior, or its absence. People learning to express their emotions and be vulnerable in meeting will lower the *Trauma/Affect* and *Life Stressors* factors of their profile by processing their emotions in a supportive context. Feeling empowered after a meeting can lower the *Psychological* factor of their profile by increasing their self-efficacy to make efficient judgments on their behaviors, which in turn reduces impulsivity. Then attending weekly meetings and spending time with others who are living a healthy lifestyle will lower the *Environment* factor by creating a healthy structure in one's life with fewer opportunities to misuse substances.

Other processes of meetings can directly target the behavior through M.E.R. Hearing people discuss the consequences of their addiction, as well as the benefits of living life soberly, is a form of Cognitive Reappraisal. This will target the cognitive processes and associated physical actions of the *Mindfulness* component of behavior. The healthy cognitive processes will be activated when hearing this at the meeting. But a person can also intentionally stimulate these cognitions after the meeting, if they experience cognition that motivates addictive actions. While sharing at a meeting can target the Trauma/Affect and Life Stressors developmental factors, sharing can simultaneously target the *Reinforcement* properties of M.E.R. if a person uses substances to cope with stress and difficult emotions. Many people's *Reinforcement* properties to use substances are socially motivated. So going to meetings can be a useful alternative behavior to fulfill the social desire. I know a lot of people who don't get much out of the actual content of meetings. But they enjoy the social aspect of the group. They view meetings as being a social get-together, where they mainly enjoy the before and after of a meeting. Many people have "home groups," where they attend the same meeting on a weekly basis because they have developed a social connection with the people who attend the meeting regularly. Some meetings include "fellowshipping" afterwards, where they may go out to eat every week after the meeting. When I was involved in A.A., I went to an 8 p.m. meeting on Saturday, where we would go out to eat afterwards and then make further plans to go dancing or find live music. So, obviously, placing oneself in these environmental contexts with others who are not actively abusing substances will directly target the *Exposure* component of substance-use behavior as well.

During "speaker meetings," the speaker typically shares, "What it was like, what happened, and what it's like now." This is the standard format when a person shares their story in a 12-Step meeting. A person shares a narrative about what their active addiction was like, what happened for them to want to start changing their behavior, and then how their life is now after their addiction. Our brains do a great job at sharing stories about others, who we are, and what we did. Tapping into clear and coherent narratives about our self and experiences of our life has shown to create balanced neural integration between various networks in the brain, which further strengthens emotional regulation and enhances our self-identity.[2] When I used to listen to clients who came in for substance abuse treatment during their intake assessment, their narratives about their substance-use behavioral experiences seem to be more fragmented. They had no coherent flow, and their narrative included a lot of emotional activation that kept their story disjointed. When the same people share their story a year later, or even several weeks later, they seem to have more of a coherent and clear narrative about their story of addiction. Early on, a person may be experiencing a lot of shame and be distraught due to their recent addiction. This emotional experience overpowers their brain, dampening the language networks that construct a regulated narrative. When a person has had some time to process their addictive experiences and work towards a healthy life, they are able to construct a coherent narrative. They tap into the linguistic parts of their brain that allow them to view their addiction and emotional experiences in an objective manner, as nothing more than something of the past or simply part of their life story.

So when a person is sharing their story in a meeting, something powerful is happening biologically in the speaker's brain. Areas of the brain, such as the dorsolateral prefrontal cortex (DLPFC) and the orbital medial prefrontal cortex (OMPFC), become activated, enhancing neural integration between the hemispheres of the brain when a healthy narrative is produced.[2] Too much activation of the DLPFC during narration may correlate with rationalizations and defense mechanisms that spin a story, while too much activation of the OMPFC can impact decision-making that it is solely based on emotion.[2] But both working in harmony can make the difference between the narrative that is shared during an active addiction, and one that is shared when a person tells their story after overcoming their addiction. If you ever notice a person with some sober experience share their story, they have bit of a realistic outlook on their own story, while still expressing enough emotion to manifest inspiration. Then when others hear the speaker's coherent story in the meeting, they can think about their own story in terms of this coherent narration. This will activate the pertinent neural networks that will exert control over their behavior, and be later used as a form of Cognitive Reappraisal that targets the *Mindfulness* component of M.E.R. Narrative Therapy utilizes this process by helping people develop a story about their life history, about who they are and what they want their story to look like as they continue their life. Therefore, a fresh self-narrative will drench a person's Vacuum System by lowering the pertinent Five Factors, and inhibit substance use altogether or maintain healthy substance use that aligns more with wanted long-term narrative of who they are.

One of the last psychological processes of 12-Step meetings is Social Learning through *modeling*. Humans learn behaviors through various processes, and one of the major processes is through modeling, or imitating, other people's behavior. We may model people's behavior that we perceive as being rewarded or having "resources." These resources may consist anything from money to status, likability, respect, or them living a life that is desired. People earlier on after their addiction may start to take on actions and skills that other people who live a healthy lifestyle share or present at a meeting. This is a regular learning phenomenon. Children are experts at learning through social modeling, from the use of language that adults speak, to "playing house" with other kids. We engage in modeling when we begin a new job, cook a new recipe, or become educated about how to modify a behavioral health issue. Then people will model our behavioral execution without even realizing it. This will continue the supportive dynamics in these social settings. Earlier on when I first got sober, I watched others have fun and get on with their life without abusing substances. Then Social Learning can become more personalized if we work "one on one" with a sponsor who has long-term sobriety.

Most of the effects of utilizing a sponsor in 12-Step programs are Social Learning in nature. A sponsor is a person who has some experience living a healthy sober lifestyle by working a 12-Step program. Sponsors merely lead as an example, while the person who is getting sober may incorporate or even leave behind in some cases behaviors that they observe in their sponsor. Working with a sponsor may also help enhance interpersonal communication skills through self-disclosure. Some sponsors may be the first person that was told about a traumatic experience. So the person may learn how to be vulnerable with people for the first time, and utilize a support system as coping tool. Just like substance use can encompass a *Reinforcement* component of alleviating emotional pain, utilizing a support system like a sponsor can be negatively reinforced as a healthy alternative behavior, since removing the unwanted experience of emotional pain rewards the social behavior. Accumulating experiences of reward from using a support system will further shape cognitive "expectations" under the *Mindfulness* component, which become rigid during active addiction, like a person feeling depressed who *expects* that substance use will be the only thing that will help them feel better. After a while, utilizing a support system will help the person experience more realistic expectations that substance use will only provide a temporary relief, while talking to others about what's bothering them as another option can deliver effective relief.

A major aspect of having a relationship with a sponsor is working the actual 12 Steps with a person who has already worked them themselves. The Steps are basically a self-help application to enhance one's being after an addiction. Many will disagree, but I believe the 12 Steps can be worked through and applied alone without a sponsor. We already know that people don't even have to be involved with a 12-Step program to live a quality life after an addiction, anyway. So working the 12 Steps can just be an additive exercise in a person's life, whether if they're abstinent or use substances at healthier levels. But working the Steps with a sponsor can be highly beneficial to process different things, while getting feedback from others at meetings who have experience with the Steps. The Steps have a "spiritual" basis to them, which we will discuss. But ultimately the Steps have self-discovery and behavioral enhancement components.

The **First Step** of the 12 Steps is the initial stride that approaches the problematic substance-use behavior with objectivity. We will discuss the major flaw that the first step encompasses later. But the essential idea of the First Step is recognizing the challenge and problem of the substance-use behavioral pattern for what it is. This is when the process of Motivational Interviewing (MI) comes in from Chapter Six. MI helps us examine the discrepancy between autonomous behavioral goals and the current problematic behavioral pattern.

The core of the **Second Step** is simply recognizing that there are many options for addressing the problematic substance-use behavior.

Then the **Third Step** is about taking the pertinent actions from those options to start changing the unwanted behavior pattern.

The 12-Step philosophy meshes Step Two and Three together. The major focus of these two steps is developing a spiritual foundation through the use of your own concept of a "Higher Power" to help change the behavior. Many people debate whether or not A.A. and other 12-Step programs are "religious" or "spiritual" programs. It is not up to me to decide and to conceptualize 12-Step programs in this regard. But individuals should reach this conclusion for themselves. All 12-Step programs use the term "God" as a convenient way to identify a Higher Power. But the nice thing about these programs is that individuals are able to identify their Higher Power however they wish; in fact, they are not ever required to identify one. This lets people tap into their own creativity, and believe in whatever they want to believe in. Some people activate their spirituality through actually praying or just thinking about something greater themselves. This will help shift their perspective, and further enhance healthy behaviors. I worked with a person who identified as an atheist, but would tap into his spirituality or "Higher Power" by watching videos about the universe and fifteenth-century history. This was just another form of Cognitive Reappraisal, which made issues that he would have used substances over seem very small and insignificant. There are many people who are really turned off by the spiritual or religious component. If so, they can simply discount it, attend the alternative S.O.S. (Secular Organizations for Sobriety) program that does not recognize the concept of a Higher Power, or attend S.M.A.R.T. Recovery, which focuses more on coping skills. Whether we use a spiritual concept of a Higher Power, focus on "rational decision-making," or use Cognitive-Behavioral Therapy (CBT), these strategies will target our Vacuum System accordingly. Steps Two and Three, and the spiritual component of 12-Step programs, are basically used like any other coping strategy or tool to modify our immediate mental and behavioral states.

So once we have our immediate coping strategies set up, we can then embark on the **Fourth Step,** which involves a "personal inventory" about our self. The fourth step is when we begin to explore a deeper understanding of ourselves, and observe how different aspects of our self drove our active addiction. This is a journaling process, where we write about various events from our life, along with different aspects of ourselves to clean out and process through. We can write down earliest memories or significant events that happened to us, current unresolved resentments, things that we feel ashamed about, fears, what we dislike and like about people close to us, and our personal strengths. Then we identify how and in what ways these experiences or characteristics have impacted us, and further identify how these aspects of our nature impact our behavior. The purpose of this Step is to resolve any unfinished business from the past, and develop insight into how earlier experiences shaped our behaviors and who we are. This process can really promote neural integration in the brain to enhance our self-narrative and understanding of ourselves.

Then doing the **Fifth Step** involves sharing our Fourth Step with another person who we trust, possibly a sponsor. This Step taps into the emotional-linguistic parts of our brain to further process our experiences at a more robust neural level. Some people may benefit from doing the Fourth and Fifth Step more than others. On the other hand, many people may not find it necessary for their behavioral health. Many people with extensive trauma history may benefit greatly from this process, especially if the *Trauma/Affect* factor of their profile is high. These couple of steps can rigorously uncover and target our Five Factor Profile, which in turn modifies the long-term substance-use behavioral pattern.

Step Six and *Step Seven* focus on re-engaging our authentic self. After we complete a personal inventory, we are now able to look at our behaviors from a more flexible standpoint. We can observe ourselves from a bird's-eye view. We realize that our past behaviors and habits are not fixed ways of acting. We can deviate from our habitual thoughts and actions more readily once we enhance our insight into ourselves through the previous steps. If stress occurs, boredom happens, or people are using substances around us, we can create some separation by being mindful of our behavioral processes. Then we can act in ways that align more with our deeper values and authenticity. Or, if we absorb fear like a sponge, we can act in new ways like a spontaneous and joyous child. Working these steps can target our Five Factor Profile directly in diverse ways. We can use them in the form of "Behavioral Activation," which is a concept in Cognitive-Behavioral Therapy (CBT), to overcome depression and elevate our mood. If a person is depressed, they may typically isolate themselves or lie around and vegetate. But Behavioral Activation involves committing to scheduled behaviors that break up the cycle of depression, such as going for walks, doing something productive, or using a support system regularly. The enactment of these steps can also directly target the three phases of substance use actions of the *Mindfulness* component within M.E.R. We can inhibit the actions altogether, or not consume the substances as impulsively. Many people get caught up in the use of "God" with these steps. But the main focus is to capture the psychological essence of the steps, and how they target our organic behavioral experiences.

Step Eight and *Step Nine* are great for people who may want to put away the guilt and shame over how their addiction affected people close to them. Once a person has been making great strides in developing new lifestyle habits through the first seven steps, the person can really hold their past substance misuse accountable now by expressing it to people close to them. It may not be appropriate to acknowledge the full extent of your problematic behavior with other people until you've established the self-efficacy to modify the behavior through the initial steps. Not only does this process address shame and guilt, it also provides practice in interpersonal skills and other assertiveness-related behaviors that can beneficially filter through a person's Vacuum System in individualized ways.

Then **Step Ten, Step Eleven** and **Step Twelve,** the last three steps, involve approaching issues that come up in our life head on, refining our coping tools, and then helping others with addictions through our knowledge of this process. These are the Twelve Steps in a nutshell, and anybody reading them can interpret them in countless ways. The importance lies in how they can directly or indirectly modify our substance-use behaviors, and help us achieve overall behavioral health. Any person can benefit from working the Steps in some way, and wouldn't need an addiction to do so. Plus many of us already use coping strategies or simply engage in behaviors that share common psychological threads with the 12 Steps. "Working the Steps" is just a formal process of doing so. The program emphasizes that the Steps should be continuously utilized. This is no different from continuously engaging in the many behavioral habits that maintain mental and behavioral health in our life.

Then we have 12-Step literature. A.A. has the *Big Book*, which is used has a self-help personal application. The Big Book includes the framework of working the program, along with success stories of people with prior addictions. The stories are pretty diverse, with people from many backgrounds. Stories help people identify their own experiences, and enhance hope and universality so they feel empowered to modify their own behavioral pattern. There have been a lot of slogans and concepts derived from the Big Book that have been infused into meetings and other practices of the program. The concept of "One Day at a Time" has been a fixture in the program, along with "Keep it Simple." Concepts like this target the *Mindfulness* component of substance-use behavior, and have many other universal applications for habit modification.

"Service work" is not only a facet of working a 12-Step program, but is also needed to maintain the life of meetings and the program in general. Service work can be anything from making coffee, to being a greeter at a meeting, to chairing a meeting, to being part of an event planning committee for a weekend conference. The mechanism behind engaging in service work for the individual is to possibly reduce shame early on, enhance social connection, improve behavioral discipline, and strengthen ego defenses through altruism. It can work the same way as what people get from volunteering at an animal shelter, or making their bed every morning.

Many people have benefited from the different features of 12-Step programs for many decades now. Its social component has been the primary driving force. Also, one of the virtues that 12-Step programs have demonstrated over the years is that there is no exclusive authority, and the program's layout has not changed since its early momentum. While this timeless factor has kept 12-Step programs pure in their own right, it unfortunately has not kept up with our updating understanding on behavioral health and addictive processes.

When evaluating 12-Step programs and self-help groups for addiction, we need to also look at some of the pitfalls that can impact people. Being able to call "balls and strikes" will actually help maximize the use of self-help groups for the individual need. One of the biggest critiques of 12-Step programs relates to its dated understanding about addiction and its behavioral process. We already addressed the fallacy and the unnecessary conceptualization of addiction being a *disease*. But 12-Step programs also indicate that people with an addiction are *powerless* over alcohol or drugs. This is a major misrepresentation of substance abuse behavior. Powerlessness implies that a person with an addiction has absolutely no control over their behavior, or they're helpless to act. But people make the decision to discontinue their substance misuse all the time. This happens when people go to detox, before going to treatment, when they experience enough consequences, or life offers a more appealing alternative. If a person uses less in a given day or they wake up in the morning deciding to discontinue their substance use, something is occurring in their cognition that is inhibiting their physical actions to continue to use. This can be happening naturally, depending on the context, or a person can be intentionally using a cognitive tool to modify this process. If a person was truly "powerless" over substances and their associated behavior, none of this could ever happen.

Remember that M.E.R. explains that there are three phases of physical actions that *every* substance-use behavior encompasses: substance-seeking, preparing, and then consuming. The first two out of three phases of these actions don't even involve ingesting the substance yet. There are many action sequences or rituals that lead up to the actual consumption of the substance.

So there is a lot of room to deviate from the path to an addictive pattern. Also, a person still has room to slow down their physical actions, even if they're at the consumption phase of their behavioral process. Addictive substance use is not as procedural as behaviors like chronic nail-biting, and even nail-biting still has a voluntary component to it that can be managed. I've worked with many clients who were in treatment with several months of sobriety, and "relapsed" for only one day. They used a quarter bag of heroin, or only had two drinks at dinner, trying to get past the facility's drug test. They express so much guilt and shame to me. But I point out how they have misused substances for months or even years consecutively prior coming to treatment. Now, they just used for one day with a much lower dose. That's progress! If they were powerless, they would not be able to stop after their initial dose or after the one day. There are so many physical actions in the whole behavioral sequence that it's impossible to be powerless over our substance-use patterns.

Alcoholics Anonymous talks about the "allergy" of craving and obsession of the mind if a person has a single drink. People can experience various craving responses and cognitive processes that are obsessive in nature after they start using substances or before they even touch the first. But do they automatically engage in the physical action process when they experience this "phenomenon of craving"? No. If it were so, then people would use substances *every single time* they experience cravings in any context. Of course as we know that there are neurobiological processes in the brain that produce a craving when a context activates our memory systems. This further enhances cognitive processes that try to motivate the physical action sequence to achieve the reward, especially if substance use is higher on our implicit reward hierarchy, as seen in addiction, or people using substances more prevalently. So sure, substance-use behaviors themselves can be a challenge to modify and overcome. But we know people reappraise their cognitive processes and inhibit their associated physical actions to use substances all the time if they crave it. The First Step does recognize the potential challenge for overcoming addictive behaviors. But that we're "powerless" over substances is a misconception in 12-Step philosophy.

Nonetheless, many people who have autonomous goals for long-term abstinence can benefit greatly from the various aspects of 12-Step programs as we examined earlier. If people are interested in these programs, they should use the programs to fit their individual needs, based on their Vacuum System. Some people who measure higher on the *Environment* factor compared to the other factors, may not benefit from a sponsor as much. But they may benefit more from finding meetings they like that create structure in their week. Whereas a person who measures higher on their *Psychological* factor due to being an extrovert and other personality traits, may benefit more from finding meetings where people go and do fun things afterwards. Then people may benefit from different aspects of a sponsor if they were to use one. It's always emphasized that a sponsor has a list of requirements for their sponsees, such as calling them every morning at 7 o'clock, not dating for the first year, participating in service work, only read up to page 86 of the Big Book, etc. But just as they have requirements, the person seeking out a sponsor should also have just as many requirements and expectations for their potential sponsor. If I have a client who is apprehensive about getting a sponsor, I tell them all the time if they just want a sponsor to work the 12 Steps with and they do not want to do all of the extra tasks, they should be able to get that. There is a lot of focus on the idea that a person needs to rely on a sponsor to guide their thinking and decision-making. This demeans personal autonomy, and takes away the person's self-efficacy over their behavior.

Unfortunately, many sponsors in 12-Step programs can deliver shaming messages to others in the group. They may mention to other members how much sobriety they have, and then tell them that if they want to go to any lengths to stay sober, then they will do exactly what they did. The person may start to feel forced, and then feel guilty or discouraged altogether if they don't commit. People in 12-Step programs may falsely believe that they know what is best for every person with an addiction. But if we look closely at a person's Vacuum System, we will be able to see how a person can benefit differently from any program or behavioral health method that is available to them. People are diverse in diverse ways. If a person regresses back into their addiction, then some people in the program may focus on the various tasks they did not follow through with in the program, such as not going to enough meetings, not working the steps as honestly, or never committing to service work, yet not once consider what the actual processes were that motivated them to regress back into their addiction, and what various *tools* could have been used to plug into these processes to prevent it. Just throwing a 12-Step blanket over the person does not help them address their substance-use behavior and strive for a quality life with precision.

I've heard many friends say things like, "man, I feel like shit. I need to get to a meeting." Then I would challenge them asking, "What's making you feel like shit?" Sometimes it would be related to the stresses of work or a relationship, and we would talk about the various ways they can go about addressing what was bothering them. Just going to a meeting can sometimes put a Band-Aid over the problem, without addressing the issue directly. But then many times they say that they feel like shit because of some guilt for not going to enough meetings, or they're not "working a program" as well as they used to. I would ask them how their quality of life is right now, and they would typically express that is has been good. Then I point out how this is all that matters. They feel guilty because of the universal assumptions of 12-Step programs, and the shaming messages that get received if "x, y and z" are not done.

We discussed how modeling and behavioral imitation in self-help groups could be highly beneficial after an addiction. But these social psychological processes can be highly detrimental instead, if they become fused to group-think. So while we can experience a lot of healthy social emotions in 12-Step programs, like empathy and compassion, more difficult social emotions like guilt and shame can manifest if we do not engage in every expectation that a sponsor or the 12-Step group sets out. The silly thing about all of this is that a person can be living a healthy and satisfying lifestyle, but feel unnecessary guilt because they're not meeting the expectations of a group they're involved with.

It's not explicitly stated, but there is a social hierarchy in 12-Step programs and addiction culture, whether people want to recognize it or not. If you bring a group of humans together for any purpose, a social hierarchy will always appear, generally based on personality dynamics and knowledge of the subject. In 12-Step programs, the social hierarchy may form based on the amount of sobriety a person has, the sponsor or sponsee role, how much you know about the literature, and how powerful or rough your story is. Many people with a higher implicit social status in the program can be more impactful with the shaming messages they send to other members who are not meeting the group's expectations. These expectations are derived from the program's set of beliefs about what is required to overcome an addiction. Confirmation Bias is a regular cognitive bias that is projected in the program. It's activated when people focus on, look for, or interpret situations that fit their own belief systems. If people express the slightest emotional or behavioral deviance, then their deviance becomes the focus, what they're *not* doing in the 12-Step program. If a person leaves a 12-Step group, then people automatically assume that the person is back using. Then if a person was known to have used, then people will believe that their behavior is already destined for a progressive addiction.

No self-help support group is required to overcome an addiction or modify a substance-use behavioral pattern, as long as we address the fundamental components of our substance-use behavioral process. But many people are pushed into 12-Step programs after an addictive pattern because they are so prevalent in our culture. If these people have autonomous goals to use substances at healthier levels, then it is recommended that they just use the 12-Step program as a launching pad into the life they truly want. The emphasis should be placed on how their behavior can be modified through the mechanical components of the program, and not so much being fixed into the 12-Step fabric and fused to the social pecking order. We need to take our time figuring out what aspects of 12-Step programs people can benefit from personally, and focus on plugging those methods into their Vacuum System. Then a person can find the right groove as to how much 12-Step involvement they need to get them where they want to be. If they develop a healthy life with substance use in it, then 12-Step may not be needed any longer. Even so, I've known many people who continued to attend A.A. despite them using cannabis, because they enjoyed the social aspects of the program.

A person drinking after their addiction and involvement in the 12-Steps will turn a lot of heads due to our culture's beliefs about addiction and treatment. Many people's friends and family may jump the gun and overreact, making a person feel like they have failed if they were to start using substances at healthier levels. This is one of the main challenges that a person may face if they decide to integrate healthy substance use back into their life, especially if they have developed various relationships from 12-Step programs, and their family holds similar cultural beliefs. A person may feel isolated, shamed, and not supported, even if their substance use is at healthier levels. I've had many good friends from A.A. who simply stopped talking to me because I use alcohol, despite living a healthy lifestyle. We quickly forget why we decided to get involved in 12-Step programs in the first place. We wanted to overcome an addiction, and get support so we could all achieve a quality life. But some of us who begin to use substances as a healthy part of life do not receive support anymore because our behavior is not fitting into the belief system of 12-Step culture. I encourage people in 12-Step programs to continue to provide support and share friendships with people who engage in moderate substance use, and not automatically assume that they have regressed back to an addiction.

If you find yourself enjoying your involvement in 12-Step programs and want to continue long-term abstinence, then you're highly encouraged to keep it up. Then there are many people who may continue abstinence, but do not find the need to continue with 12-Step. So they may naturally engage in alternative social circles with people that provide them the healthy social fulfillment they desire. Some people may become more involved with their family, engage in hobbies with co-workers, play and/or watch sports, attend a martial arts community, poetry club, Church, or a combination of a few of those. I recommend that anybody overcoming an addiction develop a diverse set of healthy social circles, whether you're involved in 12-Step or not. Some research has shown that people who are more connected to a wider range of social groups have greater well-being after an addiction.[3] So let's say you decide to integrate substance use back into your life, but your 12-Step group is not accepting of that. Then it can be an easier social transition into other *healthy* groups that use substances at moderate levels or never used in the first place. A person can feel very isolated if they're too fused to a 12-Step program and decide to engage in healthy substance use. Then they can be more at risk to regress back to their addiction due to the shame and isolation. Their Five Factor Profile may start to rise accordingly if other healthy social circles are not put in place. We need to look at all of our social circles for what they are, including 12-Step. Placing all our eggs in one basket can set us up for disappointment if we don't meet the expectations of *any* group. We're autonomous, unique individuals who find ourselves in many social groups throughout our whole lifespan, and need to engage with the ones that enhance our utmost behavioral health.

The 12-Step programs and their related approaches need to be used judiciously in treatment and when helping others with addictions. We need to first understand the exact processes of how addictive behaviors work, validate the diversity of autonomous behavioral goals, and recognize the nature of self-help groups themselves. I've stopped recommending 12-Step programs for clients who would think about using substances, after hearing constant war stories of prior addictions at meetings. Then there were people who simply wanted to stop going to meetings because they just wanted to completely move on from their addiction. They did not want rehash it every time they went to a meeting. I would never take the initiative to recommend a 12-Step program for a person under twenty-five years old with an addiction. If you're under twenty-five with an addiction, you're at an interesting developmental stage where there are many dynamics that can be driving the addiction, which could be ironed out naturally with age. If you look at the Five Factor Profile of someone in that age range, their *Psychological* factor is naturally higher because their brain has not fully developed yet. So they can be more impulsive and sensation-seeking in nature, which can further complement their emotional dysregulation under the *Trauma/Affect* factor. They experience unique *Life Stressors* related to going to school, peer pressures, becoming an adult, and taking on new responsibilities. Also, an environment where other friends are engaging substance misuse as well keeps the *Environment* factor higher. So it would not be appropriate to recommend that an adolescent or someone under twenty-five attend a 12-Step program. It would be very difficult to predict the trajectory of their addictive behavior, since they're at a narrow developmental window where substance misuse is not completely out of the ordinary.

We have a lot of conflicting messages in the addiction culture in the twenty-first century, between traditional approaches based on 12-Step programs and the innovative behavioral neuroscience movement. Since our understanding about addictive behavioral processes continues to update, self-help approaches need to be withdrawn as primary treatment models and regarded as being completely separate entities from clinical platforms. This is important, because many of these self-help programs have different views on what addiction *is*, which can be dated and misconstrued when it comes to the reality of the behavior in treatment. So the problem occurs when people keep returning to treatment with false ideas of what their addictive behavior is. This can impact a person's ongoing addiction cycle through the confirmation bias, and believing that maybe they do have a disease after all. Then they may become resistant to new ideas and various methods that can really target their personal behavior patterns for long-term change. So in some instances people may need to be *deprogrammed* of their misconstrued beliefs about their substance abuse behaviors in order to help them get out of their addiction cycle. When innovators introduce new approaches in the field, many people who hold traditional beliefs claim that we are "killing" people. But we're actually recognizing multiple routes for all people with substance misuse issues, including many who get neglected with no alternative options that match their autonomous goals. We're actually empowering people by giving the power back into them through infusing knowledge about their own behavior, and how the assorted strategies we use to achieve behavioral health target its processes.

The various self-help programs like 12-Step, S.M.A.R.T , or S.O.S., should be used as optional resources, and prescribed according to the individual. But let's say we're on a stranded island with an unlimited reservoir of drugs, and we have autonomous goals for abstinence. With other people absent on the island and no support groups available, how do we consolidate this whole scenario? Many traditional beliefs will say that the person could not stay sober alone, and that they *will* relapse back into their addiction. Yes, a person's Five Factor Profile under these circumstances can put them at more risk to re-engage in their substance abuse pattern, but it's not automatically pre-destined. So I believe that people with knowledge about substance-use behavioral processes and practice modifying their behavior have a very high self-efficacy, without depending on other people or programs under any circumstances. Many people will say, "I'm just speaking for me, but I need others and the program to stay sober, or else it's only a matter of time until I will use and die because I'm that type of addict." First and foremost, if a program enhances your quality of life, then that's all that matters. But the reality is that our past behaviors do not have to dictate future behaviors. Plus, humans hold many internal resources that have helped discontinue unwanted behavioral patterns time and time again, and we carry these tools wherever we go and whomever we're with. So all that self-help groups and other social circles are, is *support*, and not a required agent for change. But *healthy* social supports can be very helpful throughout the process. It does not matter what the social groups are, as long as they can generally reduce our Five Factor Profile, renovate our Dopaminergic System, and regulate M.E.R.

Our current addiction culture seems to imply that the only way people can celebrate the overcoming of their addiction is being completely abstinent or involved in a recovery program. But anyone should be able to celebrate their personal "recovery" without identifying as a person "in recovery," involved in a program or not, and abstinent or using substances at healthier levels. None of us should be forgotten, and we're all able to learn something from one another in regard to our behavior. The chief purpose is to overcome an addictive pattern at any level, and achieve a quality life no matter what that looks like to society. Sobriety dates are so embedded in our culture for celebrating recovery; I had a peer that I was in IOP with go as far as tattooing his sobriety date on his body. But, unfortunately, he started using substances not too long after. Whether we get back into our addiction or simply start to use substances more socially in the future, our values continue to reshape throughout our lives. What I believe today may change tomorrow. So sobriety dates are not the pinnacle of celebrating recovery. This is something like people who overcome trauma not being attached to the time of their traumatic event. They're not living in that time period anymore. It was simply a situation or set of circumstances that occurred sequentially in their life narrative. They're now free from it. To celebrate recovery means to feel free from an addictive place and time. A "sobriety date" is not fused to who we are today, and regular substance use does not have to violate our celebration. So whenever Indian Summer flourishes and October Baseball ensues, I can celebrate the conclusion of my addiction through my personal reflection with an ice tea or a beer raised to the sky.

chapter 9

Prevention

How do we never have to go back?

I GOT SOBER IN DECEMBER of 2010 and slid back into the swamp of addiction six months later. When I was sober for those six months, I was attending college during the day, hitting the gym a few nights a week, and hanging out with good friends that did not use drugs or alcohol. I'd been discovering my joy in psychology. Life was good. I finished a summer course in late spring of 2011, and then moved into a house with four other guys near campus before visiting home in Illinois.

When I was back home, I was driving with a friend who was rolling a cannabis blunt. I'd been feeling detached from my family over not being able to bring people together for a holiday. But I was feeling accomplished that I had achieved six months of sobriety, completed the year of school, and was going back to school with healthy roommates. I didn't have to see my probation officer for a month, and now a friend of mine was rolling a harmless blunt in my car next to me. This whole context activated the memory systems in my brain, and dopamine began to flush from sub-cortical levels to higher cortical regions to enhance craving and the associated cognitive processes. This contextual process elicited a "consideration-desire" level of a craving, where I simultaneously experienced cognitive processes in the form of attention salience on the weed stimulus, thought content of glamorizing the effect, and "reward outweighing the risks." Through these cognitive processes I gave myself the final permission, which concurrently dictated my physical actions to verbalize to my friend that I would just take a few hits from the blunt and I would be done. I took a few hits, and I did not use anymore substances for the rest of the day. The reinforcement properties took the form of social camaraderie with my friend, feeling attuned to the music while driving, and having a little escape from everyday life. During this initial episode after six months of continuous sobriety, my M.E.R. represented a relatively healthy substance-use behavior, at face value. This behavior was not much different than if I were to just have a couple of drinks at a restaurant. This substance-use behavior was filtered out by a corresponding Five Factor Profile. You probably have an idea what my profile looked like in that moment, based on the brief information I have provided.

The next day, when I saw some more of my friends back home, I talked myself into smoking a small dose of weed, even though had I told myself the day before that it would be the only time I would use cannabis until I saw my probation officer. A few days later, a good friend of mine invited me over to his father's place to share a case of beer around a fire in the backyard. My cognitive processes flowed according to the context, and I gave myself the final ruling that I deserved it. Looking back, I did deserve it. Why not? I drank eight beers in a five-hour span, while enjoying the summer night and a good conversation with a friend. I was able to drive to my mother's the next morning. Then I went back to Minnesota to start my next summer course. I had three more weeks until I had to see my probation officer. So having a couple of beers and smoking a little weed with a friend on the lake wouldn't show up on a drug test. But after that day, I was not going to smoke any more weed until after my appointment. However, "substance-use behavior" began to escalate in the implicit reward hierarchy of my Dopaminergic System. So when I was exposed to the relevant context later in the week, it became easier to talk myself into smoking more weed, with just two weeks to my probation appointment. By then, I was starting to *feel* like I couldn't stop my substance use. As substance use moved to a higher rank in my implicit reward hierarchy, my cognitive processes become more rigid in their attention, content, and speed, motivating reward achievement when exposed to pertinent contexts.

The day came that I smoked weed, again, and I had to now see my probation officer in two days. My cognitive process of "risk-reward evaluation" was starting to be very much outweighed by the risk of using cannabis, due to the context of seeing my probation officer in a couple of days now. This inhibited my physical actions to continue to use. I talked to a guy at the gym, and he guaranteed that I would clean out my system in two days if I drank three gallons of water, two jugs of cranberry juice, and topped it off with pickle juice. Now I had to see my probation officer the next morning and there I was, trying to finish off the remedy. But a few people told me there was a lake party that night just forty-five minutes away. I didn't even consider staying in for the night. But I wouldn't use any cannabis, that's for sure. I'd just use alcohol, as I drank the rest of my remedy, so I'd be clean for my appointment tomorrow. I was playing "beer pong" with a bottle of Chardonnay in my hand, while I chugged my gallon of water and cranberry juice in between turns. I was drinking every alcoholic beverage that came my way, feeling bulletproof since I was cleaning out my system simultaneously.

I have a history of either being the first person to pass out or the last person standing, keeping everybody awake, during my earlier drinking days. The cognitive process that used to be most active during the context of a party was the "expectation" that the night would be more fun than anything else, and that these are the greatest times you can have with other people. Being unrealistic expectations, these cognitive processes would dictate me to drink more impulsively in these social contexts in the past. This particular time, we were drinking all night, and I polished off my cleansing remedy by drinking the pickle juice by the early morning. The whole night I was trying to detox my system, while simultaneously intoxicating my system. Now I had to see my probation officer in six hours. I went to sleep, and woke in time to drive back and see her. She didn't even drug test me.

I left my appointment feeling relieved, and began to think about the next time I was going to smoke some weed. This experience was dictated by my "attention salience." Since December 2010, I told myself that I would never touch pills or other drugs again. I'd been sticking to that. But now I just wanted to relax on the lake and have some weed. So I continued my pattern, but then I noticed that I was feeling grumpy when coming down from a buzz or if I wasn't using at all. I was rushing through my summer course work, and I ended up getting a grade that did not meet my potential because I was rigidly focused on seeking, preparing, and consuming substances. The *Psychological* and *Environment* factors of my Five Factor Profile spiked due to the mere circumstance of using substances after six months of sobriety. But now the *Life Stressors* factor was increasing, due to not doing as well in school, and having difficulties with my intimate relationship. Plus, the *Trauma/Affect* was rising because of my lowered self-worth, and I was feeling more detached from my roommates and family. This Five Factor Profile filtered out more cognition that motivated more frequent physical actions of substance use. It was also covering a wider array of contexts, and more reinforcement properties than my initial pattern. As I continued to engage in the behavior, my Dopaminergic System became further adjusted, taking substance use to a higher ranking in the implicit reward hierarchy. My whole Vacuum System was updating, and starting to shape in the direction of an addictive pattern.

After my last summer class I visited home again in Illinois. An acquaintance told me that he had some Klonopin. What's wrong with taking a couple tablets? Well, by the end of my visit, I got my second D.U.I. and felony drug possession with morphine. My heart sank when the police lights flashed in my rearview mirror at two in the morning. I never made it to my next appointment with my probation officer in Minnesota. I was out on bail, and now I was driving a U-Haul to Minnesota to get my belongings with a half ounce of weed on me. I wasn't supposed to leave the state, and my sister got me the U-Haul because my license was revoked. She didn't know. I was planning to stay the night and go back to Illinois the next day. But I thought my roommates were going to have an intervention for me by the look on their faces. At the time, I felt I needed to get the hell out of there. So I drove back the same night, as soon as I had packed up my stuff. A month and a half later I was selling weed out of a house I was living at, using an assortment of prescription drugs, alcohol, cocaine, and heroin. After this second arrest, my Five Factor Profile turned upside down. My Dopaminergic System further formed the motivation of the addictive pattern, and M.E.R. expressed these finished processes overtly. My sense of reality was lost, and I had a full-fledged relapsed.

On paper, a person may say that this whole experience was the progression of my "disease" of addiction. Yes, there was a progression of some sort. It was a progression of a relearned behavioral habit. A "progressive disease" is a mischaracterization, because this description implies that if a disease progresses it can never be readjusted and it stays chronic. So if I was to ever use substances again, I was told that I would use substances just like where I left off. But this was not true, and it is not true for many people. When I used alcohol after five years sober in A.A., I never started to abuse it regularly or engage an addictive pattern like I was told I would. Sure, there are many people who abuse substances from where they left off, or reengage an addictive pattern after a period of sobriety. But it's not due to a "progressive disease." It's due to the accumulated nature of their Five Factor Profile and adjusted Dopaminergic System, and then not implementing the tools with intent and precision. When people feel the guilt and shame due to the Abstinent Violation Effect or the phenomenon of the Self-fulfilling Prophecy after the initial use, these elements may raise the *Trauma/Affect* and *Psychological* factor respectively. Consequences of the initial substance-use pattern can increase the Five Factor Profile (or decrease, depending on the significance of the consequence), filtering out an updated behavioral pattern. The behavior can adjust the Dopaminergic System due to its rewarding nature. This can further generate a feedback loop throughout the whole Vacuum System to sway the progression of the behavioral pattern.

So as I initially engaged in the substance-use behavior, based on my Five Factor Profile, my Dopaminergic System began to adjust minimally. This further spiked areas of my Five Factor Profile, and the behavior pattern continued to form. The "progression" was the learning and solidification of the wiring in the brain that filtered out the enhanced cognitive processing combined with the craving responses that motivated the actions of the behavior to achieve the reward.

The consequences became significant enough in my life, that they targeted the "punishment" properties of M.E.R., lowering my Five Factor Profile accordingly, leading me to discontinue my substance use in September 2011 without much intentional effort. When I stayed clean for five years, I created neural wiring for new behavioral patterns that became reinforced without substance use. My new behavioral patterns and the tools I used to inhibit my substance use further shaped my Five Factor Profile. Then in turn my Dopaminergic System adjusted to be more motivated for alternative behaviors and averse to substance use. So when I drank again, the substance-use behavior was pretty low on the implicit reward hierarchy. Plus, my Five Factor Profile was very different, naturally preventing the regression to an addictive behavioral pattern. So M.E.R. represented a new healthy form of substance use. Developmental psychology and neuroscience reminds us that people are like streams of water, we're very similar from the moments before, yet we're always changing.

After my first D.U.I. in 2010, I was court mandated to complete substance abuse education hours. The total regimen included watching two hours of film a week about the intoxicating effects and health consequences of different classes of substances. This intervention was used in hopes of scaring me straight into "just saying no." Obviously this traditional intervention was not effective, since I ultimately slipped back into an addiction and received another arrest. I never received any tools or the mechanical understanding about substance use that would have helped me slow down my behavioral. I never had a chance. But what's worse, is that a person then goes to treatment where they're taught they have an incurable disease and they have absolutely no control over their behavior. Then doctors, therapists, other professionals, and society reinforce their beliefs and behaviors that align with this dated outlook. Also, the person is shamed and neglected if they don't abide by these beliefs. A person could be set up for failure to never be able to manage their behavior under any circumstance. Instead of scare tactics, I wish I had been taught about the precise processes from the developmental, neurobiological, and overt behavioral levels to better understand what I was experiencing at the time so I could address my behavior with more awareness. If I had known how the Dopaminergic System and the implicit reward hierarchy worked, I could have more readily deviated from the substance use and committed to alternative behaviors. This approach would have disrupted the habit formation and kept it lower on the hierarchy. Understanding how craving coupled with cognition dictates the physical actions rooted by networks in the brain, would have helped me create space from my cognition, understand that these experiences were to be expected, and not put so much power into these processes in order to prevent me from acting out of impulse or habit.[1] Then, appreciating the developmental processes revealed by the Five Factor Profile, would have helped me understand what was driving my behavior at each moment, and how I could have addressed various parts of my being to keep the course of my behavioral process well regulated. Not only is the human developmental process about aging and external events occurring, but our own behaviors in the present also shape our course of development, making the Vacuum System function like a feedback loop. This is the reality of our behavioral patterns throughout our entire lifespan. As *time* is a linear process that does not stop for anything, our behavior at any form moves along with the trajectory of time. I didn't know where the brake pedals were. But now I do know clearly where the gas and brake pedals are for my substance-use behavior.

The traditional definition of *relapse* is simply returning to substance use after a period of abstinence from a previous addiction. One of the flaws of this definition is that "returning to substance use" can often be taken out of context. A person returning to substance use by having a single alcoholic beverage or even engaging in cocaine use for the night may not have necessarily "relapsed." So the traditional definition has added the concept of a "slip," to describe a less severe case of returned substance use after a period of sobriety. While this concept is progress, it continues to have the negative connotation that any form of substance use after an addiction is wrong or a mistake. As we examined my personal relapse, and we hear many stories of others, relapse is a more drawn-out process and progression of a behavioral pattern. Nobody relapses overnight. If I got out of rehab this afternoon and used heroin tonight, I wouldn't necessarily consider that a "relapse," especially if I woke up the next day motivated to engage in more healthy behaviors that I learned from treatment. It can be difficult to identify at what point of a person's behavioral pattern they're considered relapsed, since behavior is a very fluid experience. The line is very blurry. But does it matter? What matters most is the context of the behavior and how it's impacting the quality of life at each moment. My definition of relapse is: regressing back to an addictive behavioral pattern that creates significant negative consequences. It's not so much about whether a person is using substances or not in itself. But as we know, the initial behaviors or substance-use behaviors in general *can* stimulate the chain reaction of habit formation and relapse later in time if not addressed with precision. We will now discuss the various elements and experiences that influence the progression and reformation of addictive behavioral patterns.

Believing in the traditional definition of relapse can actually contribute to the onset of a substance-use relapse through the cognitive error–Abstinence Violation Effect we spoke of earlier. If a person uses one substance, they can feel ashamed and defeated to the point where they will continue to use substances to cope or fulfill this experience. This shameful experience due to the cognitive error will spike the *Trauma/Affect* factor of a person's developmental profile. So the person is starting to form their behavioral habit, and they're further confirming the identity label of an addict or alcoholic that culture sets out for them. Then this fixed identity will spike the *Psychological* factor, which is associated with personality dynamics. These experiences may lead people to believe that they can "never just have one." Then during each initial substance use, they suppose that they have lost all control again. So the belief in defeat, coupled with the fixed image of an addict, influences the continuance of their substance abuse. Subsequently the idea of, "relapse becomes more severe each time," is reinforced in the person's identity and some may consider themselves a "chronic relapser." I've worked with a man who had a history of daily alcohol use with blackouts. He held many of these traditional beliefs, which impacted his understanding about substance-use behavior. He had several months of continuous sobriety until he drank one pint of liquor in a single night. He checked himself into the hospital because he was worried about potential health risks due to getting drunk after not using alcohol for some time. He said to me, "I went to the hospital. That's how quickly my disease progressed this time around." But I had to educate him that there was no progression in a behavioral pattern just because he went to the hospital. It was simply a health judgment on his part to go to the hospital as a safety precaution. Then he made the choice to continue his sober lifestyle the next day. So in reality he had made significant progress with his substance-use behavior by not continuing his use into addiction territory after his initial consumption.

The primary goals are to not let these misbeliefs and fixed ideas of identity dictate the physical actions to continue substance use that lead to addictive patterns. The Mindfulness–cognitive-based tools that we discussed in Chapter Five can help create space with these cognitive errors and fixed identity to allow us act in new ways that deviate from the habit formation of substance use. It would help us view our initial substance-use behavior in a realistic light, and continue to choose healthy alternative actions that surround the substance-use behavior. So the person may only have two more drinks for the night, or simply discontinue their drug use the next day and engage in behaviors that align more with their values. If a person engages in initial substance use after a period of abstinence, they don't have to view themselves in the context of an "addict." They can view themselves more as a human being that has many more facets and value to them. We cannot be fused to thoughts like, "I can't just have one," because this belief does not create space to act in new ways. This is especially the case if we do have intense cravings to continue to use substances after just one day or one week of using.

I'm not saying people cannot relapse or go on to develop an addictive pattern if they use one substance. But the reality is that it's not an automatic occurrence, and that it's much easier to manage our behavioral patterns if we have knowledge about its processes. Although, there is a learning principle known as the **Reinstatement Effect**, where a person's previous behavioral pattern can be reinstated if they are presented with the stimulus. Simply put, if a person ingests a substance and experiences its effect, this can bring on new intense cravings to want more, potentially reinstating the previous behavioral pattern down the line. This is why it's a "no-no" in traditional approaches to use mouthwash or eat food with alcohol in it, or take opioid pain medication if a person had a previous addiction. The common belief is that a person has absolutely no control over their behavior once they ingest the substance or a substance that mimics the effect. So a person can start to experience more cravings and motivation to use the substance once they ingest it. But relapse prevention 101 emphasizes the skills to manage cravings under *any* circumstances. So logically, a person can start and finish using substances at any rate they wish as long as they plug the tools into their Vacuum System. However, we cannot unlearn behaviors completely in the brain, especially if it was a behavior that released a significant amount of dopamine. Once we have one substance, implicit memory systems in the brain associated with previous reward are triggered, manifesting the motivation to continue to engage in the behavior. This can be *a* reason why a person "picks up where they left off" or develops the pattern quickly if they begin using after a period of sobriety. But this phenomenon occurs if a person's Five Factor and Dopaminergic System reflects compulsive substance use, and the tools are not utilized.

Another learning theory phenomenon that needs to be considered with relapse is the **Renewal Effect**. The Renewal Effect occurs when the behavior reemerges when the context has changed. I've worked with many people who quit smoking cigarettes when they were in jail or attended a hospital program to quit smoking. But they engage in their previous smoking pattern as soon as they leave jail or the hospital. The Exposure component of M.E.R. sheds light on this learning principle, but it needs to be emphasized in the context of relapse prevention. Many people may completely change their environment by going away to treatment for ninety days. But once they come back home they may insidiously move back into their previous behavioral pattern. This is why exposure strategies and treatments with people's natural experiences can be highly effective.[2] In this way, a person can learn to manage their cravings and behavior with more precision, and not let these influences dictate their actions in the direction of addiction.

Developing a tolerance for a substance is a major phenomenon that can nudge a person into relapse. Tolerance begins to occur when a person has to take more of a substance to get the same effect that they desired from a smaller amount. Tolerance can increase very subtly. A person can use a substance two days in a row, but may need to use a little more on the third day to get the same effect they wanted. So if they smoke a joint or have a beer on the following day, the chemical effect may feel stale and not as desirable. So they may double the dosage to chase the effect. Then if a person continues this rate, they can reach the threshold of becoming chemically dependent and experience withdrawal symptoms if they don't use the substance. Therefore, the person will continue to use the substance and enhance their behavioral pattern to prevent the experience of withdrawal. The experience of tolerance can move from chasing the original desired effect from a small dose of a substance, to continuing to use to manage discomfort without the substance. Tolerance is also associated with depletion of dopamine in the brain, so that people chemically dependent to substances may have difficulty experiencing pleasure from natural rewards and alternative activities that don't release as much dopamine at a baseline compared to substances. This is known as *anhedonia*. When a person builds up a tolerance, dopamine release is less responsive to the substance, while also making it difficult to release a significant amount of dopamine to alternative activities. Therefore, developing tolerance and dependence can influence a person to continue to use substances at significant levels to compensate for their depletion of dopamine and to override the effect on alternative behaviors. Even though brain scans show the changes in dopamine activity between people who have developed a chemical dependency and a non-dependent group, this is not evidence of a disease. This is just a natural biological process that occurs if we ingest a substance repeatedly over time, and tolerance will decrease back to a baseline level as we discontinue the particular substance.

This relates to the experience of the Wall Stage of abstinence, which may generally occur six months to a year into sobriety with people who had previous moderate to severe patterns of addiction. What happens is that when a person discontinues their addiction, they are depleted of pertinent neurochemicals. They're experiencing withdrawal symptoms and feeling lousy. But then once they are finishing up with detox, their neurochemicals begin to naturally rise back to baseline over time. So they are naturally starting to feel good. Plus as they continue to stay sober, they may be receiving external rewards, such as getting their job back and their family starts talking to them again. So they're feeling very good at this point, and possibly experiencing the Pink Cloud Effect. But then what happens is that they hit a *wall* around six months to a year of sobriety. Their neurochemicals have reached their maximum baseline, and they settle back into their life and routine. So now the person may start to want more out of life, and feel bored or dissatisfied. This can make them feel more attracted to substance use, where they slip back into an addictive pattern and chase the associated pleasurable experiences.

We need to incorporate a theoretical tolerance meter in our mind to help prevent the risk of entering relapse territory and reaching the chemical dependency threshold. It's difficult to measure our biological tolerance with a particular substance. But you can learn to at least ballpark it to manage your behavioral pattern. We can measure our tolerance meter by identifying the nature of our substance-use pattern recently, and observing our attitude to the effect of the substance's dosage. I may have used cannabis four days in a row and used it from mid-morning until I go to sleep. So I start to notice that I need to use more to get the same euphoric feeling, and feel somewhat irritable and constantly foggy in between dosages. I will be able to observe that my tolerance meter is increasing, based on my pattern and general attitude. So with this understanding of how substances affect our biological system, I would cut down on my behavior and engage in alternative behaviors to lower my tolerance meter. But some of us may not care if we develop tolerance, and just continue to chase the desired effect. So we have to use cognitive strategies, reminding ourselves, "If I continue, I'm not going to enjoy the substance as much as I used to. I'm wasting more money. I have to accept that my biology does not have an unlimited reservoir of pleasurable neurochemicals." The person may need to also think long term in regard to engaging in alternative behaviors right now to lower the tolerance meter, so they can enjoy and appreciate the substance at a later time. Using the tolerance meter can be a mindfulness skill and approach in itself. The person may need to develop cognitive strategies and alternative behaviors in conjunction to lower the tolerance meter to a desirable level. Being a "lightweight" is actually a good thing, and nothing to be embarrassed about. Being a lightweight just means your tolerance is low due to not using a substance as much, and a smaller dose of a substance does the trick.

When it comes to addressing the Wall Stage, the primary tool to address this experience is patience and time. While patience and time can be dissatisfying, it's the price we pay for being human and discovering chemicals that do a great job of providing pleasure and comfort. But with that patience, we are creating an opportunity to sharpen our skills for delaying instant gratification and enhancing new healthy habits that create a sober foundation.

We have covered how general experiences can contribute to the process of relapse. But we need to always examine the individuality of a person's Vacuum System, and how it can allow an addictive pattern to re-emerge. I worked with a person who had several months of sobriety until he engaged in a two-week alcohol binge, from which he needed medically monitored detox. When you take a closer look at his behavior, he didn't necessarily relapse due to his initial use. The first night he drank he went out with a girlfriend, and he had two alcoholic beverages with dinner and stopped. So we can imagine that his Vacuum System at the time was functioning smoothly to create this particular behavioral occurrence. But a couple of hours later when he got back to his sober living home, he tested positive for alcohol. He was exited from the program that night, and was not allowed to come back until he could test clean. So now this situation completely turned his Five Factor Profile upside down. His *Life Stressors* spiked dramatically, due to the circumstance of not being able to go back to where he had been living, not having any other place to live, and now facing challenges to get re-admitted around his work schedule. Plus his *Environment* factor had started to increase because he was going to stay with a friend who drinks, and now he didn't have to worry about being clean, since he was not staying at the sober living home in the meantime. His particular *Psychological* factor was higher at baseline, which primarily drove his previous drinking patterns. But now it spiked, due to the synergistic effect of the *Life Stressors* and *Environment* increases, based on the present circumstances.

So his Five Factor Profile created the thought that he had no other options but to get a bottle at the liquor store and go to his friend's for the night. The next morning he experienced a spike in his *Trauma/Affect* factor, due to feeling the shame and guilt of his changed lifestyle circumstances. So his high Five Factor Profile and lack of prevention skills made him feel like he did not have any option but to continue to drink. Now he was in a perpetuated cycle where his substance-use behavior, represented by M.E.R., was continuing to impact his Five Factor Profile, and his profile, filtered by the Dopaminergic System, was shaping his substance-use pattern. So his tolerance was increasing rapidly, to the point of developing dependence to alcohol. Tolerance is associated with the *Psychological* factor due to the depleted dopamine and longing to experience a desired effect. At the same time, dependence is associated with the *Life Stressors* factor, due to the circumstantial discomfort of experiencing withdrawal. When I met with him upon his return from detox, we reflected on how his Five Factor Profile at dinner influenced him to only have two drinks and stop. But then we looked at how his Five Factor Profile completely shifted once he was ejected from the program, which influenced the chain reaction to relapse. He said, "At the time, I could have just sat at the bus stop for an hour and then come back. I would have been clean, and wouldn't have had to go through all of this."

Some people's Five Factor Profile may not be as apparent in their behavioral pattern as the example above. I worked with a woman where it took us a few weeks to uncover the underlying factor that drove her binge use, whereas under other circumstances she used alcohol at healthier levels. We uncovered that a core belief of "needing to be perfect" stemming from her childhood impacted her binge use when she felt depressed or detached from other people. We had to examine multiple binge episodes during different periods of her life to uncover this core belief. Her core belief obviously increased her *Trauma/Affect* factor when activated. It's not that "negative" emotions cause substance misuse behaviors and relapse. It's the belief that we don't have any other options besides using, or that it's our best option when we're experiencing challenging emotions.

This is associated with the "expectation" cognitive process from the *Mindfulness* component of M.E.R. It says something like, "I *expect* that drinking is the only thing that will give me relief in this moment, and doing a "daily thought record" is a waste of time." The concept of *options* can also be related to our patterned behavior. Suppose someone experiences mild consequences due to their substance-use behavior, but then they use more to cope with these consequences, which creates a cycle of more severe consequences. It's fine to use substances when we're experiencing stress or difficult emotions, as long as we don't believe it's the *only option*, and that we engage in other healthy behaviors in combination. So then we can associate new behaviors with challenging emotions, so as to eventually adjust the cognitive process of "expectations" that coincides with substance-use actions.

An element of the *Trauma/Affect* factor that is a major challenge is the "fuck it" attitude. The "fuck it" attitude is a challenge because the person absolutely disregards their true values, and does not care about the consequences of their substance-use behavior in that moment or for an extended period of time. They are ultimately self-sabotaging their life. Then there are some people who may be addicted to the addiction cycle itself. They engage in the addiction until it lands them at the bottom. Then they get pleasure from rising above it and getting their life back together, as people in their support group are patting them on their shoulder. They do this until they reach a plateau at six months and then deliberately re-engage back into the addictive pattern to start the cycle over again. Other people's addiction can be maintained by assimilating a self-image of a famous rock star that abuses substances because it's edgy. This presentation can spike the *Psychological* or *Trauma/Affect* factors, depending whether the assimilated self-image is merely a tool to justify the substance use or due to a person's self-esteem being disrupted. People with these underlying concerns may benefit more from thorough therapy or coaching, where they can work on exploring any unresolved interpersonal strains from their past, and enhance their social support, self-esteem, and purpose.

To be clear, just because a person uses a single dose of a taboo drug like heroin or methamphetamine, doesn't mean all of their Five Factors are high on their profile. Some can be higher to motivate the initial use. But the Five Factors can start to generally increase accordingly, if the person is starting to form a behavioral habit and enter relapse territory. Many people's relapse or behavioral patterns in general can primarily hinge on the fluctuation of the *Environment* factor. A person can be measuring high on all of the Factors, but if their *Environment* factor is absent or extremely low, the substance-use behavior will not occur due to the lack of access to substances or having other commitments in that moment. But then if the same person experiences a spike in the *Environment* factor, they will need to implement tools to lower the other four factors or target the M.E.R. processes to prevent the regression to addictive states. People generally have a fixed baseline for the *Psychological* factor, since this factor has more features that are difficult to change than the other factors. But other factors like *Environment* or *Life Stressors* can influence the *Psychological* level. Preventing relapse lies within the individual nature of a person's Vacuum System in the moment, and how it fluctuates across a period of time to either form an addictive pattern or disrupt the pattern formation.

Strategies to prevent relapse can come in two general forms, such as "acute" strategies and "lifestyle" strategies. *Acute strategies* are the tools that are used in immediate situations to help manage or inhibit the behavior itself. They are our frontline defense. These strategies typically target the M.E.R. processes of the substance-use behavior in the moment, whether we want to maintain sobriety or use substances in a healthier manner. On the other hand, *lifestyle strategies* for relapse prevention don't necessarily address immediate situations associated with substance use, but rather circumstances that indirectly make a person vulnerable to relapse. These circumstances can range from having a support system in place to having weekly structure, taking psych medication, or having alternative hobbies. So these lifestyle strategies will primarily target our Five Factor Profile and M.E.R. simultaneously, depending on the strategy and its relationship to the actual substance-use behavioral process. Keeping this distinction in mind will help us understand how relapse prevention skills plug into our Vacuum System, and make our behavioral pattern function.

If we are already using substances, the crucial aspect of relapse prevention is to catch the habit as it progresses, once we *initially* desire a changed behavior. It will take observation on our part to look at our behavioral pattern, and begin to implement some strategies once we notice that the habit is forming and that we're starting to experience mild consequences. Relapse is not a black-and-white occurrence; a lot of gray area is involved, since behavior is fluid. No one wants to experience the consequences of substance use, nor do we want society to tell us how to behave. So that's when we become the executive of our own behavior. We need to pay attention once we desire some kind of change in our behavioral pattern, and adjust the Vacuum System accordingly to work towards our autonomous goals.

When many people get sober, they say things like, "I don't want to go back to using." What they're truly saying is that they don't want to go back to the previous addictive pattern and its consequences. This can be a cognitive process to motivate sobriety, and the same thinking can motivate more moderate substance use, if that is what is desired. Another major component of relapse prevention is teaching people to be more sensitive to the consequences of substance use. It takes a mindfulness skill. An interesting study from 1998 showed that people who abused heroin were more focused on immediate gains at the expense of experiencing increased punishments in the future during a card ask.[3] This implies that people with addictions may be less sensitive to future consequences.[4] If we learn to become more sensitive to mild consequences, such as hangovers, increasing tolerance, or low self-esteem, we can tweak our behavioral pattern accordingly to help prevent experiencing more severe consequences and habit formation. We can learn a lot from people who use substances without a history of addiction, by looking at the cognitive processes that regulate their behavior and how sensitive they are to consequences, if they occur. An image I like to use to be more mindful of substance-use behavior is imagining that you live in a black-and-white world, where only substances are in color. This can help turn our mindfulness switch on, to become more sensitive to our substance-use behavior. We have less control over our motivations, which are embedded in our Dopaminergic System, but more control over the individual actions that are directed towards our motivational system. Relapse prevention is about opening up the behavioral options that are entrenched in our values, which the values align with our motivational system.

Coaching can be a very useful resource for relapse prevention with substance-use behavior. There are many different kinds of coaches, from wellness coaches and business coaches to life coaches. Coaches for substance abuse fall under the realm of "recovery coaching." Coaching is different from psychotherapy or counseling, especially in terms of the interpersonal dynamic in particular. In psychotherapy, the therapist may play a role as an emotional corrective experience that the client may never have received from their family of origin, where the members of this therapeutic relationship uncover and process unconscious material that unfolds in session. Coaches, on the other hand, may be more direct about providing expert knowledge about an identifiable problem, and are more "hands on" in guiding a person to develop the skills to solve the problem.

Many life coaches direct people to take action in various areas of their life to enhance overall lifestyle functioning and purpose. The Cognitive-Behavioral Therapy (CBT) concept of Behavioral Activation that I introduced earlier is a primary mechanism behind life coaching. Life coaches flood their clients with the direction to take a lot of positive and healthy actions, to the point that these behaviors will influence healthy thought patterns and emotions. So then these new thought patterns and emotions will maintain high motivation and influence the person to continue to take more action to create the lifestyle results that are desired. Then the life coach becomes just a guide to empower and monitor the person's progress towards their specific goals. The person may only need the coach until they have developed more adaptive behavior, goal-oriented thinking, and improved sense of self-efficacy over their life. A 2012 study of a thousand smokers found that people with lower measures of self-efficacy progressed further into relapse with smoking than people who measured higher on self-efficacy.[5]

So coaching for substance-misuse behaviors can give people the boost to learn the skills to manage their behavior and adjust their Vacuum System, like a surgeon's efficacy with a scalpel. A recovery coach may escort people home from residential treatment, and be used as an early safety net to walk a person through cravings and help them develop a healthy lifestyle after an addiction. The coach may be available in person at various locations or on call at numerous times throughout the day as a guide to help the person through challenging situations. Receiving direct assistance from a person who has the knowledge and tools to regulate substance-use behavior can help us experience the self-efficacy to address the behavior under any circumstance.

Recovery coaching has been traditionally focused on helping a person maintain total abstinence and integrate them into a "recovery" lifestyle. But since moderation management and other related autonomous goals are becoming more popular and desirable for substance-use behavior, the scope of coaching will expand. Many people with moderation drinking goals in particular can benefit greatly from using a "drinking companion" coach. After they experience their period of initial sobriety, it would be highly recommended to have some drinking episodes with a coach before they were to take on drinking alone. A coach can help the person slow down the whole drinking experience, whereby the person can learn to drink more mindfully through observing the M.E.R. processes, and learn to enjoy the substance-use experience without letting the substance become the primary focus in the situation. The coach may guide the person to let the alcoholic beverage last fifteen to forty-five minutes. Then, while drinking, the coach will have the person focus on various aspects of the present experience to practice getting their mind off the substance. They may focus on what's on TV, the conversation with the coach, observing other social encounters, or engage in other activities in the present that do not involve drinking. After a couple of drinks the coach may have the person pause and place their attention on the present intoxicating effects, so the person can become more aware of the desired effects and reduce any impulsivity to further drink at frequent levels. Many times, the person will reach their desired level of intoxication a lot earlier than they expected. Then the next day, the coach can check in with the person to help process their experiences and work through any cravings they may have on that following day. The person will be guided to engage in more alternative behaviors that align with their values to prevent habit formation of the substance-use behavior. The coach can anonymously attend weddings, company parties, or other social settings as a direct aid in checking in with the person. This can help the person work through any challenges they may face with using alcohol in these various settings, until they feel the confidence to manage their behavior on their own. The drinking companion coach is just another voice of reality to help the person place their foot over the brake pedal and nudge them in the direction of their autonomous goals. There has been some evidence as early as the late nineties that demonstrated significantly reduced drinking outcomes after a six-month followup with problem drinkers who were coached by therapists through multiple drinking episodes.[6] I've worked with problematic drinkers in a intensive outpatient program who used the group as a scaffolding agent by bringing in their weekly alcohol use pattern to adjust it to the healthy pattern that they desired. They found what worked and what didn't. Since addictive behaviors can be challenging to modify, coaching can accelerate the learning process to effectively implement the tools.

Instead of just sending a person back through the revolving rehab door after a relapse, we need to use a magnify glass to really look at a person's behavioral pattern and identify the processes that contribute to the addiction. I've heard many people say that they can start off drinking casually, but after a while they just can't have one. When I ask, "why?," they give me an astound look and say because they're an "alcoholic." But that's not explaining enough. I want to find exactly what is happening between one beer and six, and then between one binge use and the next. The individualized Vacuum System can explain what is occurring, and what processes we need to tap into to create a healthier stream of behavior. It helps to evaluate our substance-use behavior throughout our lifespan to see how the behavioral pattern has changed according to the fluctuations of the Five Factor Profile. The medical industry and the behavioral health industry share a very similar practice sequence. The professional does an assessment or examination to evaluate a problem, a diagnosis is made, a treatment or intervention is implemented, and then the problem is monitored to reach the desired outcome. Professionals like dentists and physicians may have a quicker practice protocol, since they are dealing with direct biological processes that can be easier to measure and observe. Then they use treatments that deal more with chemistry and biological mechanics that may have a faster-acting effect, while behavioral health practices need to evaluate a wide range of abstract factors and metaphysical areas of a person to understand their presenting behavior. Then the treatment needs to target these multiple facets of the person. Behavioral health professionals exemplify the art of conducting a thorough practice on a single person. The Vacuum System, being a comprehensive model, can help evaluate the complexity of substance-use behavioral processes in a concise manner.

We hear things like, "For me, if I drink, it leads to everything else," or "If you stop in a salon enough, you'll get a haircut." These beliefs imply that the addictive pattern is inevitable under particular circumstances or if an initial substance-use behavior is engaged. But that doesn't have to be the case! Some people may have more challenges than others when it comes to overcoming their addiction. But the behavioral processes need to be understood more objectively, and targeted with precision. Sometimes we drink a little more than we intended, or used a drug that we wish we hadn't. But that doesn't have to be the end of the world. Many people will say, "Why would you risk opening up that door anyway? Abstinence and sticking to the program is the safest route." First of all, this attitude in itself creates low self-efficacy in the belief that people have no influence over their own behavior, and second, abstinence does not meet every person's autonomous goals. People need options, whether it's abstinence, moderation, or somewhere in between. We know that addiction consists of an accumulation of moment-to-moment substance use occurrences. This reminds us that our primary focus lies in the quality of actions in the *now*.

The problem with the traditional outlook on relapse prevention is that it elicits fear and implies low self-efficacy to manage the behavior. "Relapse prevention plans" are placed as some magical guide that is necessary for long-term change, while less reliance is placed on behavioral autonomy in the moment. A lot of prevention for substance abuse is embedded in "just say no" rhetoric, and having adults prevent adolescent substance use at all costs. We don't want to

encourage adolescent substance use, of course, but we don't want a zero tolerance attitude either, since people will always use substances. A lot of prevention
is based on scare tactics in regard to the consequences of substance use, and not
built around behavioral modification. Of course people need to be educated
about the risks of substance use, such as not mixing opioids with sedative-hypnotic drugs. But relapse prevention needs more of an emphasis on performance
psychology, where people with substance use issues need to develop an athlete's
mindset. So then they're able to really zone into their action-oriented experiences to create the most favorable behavioral outcome to achieve their desired
lifestyle. *Substance-use health and prevention should address the potential risks
and addictive nature of the behavior, at the same time, promoting the pleasure,
appreciation and overall well-being of using substances with a healthy perspective.*

It's time we stopped giving addictive patterns and substances more power
than they deserve. What if we just took all the power out of our addiction and
set it aside?

What would we say to that addiction or substance? What would it say to us,
and how would we respond?

Then if we put that power back into **us**, how would we use it? The "power"
of addiction is truly an illusion, once we recognize the neurobiological and
behavioral processes that make it *feel* powerful. But in reality it's not any more
powerful than the potential of our whole being working together to shrink the
behavior.

I asked a woman in treatment how her thirty-four-year-old self saw her
drinking. This question made something click for her, and she started to cry.
The power of her ideal self as a thirty-four-year-old had a completely different
outlook on her behavior. She was able to see her old self from the perspective of
an outsider looking in. So this spark eased her into the change process. Making
personal changes to substance-use behavior will naturally improve overall
self-esteem and autonomy. In turn, the implicit memories that once brought
out cravings and obsession about substances will be modified, and new conditioning for a more satisfying lifestyle can be restored. These improvements shift
the perspective about personal substance use and our overall relationship with
substances. This is just the beginning to transform our life and find our purpose.

chapter 10

Beyond

What is it all for?

WE'VE SPENT THE MAJORITY OF the time examining the nature of sub-stance-use behavior. We broke down the developmental, neurobiological, and behavioral components that embody the whole organic process. We need to understand these fundamental properties of substance-use behavior, and how to modify the behavioral pattern when necessary. This is the foundation of overcoming our addiction. However, living a quality lifestyle goes well beyond the substance-use behavior itself.

Substance use is a single behavioral experience that flows within the stream of behavioral patterns that make up our existence. Using substances can enhance our lives in many ways, from casual social bonding to relieving imme-diate symptoms of trauma. If we are to use substances, the goal is to maximize the benefits of using them, while minimizing the potential negative impact. Many people find that they actually enjoy life more without using any sub-stances. But some people will always value substances, from caffeine to can-nabis. Regardless of whether substances are used or not, substance use is an *insignificant* part of life. The significance of life is tapping into our purpose and mission to seek meaning. Achieving this life task can override any addictive pattern. Our personal meaning of life drenches the Vacuum System in magnifi-cent ways that quiet down the substance-use behavior.

When we initially get sober or reduce our substance use after an addiction, we're just trying to escape the pain and consequences of the previous behavioral pattern. Our neural chemicals are replenishing, and our lifestyle is resetting itself back to normalcy. Many people sustain their sobriety or reduce substance use initially to evade the consequences of the behavior. However, people will need to eventually switch from just managing the consequences to creating the benefits of new behaviors and a larger lifestyle. This shift will happen over time. We need to first learn how to shape our substance-use behavior by directly targeting the behavioral properties of M.E.R., and the underlying Five Factor Profile that generates the behavior through the Dopaminergic System. Building up the self-efficacy to influence the substance-use behavioral pattern at will is a monumental goal: so the addiction can be stopped in its tracks and never manifest again.

Beyond the behavior's impact and "relapse prevention," we learn to develop intrinsic motivation to maintain a lifestyle without excessive substance use. We start to find natural rewards that are alternatives to substances. The famously cited Rat Park experiment demonstrates how alternative rewards and stimulation can help override the reinforcing effects of substance use.[1] The study found that rats in a small cage drank the morphine solution significantly more, compared to when placed in a environment where they had toys, tubes, and other rats to interact with. Even though the morphine water was available to them in the stimulating environment. This experiment has become so popular due to its related application with humans. The goal is to develop environments in our personal life that are stimulating and provide purpose to the point where we naturally choose that over mere substance use. Addictive behavioral patterns constrict our potential and keep us trapped in the cage. The use of *contingency management* in treatment for substance use plays on an alternative reinforcement mechanism similar to Rat Park experiment. Treatment programs use contingency management by giving clients gift cards or monetary vouchers if they provide negative urine analysis during treatment to help motivate them to stay sober.[2] While this can create motivation to live a healthy lifestyle early on after an addiction, people will eventually need to develop their personal contingency management through their purpose and an overall lifestyle they can enjoy. How do you visualize your life being if there wasn't an addiction? What does your life look like without it? What would you want it to look like? What would be in your life, and what would you subtract from your life? What is it that you want in your future life six months, one year, and five years from now? How can you get started toward that today?

Many of us basically live our life in weekly intervals. The week starts over after the seventh day. We work a set number of hours in a week. We often get paid on a weekly basis. Many of us have the same days off every week. We have weekly activities, and maybe go on one date each week when we meet a new person. So when developing a lifestyle after an addiction, I coach people to set activities and tasks that they can engage in on a weekly basis. Maybe the person will start going to the gym twice a week, have one social activity a week, eat an expensive meal, or take piano lessens one day out of the week. The goal is to place activities in our life that stimulate different parts of our being, such as creativity, relaxation, challenge, achievement, and the social brain.

I use the week as the basic interval because it can make our lifestyle more manageable. Life can be typically run on weekly intervals that constantly restart. Then we can have something to look forward to all the time. Some people may feel overwhelmed after an addiction when they start to engage in the goals that they have neglected. But just focusing on weekly activities can help us get started and work on short-term goals. If I wanted to get back into a web photography blog, I could focus on just one blog post a week, drive to a destination that would challenge my photography skills weekly, or just read about photography for one hour each week. Something that starts off as a weekly activity that we enjoy can grow into something that brings inspiration and meaning to our lives. Weekly intervals also keep things simple and structured in our lifestyle. A lot of people say they want to travel more or maybe try an activity like skydiving. Activities like these are great and all, and give you something to look forward to in the future. But activities like these can be infrequent and unrealistic. We need to first develop activities that we can start engaging in and focus on daily or weekly that will assist in developing a lifestyle.

When we're in active addiction, we're constantly looking forward to the next buzz or excitement with substances. We need to tap into this natural desire for anticipation. Having a number of varied activities that are challenging, creative, social, and relaxing can help fulfill this natural desire and lead to a larger purpose in life. This is when we start to feel truly free from our addiction, and that it wouldn't make sense to use substances like we did before. Neurobiologically, the substance-use behavior will rank lower on the implicit reward hierarchy. So we will have a bunch of new behaviors and activities that will rise toward the top of the hierarchy. Individually, each single activity or interest may not hold as much dopamine weight as substances once did in our lives, but we will have an accumulation of activities making up a lifestyle that pushes substance-use behavior farther down the hierarchy. Go ahead, engage in the pleasures of the world.

I worked with a younger guy who had a habit with heroin, but had never had any issues with other substances. He lived in a sober home and often expressed frustration because he couldn't go out and have a drink with his co-workers. He had no desire to use heroin anymore; he just wanted to live his life like a regular thirty-year-old and move on from addiction-recovery. He felt despair, detached from people and trapped in a "recovery" cage. Traditional approaches would say that he needed to explore why he had to drink with his co-workers, and learn how to live a life without using any substances. But that would be missing the point. Unfortunately for young people, substance use permeates the culture. People can feel isolated if they're restricting their behavior solely based on their culture's misbeliefs about addiction. Also, for this person it's not about drinking for the effect *per se;* it's about breaking through the recovery culture, and be able to partake in a drink from time to time in a healthy social environment. This guy drinking with his co-workers would actually add a healthy social activity into his week, and provide his life with a little more interest that he perhaps tried to fulfill with heroin. Sure, he can't make alcohol use his primary focus in life. But you're telling him he can't do something that can actually help improve the overall quality of his life. Again, it's about taking a closer look at people's personal Vacuum System, and not making absolute assumptions about their behavior potential. I'd rather tell people to be "cautious" than say you "can't." It wasn't until I followed my autonomous goals that I felt truly free from my addiction.

Once we overcome our addictions, resolve our traumas, manage lifestyle stress and other impulses, we need to push ourselves into a higher dimension. We spoke earlier about values, and the importance of tapping into our values to reduce substance use. Looking at our values can be a starting point and the compass that takes us into a new dimension of our being. I coach clients to develop a values pie chart. They first identify various values ("good" or "bad") and place a percentage on each one, based on how much they value or focus on it in their present life. Substances are typically included. Then I would have them develop a second pie chart that they would desire or envision to look differently after exploring more potential values. Then an action plan is made to start engaging in activities or behaviors that align more with the high percentage values there, so the new pie chart can start to be actualized. Also, a person can continue to use the chart to assess what values they are focusing on more in their present life. It's time to move forward, create new habits, and reinvent ourselves through the things we value in our lives.

A classic model in psychology, known as *Maslow's Hierarchy of Needs,* proposed by a psychologist Abraham Maslow, is highly applicable to people's functioning during and after an addiction. The model suggests a set of universal human needs that can fall along a hierarchy of sophistication. At the bottom of the hierarchy we have basic needs: food, water, and safety. Then next up on the pyramid is where you'll find higher human needs of belonging and social desires, and esteem needs of feeling accomplished and a sense of prestige. At the top of the hierarchy is "self-actualization," where a person achieves their full potential and purpose as a human being. We cannot achieve the higher needs until we address the lower ones first. We can fluctuate along the hierarchy within a matter of minutes, days, or years, and many of us do not achieve self-actualization during our lifetime.

Maslow's Hierarchy of Needs is a nice model to use in assessing our present functioning as a human and our motivation to strive towards higher fulfillment. We can think about our own history of relapse and observe where in the hierarchy we were situated during the relapse process. Some of us relapsed when we were at the basic needs level, trying to achieve safety from trauma or dealing with unstable living conditions. At other times in our lives we relapsed because we didn't get the job promotion that we expected, or because we fell out of love that fulfilled more of the esteem needs. Now, living beyond our addictive behavior, we can monitor our human needs and look ahead to see what needs to be fulfilled. Where do we find ourselves right now in Maslow's Hierarchy of Needs? What are some actions that we can start taking to get to the next level of the hierarchy? If we're already at the level of the esteem needs, what are some healthy risks or challenges we can pursue that take us out of our comfort zone that point us towards self-actualization?

As we start to change and work towards self-actualization after an addiction, our behavioral patterns with substance use can transform for good. The substances remain the same, while our *relationship* with the substances changes. We have to face our ego head-on once we start to change our relationship with substances and explore our purpose after an addiction. When I talk about the *ego*, I don't refer to it in the pop psychology terms of grandiosity. But I refer to the ego more as our "reality principle" or "mental arena," where everything comes to be. Every person has an ego, and it's incorrect to judge whether an ego is "big" or "small." It's more accurate to view our ego as a form of *strength* or variance of *distortion*. A person who gets defensive after receiving constructive criticism for making a mistake at work is said to have weak ego strength in this context. A person who is in the denial stage after losing a loved one is distorting their ego or "reality" with the use of this defense after a tragic event. We all have ego defense mechanisms that help us shape our reality and protect us from challenging emotions in everyday circumstances.

Every person's ego defenses will just look a little bit different, depending on their experiences. Our style of defenses can also change frequently, depending on the situation and the quality of our mental health at that the moment. Defense mechanisms can fall under three general categories, known as *primitive defenses, high-level neurotic defenses,* and *mature defenses.*[3] People with early childhood trauma may develop more primitive defense mechanisms such as "splitting," where they can view people in terms of either good or bad and cannot integrate these qualities. Other defenses like "projection," placing focus of our inner unacceptable qualities onto others, and "dissociation" are also examples of primitive defense mechanisms. Defenses like "rationalization," "undoing" something, and "identification" by internalizing the qualities of others, are considered more mature defenses. The term defense mechanism has a negative connotation to it, but we all engage in ego defenses, and many defenses don't have to necessarily be "bad." The use of "humor" is a highly mature defense mechanism, and even the act of "altruism" is considered a mature defense. Many of the defenses that we use regularly were developed earlier in our lives, and we carry them forward into our adulthood to help manage our reality. The *strength* of our ego depicts how well we can take on encounters that may challenge our sense of reality and perception. The level of the ego *distortion* depicts the quality of our ego and how close to objective reality it measures up. The more primitive defenses we use, the more our reality is being distorted, to manage the present circumstances. On the other hand, the more we use the mature defense mechanisms, the more at ease we can live with the current reality of our internal and external experiences.

We are distorting our reality in some way when we are engaging in substance-use behavior. Depending on the context of the behavior, some of us engage in substance use to distort our ego that is manifesting intrusive images of past trauma or negative beliefs about the self. However, some of us slightly distort our reality just by having a good time and having a drink with some friends to unwind. In the perspective of ego distortion, this process doesn't have to be seen as negative or a bad thing. Ego distortion can vary in severity, and this can be measured along with the nature of a person's behavioral pattern in regard to substance use. The more substances a person uses, the more their ego is being distorted. After we resolve our addiction, we're facing the nature of our ego head on. So we may feel more stress, boredom, and other experiences that challenge the ego.

A challenge for exploring what our purpose is and taking on new challenges towards self-actualization is sometimes just dealing with our ego. Sometimes it feels better and safer to just create a fantasy of what we want our life to be like. It can be healthy to daydream and create fantasies, as long as we can come back to reality and take actions that align with that fantasy or value. But as we start to take actions, we hear our mind say things like, "You don't have to do it. Just give up." or "You can't do it. Remember what happened last time." If I go to Brazilian Jiu-Jitsu after work, I'm constantly battling with my ego. My ego says, "You had a long day at work. You don't have to go today. Why deal with the aggravation of getting handled and choked-out?" We often get in the way of ourselves when it comes to taking on new challenges and reinventing ourselves after an addiction. We fall out of weekly exercise routines, don't go back to school, or never pick up the instrument that we said we always wanted to try. We either don't value the activity as much as we thought we did, or our ego gets in the way.

As children, we learn to take healthy risks by trying new things, saying what's on our mind, and engaging in various types of imaginative play. As we're free and spontaneous, our ego is developing through life experiences and the memories we begin accumulating. We experience trauma, we get rejected, support is withheld or we are bombarded with emotional support, and we receive direct and indirect messages about ourselves from society and the people close to us. So then we start to hold back. We may begin to limit our potential due to the nature of our ego, which has been developed from earlier experiences by people with their own ego struggles. Going to my Brazilian Jiu-Jitsu class is a great opportunity for me to observe the processes of my ego and learn to transcend it. This opportunity can translate into other areas of my life. I can practice acting as a freer functioning human being without ego restraints, whether I'm having a disagreement with a loved one or I'm trying to market a brand for a business venture. As an adult, I can appreciate the spontaneity of children and how they make use of a playground. Adults can use the larger world as their playground to explore the various interests and opportunities that launch us towards our purpose beyond substance-use behavior.

So we're continuing to change the brain as we're reinventing ourselves by engaging in new lifestyle interests and reshaping old behavioral habits. Just as our brain can mold *into* the behavioral pattern of an addiction, the brain and its connections can mold itself *out of* addictive behavioral processes.[4, 5] Just like the brain changes into addictive patterns on the basis of reward processing, our brain transforms as substance use is inhibited and new behaviors become activated on a rewarded basis as well. We can break through the expectations of our wiring as children, society's plans for us, culture's view of substance use after addiction, and how the ego restricts us, *to be*. We're always developing and in motion with time, and behavior is a continuous flow that pours out of us. Even when we're living beyond our addictions, the Vacuum System is constantly active. This book is about addiction and substance-use behavior, so we have to recognize that the Vacuum System is always present within ourselves, creating or inhibiting this behavior. We just have to pay closer attention to it, as soon as we experience a desire to change our behavior in some way. It's just that our life and our being go well beyond a substance-use behavior, whether we've never had an issue with substances and we have been living our life beyond the mere activity of substance use, or we've been in active addiction and we have been longing for something greater than our substance use at a subconscious level. Now we can create a conscious visualization and give ourselves the chance to experience life again without an addiction.

notes

CHAPTER ONE - VISION

1. Hooton, C. (2015). Neuroscientist Carl Hart: People will always use drugs, we must learn to live with this fact. *The Independent.* Retrieved from https://www.independent.co.uk/news/world/americas/neuroscientist-carl-hart-people-will-always-use-drugs-we-must-learn-to-live-with-this-fact-10435621.html

2. Christenson, P., Roberts, D. F., & Bjork, N. (2012). Booze, drugs, and pop music: trends in substance portrayals in the billboard top 100-1968-2008. *Substance Use & Misuse, 47*(2), 121–129.

3. Clay, R. A. (2015). Treating drug abuse. *American Psychological Association* (Vol. 46, No. 2, p. 46). Retrieved from http://www.apa.org/monitor/2015/02/drug-abuse.aspx

CHAPTER TWO - ORIGINS

1. Swaab, D. F. (2014). *We are our brains: A neurobiography of the brain, from the womb to Alzheimer's.* New York, NY: Spiegel & Grau.

2. Gupta, A. (2013). Could genetic testing help doctors treat pain more effectively? *Fox News Health.* Retrieved from http://www.foxnews.com/health/2013/08/06/could-genetic-testing-help-treat-pain-more-effectively.amp.html

3. Genetic Science Learning Center. (2015). Learn.genetics. *The Science of Addiction: genetics and the brain.* Retrieved from http://www.learn.genetics.utah.edu/content/addiction/genes/

4. Palmer, A. A., & de Wit, H. (2012). Translational genetic approaches to substance use disorders: Bridging the gap between mice and humans. *Human Genetics, 131*(6), 931–939.

5. Weerts, E. M., Wand, G. S., Maher, B., Xu, X., Stephens, M. A., Yang, X., & Mc-Caul, M. E. (2017). Independent and interactive effects of oprm1 and dat1 polymorphisms on alcohol consumption and subjective responses in social drinkers. *Alcoholism: Clinical & Experimental Research, 41*(6), 1093–1104.

6. Repunte-Canonigo, V., Herman, M., Kawamura, T., Kranzler, H. R., Roberto, M., & Sanna, P. P. (2015). Nf1 regulates alcohol dependence-associated excessive drinking and gaba release in the central amygdala in mice, and is associated with alcohol dependence in humans. *Biological Psychiatry, 77*(10), 870–879.

7. Schumann, G., Chunyu, L., & Elliot, P. (2016). Klb is associated with alcohol drinking, and its gene product β-klotho is necessary for fgf21 regulation of alcohol preference. *Proceedings of the National Academy of Sciences of the USA, 113*(50), 14372–14377.

8. Bergland, C. (2013). Hyperactive dopamine response linked to alcoholism. *Psychology Today*. Retrieved from https://www.psychologytoday.com/blog/the-athletes-way/201308/hyperactive-dopamine-response-linked-alcoholism

9. Maisel, N. C., Blodgett, J. C., Wilbourne, P. L., Humphreys, K., & Finney, J. W. (2013). Meta-analysis of naltrexone and acamprosate for treating alcohol use disorders: When are these medications most helpful?. *Addiction, 108*(2), 275–293.

10. Hulse, G. K. (2013). Improving clinical outcomes for naltrexone as a management of problem use. *British Journal of Clinical Pharmacology, 76*(5), 632–641.

11. Sinclair, J. D. (2001). Evidence about the use of naltrexone and for different ways of using it in the treatment of alcoholism. *Alcohol and Alcoholism, 36*(1), 2–10.

12. Giancola, P. R., & Tarter, E. E. (1999). Executive cognitive functioning and risk for substance abuse. *Psychological Science, 10*(3), 203–205.

13. Beaton, D., Abdi, H., & Filbey, F. M. (2014). Unique aspects of impulsive traits in substance use and overeating: Specific contributions of common assessments of impulsivity. *American Journal of Drug & Alcohol Abuse, 40*(6), 463–475.

14. Vaughn, M. G., & King, K. M. (2016). Premeditation and sensation seeking moderate the reasoned action and social reaction pathways in the prototype/willingness model of alcohol use. *Substance Use & Misuse, 51*(6), 711–721.

15. MacKillop, J., Amlung, M. T., Few, L. R., Ray, L. A., & Sweet, L. H. (2011). Delayed reward discounting and addictive behavior: A meta-analysis. *Psychopharmacology, 216*(3), 305–321.

16. Amlung, M., Vedelago, L., Acker, J., Balodis, I., & MacKillop, J. (2017). Steep delay discounting and addictive behavior: A meta-analysis of continuous associations. *Addiction, 112*(1), 51–62.

17. Leonard, H. L. (2011). ADHD a risk factor for substance abuse; Cognitive deficits not a predictor. *Brown University Child & Adolescent Psychopharmacology Update, 13*(7), 1–7.

18. Lee, S. S., Humphreys, K. L. Flory, K., Liu, R., & Glass, K. (2012). Prospective association of childhood attention-deficit/hyperactivity disorder (ADHD) and substance use and abuse/dependence: A meta-analytic review. *Clinical Psychology Review, 31*(3), 328–341.

19. Genetic Science Learning Center. (2015). Learn.genetics. *Ritalin and cocaine: The connection and the controversy.* Retrieved from http://www.learn.genetics.utah.edu/content/addiction.ritalin/

20. Knafo, A., Jaffee, S. R., Quinn, P. D., & Harden, K. P. (2013). Differential changes in impulsivity and sensation seeking and the escalation of substance use from adolescence to early adulthood. *Development & Psychopathology, 25*(1), 223–239.

21. Hersen, M., & Beidel, D. C. (2012). *Adult psychopathology and diagnosis.* (6th ed.). Hoboken, NJ: John Wiley & Sons, Inc.

22. Satre, D. D., Chi, F. W., Mertens, J. R., & Weisner, C. M. (2012). Effects of age and life transitions on alcohol and drug treatment outcome over nine years. *Journal of Studies on Alcohol & Drugs, 73*(3), 459–468.

23. Furr, S. R., Johnson, D. W., & Goodall, C. S. (2015). Grief and recovery: The prevalence of grief and loss in substance abuse treatment. *Journal of Addictions & Offender Counseling, 36*(1), 43–56.

24. Moskowitz, J. T., Hult, J. R., Bussolari, C., & Acree, M. (2009). What works in coping with HIV? A meta-analysis with implications for coping with serious illness. *Psychological Bulletin, 135*(1), 121–141.

25. Habermann, A. (2016). Combating heroin addiction in Vietnam vets and what we can learn in today's epidemic. *Sovereign Health Group Blog: Addiction, PTSD, Recovery.* Retrieved from https://www.sovhealth.com/addiction/combating-heroin-addiction-in-vietnam-vets-and-what-we-can-learn-in-todays-epidemic/

26. Maté, G. (2012). Addiction: Childhood trauma, stress and the biology of addiction. *Journal of Restorative Medicine, 1*(1), 56–63.

CHAPTER THREE – BEHAVIOR

1. Pierce, C. R., & Vanderschuren, L. (2010) Kicking the habit: The neural basis of ingrained behaviors in cocaine addiction. *Neuroscience & Biobehavioral Reviews, 35*(2), 212–219.

2. Milton, A. M., & Everitt, B. J. (2012). The persistence of maladaptive memory: Addiction, drug memories and anti-relapse treatments. *Neuroscience & Biobehavioral Reviews, 36*(4), 1119–1139.

3. Houben, K., & Wiers, R. W. (2009). Response inhibition moderates the relationship between implicit associations and drinking behavior. *Alcoholism: Clinical & Experimental Research, 33*(4), 626–633.

4. Field, M., Franken, I. H., & Munafo, M. R. (2009). A meta-analytic investigation of the relationship between attentional bias and subjective craving in substance use. *Psychological Bulletin, 135*(4), 589–607.

5. Korb, A. (2016). Expectations, dopamine and Louis CK: Why everything is amazing and nobody's happy. *Psychology Today.* Retrieved from https://www.psychologytoday.com/blog/prefrontal-nudity/201603/expectations-dopamine-and-louis-ck

6. OHSU (2017). Discovery could lead to new treatments for addiction and anxiety. *Neuroscience News.* Retrieved from http://neurosciencenews.com/addiction-anxiety-7918/

7. Marlatt, G. A., & Gordon, J. R. (1985). *Relapse prevention: Maintenance strategies in the treatment of addictive behaviors.* New York: The Guilford Press.

8. Fatseas, M., Serre, F., Alexandre, J., Debrabant, R., Auriacombe, M., & Swendsen, J. (2015). Craving and substance use among patients with alcohol, tobacco, cannabis or heroin addiction: A comparison of substance- and person-specific cues. *Addiction, 110*(6), 1035–1042.

9. Jaffe, A. (2010). Craving: When the brain remembers drug use. *Psychology Today.* Retrieved from https://www.psychologytoday.com/blog/all-about-addiction/201002/craving-when-the-brain-remembers-drug-use

10. Wilson, S. J., & Sayette, M. A. (2015). Neuroimaging craving: Urge intensity matters. *Addiction, 110*(2), 195–203.

CHAPTER FOUR – VACUUM

1. Van Der Kolk, B. (2014). *The body keeps the score: Brain, mind, and body in the healing of trauma.* New York, NY: Viking Penguin.

2. Zorumski, C. F., & Rubin, E. H. (2011). *Psychiatry and clinical neuroscience.* New York, NY: Oxford University Press.

3. Keramati, M. & Gutkin, B. (2013). Imbalanced decision hierarchy in addicts emerging from drug-hijacked dopamine spiraling circuit. *PLS ONE, 8*(4): e61489.

4. Robbins, T. W., & Everitt, B. J. (2002). Limbic-striatal memory systems and drug addiction. *Neurobiology of Learning & Memory, 78*(3), 625–636.

5. Volkow, N. D., Wang, G., Fowler, J. S., Tomasi, D., Telang, F., & Baler, R. (2010). Addiction: Decreased reward sensitivity and increased expectation sensitivity conspire to overwhelm the brain's control circuit. *BioEssays, 32*(9), 748–755.

6. Baler, R. D., & Volkow, N. D. (2006). Drug addiction: The neurobiology of disrupted self-control. *Trends in Molecular Medicine, 12*(12), 559–566.

7. The Agenda with Steve Paikin. (2015, November 4). *Marc Lewis: The biology of desire.* Retrieved from https://m.youtube.com/watch?v=sRTL88ZMPBA

8. Goodman, A. (2008). Neurobiology of addiction: An integrative review. *Biochemical Pharmacology, 75*(1), 266–322.

9. Smith, D. G., & Robbins, T. W. (2013). The neurobiological underpinnings of obesity and binge eating: A rationale for adopting the food addiction model. *Biological Psychiatry, 73*(9), 804–810.

10. The Royal Institution. (2016, December 10). *The neuroscience of addiction – with Marc Lewis.* Retrieved from https://m.youtube.com/watch?v=aOSD9rTVuWc

11. Connolly, C. G., Bell, R. P., Foxe J. J., & Garavan, H. (2013). Dissociated grey matter changes with prolonged addiction and extended abstinence in cocaine users. *PLoS ONE, 8*(3): e59645.

CHAPTER FIVE – TOOLS

1. A-Tjak, J. G., Davis, M. L., Morina, N., Powers, M. B., Smits, J. A., & Emmelkamp, P. M. (2015). A meta-analysis of the efficacy of acceptance and commitment therapy for clinically relevant mental and physical health problems. *Psychotherapy & Psychosomatics, 84*(1), 30–36.

2. Luoma, J. B., Kohlenberg, B. S., Hayes, S. C., & Fletcher, L. (2012). Slow and steady wins the race: A randomized clinical trial of acceptance and commitment therapy targeting shame in substance use disorders. *Journal of Consulting & Clinical Psychology, 80*(1), 43–53.

3. Chiesa, A., & Serretti, A. (2014). Are mindfulness-based interventions effective for substance use disorders? A systematic review of the evidence. *Substance Use & Misuse, 49*(5), 492–512.

4. O'Reilly, G. A., Cook, L., Spruijt-Metz, D., & Black, D. S. (2014). Mindfulness-based interventions for obesity-related eating behaviours: A literature review. *Obesity Reviews, 15*(6), 453–461.

5. Grecucci, A., Pappaianni, E., Siugzdaite, R., Theuninck, A., & Job, R. (2015). Mindful emotion regulation: Exploring the neurocognitive mechanisms behind mindfulness. *BioMed Research International,* Vol. 2015, 1–9.

6. Tang, Y. Y., Tang, R., & Posner, M. I. (2016). Mindfulness meditation improves emotion regulation and reduces drug abuse. *Drug & Alcohol Dependence, 163*(2016), 13–18.

7. Garland, E. L., Howard, M. O., Priddy, S. E., McConnell, P. A., Riquino, M. R., & Froeliger, B. (2016). Mindfulness training applied to addiction therapy: Insights into the neural mechanisms of positive behavioral change. *Neuroscience & Neuroeconomicss, 5*(2016), 55–63.

8. Lebowitz, S. (2016). A sports psychologist who trains Olympic athletes reveals the keys to performing under pressure. *Business Insider.* Retrieved from https://www.businessinsider.com/how-to-perform-under-pressure-2016-8?r=UK&IR=T

9. Vannicelli, M. (2001). Moderation training for problem drinkers: Treatment techniques and clinical considerations. *Cognitive and Behavioral Practice, 8*(1), 53–61.

10. Heslin, K. C., Singzon, T. K., Farmer, M., Dobalian, A., Tsao, J., & Hamilton, A. B. (2013). Therapy or threat? Inadvertent exposure to alcohol and illicit drug cues in the neighbourhoods of sober living homes. *Health & Social Care in the Community, 21*(5), 500–508.

11. Loeber, S., Croissant, B., Heinz, A., Mann, K., & Flor, H. (2006). Cue exposure in the treatment of alcohol dependence: Effects on drinking outcome, craving and self-efficacy. *British Journal of Clinical Psychology, 45*(4), 515–529.

12. Vollstädt-Klein, S., Loeber, S., Kirsch, M., Bach, P., Richter, A., Bühler, M., von der Goltz, C., Hermann, D., Mann, K., & Kiefer, F. (2011). Effects of cue-exposure treatment on neural cue reactivity in alcohol dependence: A randomized trial. *Biological Psychiatry, 69*(11), 1060–1066.

13. Unrod, M., Drobes, D. J., Stasiewicz, P. R., Ditre, J. W., Heckman, B., Miller, R. R., & Brandon, T. H. (2014). Decline in cue-provoked craving during cue exposure therapy for smoking cessation. *Nicotine & Tobacco Research, 16*(3), 306–315.

14. Houben, K., Havermans, R., & Wiers, R. (2010). Learning to dislike alcohol: Conditioning negative implicit attitudes toward alcohol and its effect on drinking behavior. *Psychopharmacology, 211*(1), 79–86.

CHAPTER SIX – GOALS

1. Cutler, R. B., & Fishbain, D. A. (2005). Are alcoholism treatments effective? The project MATCH data. *BMC Public Health, 5:75*, 1–11. doi:10.1186/1471-2458-5-75

2. Bujarski, S., O'Malley, S. S., Lunny, K., & Ray, L. A. (2013). The effects of drinking goal on treatment outcome for alcoholism. Journal of Consulting & Clinical Psychology, 81(1), 13–22.

3. Paone, D., Des Jarlais, D. C., Gangloff, R. Milliken, J., & Friedman, S. R. (1995). Syringe exchange: HIV prevention, key findings, and future directions. *The International Journal of the Addictions, 30*(12), 1647–1683.

4. Ritter, A., & Cameron, J. (2006). A review of the efficacy and effectiveness of harm reduction strategies for alcohol, tobacco and illicit drugs. *Drug and Alcohol Review, 25*(6), 611–624.

5. Moderation Management. (2010). In *SAMHSA's National Registry of Evidence-based Programs and Practices*. Retrieved from https://nrepp.samhsa.gov/Legacy/ViewIntervention.aspx?id=212

6. Hester, R. K., Delaney, H. D., & Campbell, W. (2011). Moderatedrinking.com and moderation management: Outcomes of a randomized clinical trial with non-dependent problem drinkers. *Journal of Consulting and Clinical Psychology, 79*(2), 215–224.

7. Rubak, S., Sandbæk, A., Lauritzen, T., & Christensen, B. (2005). Motivational interviewing: A systematic review and meta-analysis. *British Journal of General Practice, 55*(513), 305–312.

8. Lozano, B. E., Stephens, R. S., & Roffman, R. A. (2006). Abstinence and moderate use goals in the treatment of marijuana dependence. *Addiction, 101*(11), 1589–1597.

9. Schnoll, R. A., Martinez, E., Tatum, K. L., Glass, M., Bernath, A., Ferris, D., & Reynolds, P. (2011). Increased self-efficacy to quit and perceived control over withdrawal symptoms predict smoking cessation following nicotine dependence treatment. *Addictive Behaviors, 36*(1/2), 144–147.

CHAPTER SEVEN – LANGUAGE

1. Winawer, J., Witthoft, N., Frank, M. C., Wu, L., Wade, A. R., & Boroditsky, L. (2007). Russian blues reveal effects of language on color discrimination. *National Academy of Sciences, 104*(19), 7780–7785.

2. Corrigan, P. (2004). How stigma interferes with mental health care. *American Psychologist, 59*(7), 614–625.

3. Pasman, J. (2011). The consequences of labeling mental illnesses on the self-concept: A review of the literature and future directions. *Social Cosmos, 2*, 122–127.

4. DePierre, J. A., Puhl, R. M., & Luedicke, J. (2013). A new stigmatized identity? Comparisons of a "food addict" label with other stigmatized health conditions. *Basic & Applied Social Psychology, 35*(1), 10–21.

5. Link, B. G., Struening, E. L., Rahav, M., Phelan, J. C., & Nuttbrock, L. (1997). On stigma and its consequences: Evidence from a longitudinal study of men with dual diagnoses of mental illness and substance abuse. *Journal of Health & Social Behavior, 38*(2), 177–190.

6. Best, D., Andersson, C., Irving, J., & Edwards, M. (2017). Recovery identity and wellbeing: Is it better to be "recovered" or "in recovery"? *Journal of Groups in Addiction & Recovery, 12*(1), 27–36.

7. Heyman, G. M. (2013). Addiction and choice: Theory and new data. *Frontiers in Psychiatry, 4*(31), 1–5. doi:10.3389/fpsyt.2013.00031

8. Miller, W. R., Westerberg, V. S., Harris, R. J., & Tonigan, J. S. (1996). What predicts relapse? Prospective testing of antecedent models. *Addiction, 91*: 155-172. doi: 10.1046/j.1360-0443.91.12s1.7.x

9. Brandsma, J. M. (1980). *Outpatient Treatment of Alcoholism: A review and comparative study.* Baltimore, MD: University Park Press.

10. McQuaid, R. J., Malik, A., Moussouni, K., Baydack, N., Stargardter, M., & Morrisey, M. (2017). *Life in recovery from addiction in Canada.* Ottawa, ON: Canadian Centre on Substance Use and Addiction.

11. Scott, R. A. (1969). *The making of blind men: A study of adult socialization*. New York, NY: Russell Sage Foundation.

CHAPTER EIGHT – SUPPORT

1. Yalom, I. D., & Leszcz, M. (2005). *The theory and practice of group psychotherapy*. New York, NY: Basic Books.

2. Cozolino, L. (2017). *The neuroscience of psychotherapy: Healing the social brain*. New York, NY: W. W. Norton & Company, Inc.

3. Best, D., Andersson, C., Irving, J., & Edwards, M. (2017). Recovery identity and wellbeing: Is it better to be "recovered" or "in recovery"? *Journal of Groups in Addiction & Recovery, 12*(1), 27–36.

CHAPTER NINE – PREVENTION

1. Domínguez-Salas, S., Díaz-Batanero, C., Lozano-Rojas, O. M., & Verdejo-García, A. (2016). Impact of general cognition and executive function deficits on addiction treatment outcomes: Systematic review and discussion of neurocognitive pathways. Neuroscience & Biobehavioral Reviews, 71, 772–801.

2. Sitharthan, T., Sitharthan, G., & Kavanagh, D. J. (2001). Emotional cue exposure for alcohol abuse: Development of a new treatment procedure to train moderation drinking in the context of dysphoria. *Clinical Psychology & Psychotherapy, 8*(1), 73–78.

3. Petry, N. M., Bickel, W. K., & Arnett, M. (1998). Shortened time horizons and insensitivity to future consequences in heroin addicts. *Addiction, 93*(5), 729–738.

4. Campbell, W. G. (2003). Addiction: A disease of volition caused by a cognitive impairment. *Canadian Journal of Psychiatry, 48*(10), 669–674.

5. Kirchner, T. R., Shiffman, S. & Wileyto, P. E. (2012). Relapse dynamics during smoking cessation: Recurrent abstinence violation effects and lapse-relapse progression. *Journal of Abnormal Psychology, 121*(1), 187–197.

6. Sitharthan, T., Sitharthan, G., Hough, M. J., & Kavanagh, D. J. (1997). Cue exposure in moderation drinking: A comparison with cognitive-behavior therapy. *Journal of Consulting and Clinical Psychology, 65*(5), 878–882.

CHAPTER TEN – BEYOND

1. Alexander, B. K., Coambs, R. B., & Hadaway, P. F. (1978). The effect of housing and gender on morphine self-administration in rats. *Psychopharmacology, 58*(2), 175–179.

2. Prendergast, M., Podus, D., Finney, J., Greenwell, L., & Roll, J. (2006). Contingency management for treatment of substance use disorders: A meta-analysis. *Addiction, 101*(11), 1546–1560.

3. Gabbard, G. O. (2014). *Psychodynamic psychiatry in clinical practice* (5th ed.). Arlington: VA: American Psychiatric Publishing.

4. Forster, S. E., Finn, P. R., & Brown, J. W. (2016). A preliminary study of longitudinal neuroadaptation associated with recovery from addiction. *Drug & Alcohol Dependence, 168*: 52–60.

5. Regner, M. F., Saenz, N., Maharajh, K., Yamamoto, D., Mohl, B., Wylie, K., Tregellas, J., & Tanabe, J. (2016). Top-down network effective connectivity in abstinent substance dependent individuals. *PLoS ONE, 11*(10), 1–21.

Made in the USA
Monee, IL
17 December 2019